Development of
the Industrial U.S.
Biographies

Development of the Industrial U.S. Biographies

Sonia G. Benson
Carol Brennan,
Contributing Writer
Jennifer York Stock,
Project Editor

U·X·L
*An imprint of Thomson Gale,
a part of The Thomson Corporation*

THOMSON
─────★─────
GALE

Detroit • New York • San Francisco • San Diego • New Haven, Conn. • Waterville, Maine • London • Munich

Development of the Industrial U.S: Biographies

Sonia G. Benson

Project Editor
Jennifer York Stock

Editorial
Sarah Hermsen

Rights Acquisitions and Management
Shalice Shah-Caldwell, Kim Smilay

Imaging and Multimedia
Randy Bassett, Lezlie Light,
Daniel Newell, Denay Wilding

Product Design
Pamela A. E. Galbreath

Composition
Evi Seoud

Manufacturing
Rita Wimberly

For permission to use material from this product, submit your request via the Web at http://www.gale-edit.com/permissions, or you may download our Permissions Request form and submit your request by fax or mail to:

Permissions Department
Thomson Gale
27500 Drake Rd.
Farmington Hills, MI 48331-3535
Permissions Hotline:
248-699-8006 or 800-877-4253, ext. 8006
Fax: 248-699-8074 or 800-762-4058

Cover photographs of J. P. Morgan, © Corbis; Samuel Slater, © Bettmann/Corbis; Jane Addams, courtesy of The Library of Congress.

While every effort has been made to ensure the reliability of the information presented in this publication, Thomson Gale does not guarantee the accuracy of the data contained herein. Thomson Gale accepts no payment for listing; and inclusion in the publication of any organization, agency, institution, publication, service, or individual does not imply endorsement by the editors or publisher. Errors brought to the attention of the publisher and verified to the satisfaction of the publisher will be corrected in future editions.

LIBRARY OF CONGRESS CATALOGING-IN-PUBLICATION DATA

Benson, Sonia.
   Development of the industrial U.S. Biographies / Sonia G. Benson ; Jennifer York Stock, project editor.
     p. cm.
Includes bibliographical references and index.
ISBN 1-4144-0176-0 (hardcover : alk. paper)
   1. Industries–United States–Biography–Juvenile literature. 2. Industrial revolution–United States–Biography–Juvenile literature. [1. United States–Economic conditions–To 1865–History–Juvenile literature.] I. Title: Development of the industrial US. II. Stock, Jennifer York, 1974- III. Title.

HC102.5. A2.B46 2006
338. 092′273–dc22
                                      2005016350

Printed in the United States of America
10 9 8 7 6 5 4 3 2 1

Table of Contents

Introduction

I ndustrialization is the widespread development of profit-making businesses that manufacture products on a large scale, using labor-saving machinery. Understanding the history of the development of industrialization in the United States, which took place over two centuries, involves learning about some of its technical elements, such as technology and the economy. But the history of U.S. industrialism is also a dramatic story of people rising and falling from power or struggling desperately to make the world a better place. Industrialization fueled the national culture, economy, daily life, and politics, creating such tremendous social changes that it is impossible to imagine what life in the United States would be like without it.

Though the Industrial Revolution, a period of rapid industrial growth causing a shift in focus from agriculture to industry, first began in England and Europe in the middle of the eighteenth century, industrialization did not begin to take root in the United States until after the American Revolution (1775–83). Even then American industrialization had a slow start, due to overwhelming obstacles. At the time, the vast majority of Americans lived independent lives as farmers in remote areas. For the most part, they had little connection with anyone but neighboring farmers, since there were few good roads or systems of communication. Most people did not even own clocks; time was determined by the seasons and the rising and setting of the sun. Few people worked for wages, and those manufactured goods Americans could afford generally came from Europe. The new nation had vast natural resources, such as land, timber, metals, minerals, water power, and ports, but without transportation or manufacturing it was nearly impossible to make industrial use of them.

Once begun, the American Industrial Revolution took on its own character, differing from that of other countries. This was primarily because Americans themselves had been shaped and selected by a unique set of forces. After fighting hard to gain independence from England, most Americans were passionate about the ideals of liberty and equality for all (although to many Americans at the time this meant only white males), and they were determined to create a society in which any individual could rise and prosper through his or her own efforts. They were also driven by the desire for wealth. Though many Europeans immigrated to America to find religious or social freedom, the majority came seeking riches. Many had faced bitter hardships and were prepared to take major risks to obtain wealth. Another key trait of Americans was a spirit of innovation; it had been a necessary attribute for emigrants who left Europe in the seventeenth century, for they would have to reinvent the most basic aspects of their daily lives in the New World. The combined spirit of individualism, greed, and innovation came to characterize U.S. industrialism.

In the years between the American Revolution and the American Civil War (1861–65), innovation and invention were highly esteemed by the American public. Most industrial designs and ideas came initially from Europe, but once they reached the machine makers, or "mechanicians," of American shops, they were improved until they became distinctly American, suited to the land and its people. The times produced an extremely talented group of inventors and innovators, and from their workshops, which were mainly located in the northeastern United States, the "American System," or mass production and the use of interchangeable parts, emerged. It would forever change the nature of manufacturing worldwide.

With new advances in technology, some enterprising business people built the first U.S. factories, and most of them flourished. However, from the start the stark division in wealth and position between industry owners and their workers was at odds with the popular belief in American liberty and equality. Despite early factory owners' efforts to humanize factory work, workers faced low wages and poor working conditions. Many claimed they were slaves to wage labor. It was not long after the first industrial workforces were hired that the first labor strikes took place. The conflict between employers and employees continued, and the factory owners' early attempts to create ideal circumstances for workers were abandoned. Professional managers were hired to get as much work from the workforce as possible. A huge influx of immigrants from Europe and Asia from the 1840s until the 1920s supplied inexpensive labor, but labor strikes continued.

After a slow beginning in the Northeast industrialization began to spread at a rapid pace with the nationwide building of transportation and communications systems. The construction of the transcontinental railroad spanning the nation from one coast to the other—a mammoth undertaking—signaled the start of a new way of life for all Americans. Where railroads went, towns and cities with bustling new commerce arose. The construction of the railroads spawned giant new industries in steel, iron, and coal. Railroads brought farmers' crops to distant markets and were instrumental in bringing the industrial society to the West.

For the railroads to be built and industry to advance, capital, or vast quantities of money, was required. The art of raising large amounts of capital and applying it to industry was mainly accomplished by a generation of extremely capable industrialists who built the gigantic industries that dominated the nation and ruled its economy. These legendary men, admired as the "captains of industry" by some and loathed as ruthless crooks, or "robber barons," by others, included railroad owner Cornelius Vanderbilt, steel empire founder Andrew Carnegie, Standard Oil tycoon John D. Rockefeller, investment banker J. P. Morgan, and many others. Though some of them came from wealthy backgrounds, many were born in humble circumstances and rose to wealth and power through their own efforts. These industrialists created new systems of doing business that are still in place today. Their tactics almost always included creating monopolies, huge corporations that dominated their industry nationwide and limited attempts at competition by others. As the industrialists prospered, most of the wealth of the nation fell into their hands. This period became known as the Gilded Age, the era of industrialization from the early 1860s to the turn of the century in which a few wealthy individuals gained tremendous power and influence. During the Gilded Age the power of industrialists and their corporations seemed unstoppable.

The number of U.S. companies dwindled from thousands to hundreds as the most powerful industrialists bought out or crushed their competitors. Once again, the national spirit of liberty and equality was aroused. Farmers, laborers, poor immigrants, and labor unions as well as middle class reformers sought relief from the power of the corporations, giving rise to the Progressive Era, or the period of the American Industrial Revolution that spanned roughly from the 1890s to about 1920, in which reformers worked together in the interest of distributing political power and wealth more equally. It was during this time that the strong hand of the federal government was finally felt in American industry, as it began to leave behind its laissez-faire, or non-interference, policies in order to regulate businesses, curb monopolies, and protect workers.

By the twentieth century, the United States was the richest and most powerful industrial nation in the world, but the process of industrialization continued. During the twentieth century industry was shaped by scientists like Frederick Winslow Taylor, who devised measurable methods of business management designed to produce top levels of efficiency. The best-known follower of "Taylorism" was Henry Ford, who began to mass produce affordable automobiles in 1909. The Great Depression (1929–41) and World War II (1939–45) both had profound effects on American industrialism, causing government controls and assistance to individuals to increase even more. In recent decades, computers and globalism have been the active agents of change in U.S. industrialism.

Finally, it is worthwhile to note that the development of U.S. industrialization is not finished. It took more than one hundred years for the United States to transform from a farming society to an industrial world power. Adjusting to industrialism has already taken up another century and will continue for many years to come.

Sonia G. Benson

Reader's Guide

The United States began as a nation of farmers living in remote areas, but over a period of two hundred years the country became the wealthiest and most powerful industrial nation of the world. During the American Industrial Revolution inventors and innovators created new and improved machines for manufacturing, while a new breed of American businessmen created revolutionary methods of conducting business and managing labor. The road to industrialization was not always heroic. Ruthlessness and greed were often key ingredients in advancing industry. While a few found wealth and power, multitudes of workers and farmers suffered, and small businesses were crushed by the powerful new corporations. Reformers, unions, and protestors against big business played a crucial role in the industrialization process as they pressed for the rights of workers and regulations on business to help farmers and consumers. The diverse people and events that forever changed the nation from a rural farming economy to an industrialized urban nation create a dramatic story that lies at the heart of U.S. history.

Coverage and features

Development of the Industrial U.S.: Biographies profiles twenty-six significant figures who participated in American industrialization. The biographies cover a wide spectrum of people, from the creators of the first factories, such as Samuel Slater and Francis Cabot Lowell, to inventors and innovators, including John Fitch, Elijah McCoy, and Thomas Edison. Industrialists Andrew Carnegie, J. P. Morgan, and John D. Rockefeller are profiled, as are reformers and educators such as Jane Addams, Florence Kelley, and Booker T. Washington. *Biographies* also includes labor advocates such as Eugene Debs and A. Philip Randolph. The volume features more than fifty photographs and illustrations, a timeline, a glossary, and sources for further reading.

U•X•L Development of the Industrial U.S. Reference Library

Development of the Industrial U.S.: Biographies is only one component of the three-part U•X•L Development of the Industrial U.S. Reference Library. The other two titles in this set are:

- *Development of the Industrial U.S.: Almanac* presents an over-view of the history of American industrialization. Its four-teen chapters cover the first American factories, inventors, the rise of big business and railroads, urbanism, labor unions, industrial influences in places such as the South or the Great Plains, the Gilded Age, the Progressive Era, the post-industrial era, and much more. Each chapter of the *Almanac* features informative sidebar boxes highlighting glossary terms and issues discussed in the text and con-cludes with a list of further readings. Also included are more than sixty photographs and illustrations, a timeline, a glossary, a list of suggested research and activity ideas, and an index providing easy access to subjects discussed throughout the volume.

- *Development of the Industrial U.S.: Primary Sources* presents eighteen full or excerpted written works, speeches, and other documents that were influential during American industrialization. The volume includes excerpts from the writings of Thomas Jefferson and Alexander Hamilton reflecting their debate on industrialization; excerpts from legislation regarding industrialization, such as the Interstate Commerce Act and the Sherman Antitrust Act; segments of popular novels by Horatio Alger and William Dean Howells depicting the effects of industrialization on American society; political cartoons; a popular labor song; an excerpt from an essay by William Graham Sumner presenting the concept of social Darwinism, and much more. Nearly fifty photographs and illustrations, a timeline, sources for further reading, and an index supplement the volume.

A cumulative index of all three volumes in the U•X•L Development of the Industrial U.S. Reference Library is also available.

Comments and suggestions

We welcome your comments on *Development of the Industrial U.S.: Biographies* and suggestions for other topics in history to consider. Please write: Editors, *Development of the Industrial U.S.: Biographies,* U•X•L, 27500 Drake Rd., Farmington Hills, Michigan, 48331-3535; call toll-free: 1-800-877-4253; fax to: 248-699-8097; or send e-mail via http://www.gale.com.

Timeline of Events

1780: American mechanics in the Northeast begin to apply principles learned from the English Industrial Revolution in their innovations on tools and machines.

1781: Oliver Evans invents machines to replace human labor in flour mills.

1787: **John Fitch** demonstrates the first working steamboat to potential investors.

1789: **Samuel Slater** arrives in the United States with detailed knowledge of English textile machines and helps found the U.S. textile industry.

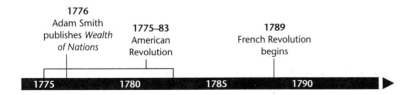

1776
Adam Smith publishes *Wealth of Nations*

1775–83
American Revolution

1789
French Revolution begins

1775 1780 1785 1790

1790: Eighty percent of the nation's population is made up of farmers and ninety-five percent of the population lives in rural areas.

1790: Congress passes the first patent law.

1798: Eli Whitney proposes to make 4,000 muskets for the U.S. government, using new machine-making tools and interchangeable parts.

1807: Robert Fulton's steamboat, the *Clermont,* makes its maiden voyage from New York City to Albany, New York.

1807: Eli Terry builds four thousand clockworks on a tight schedule using the latest principles of mass production.

1814: **Francis Cabot Lowell** opens the first textile factory that incorporates spinning and weaving under one roof in Waltham, Massachusetts.

1817: Congress authorizes the construction of the National Road, the first road to run west across the Appalachian Mountains.

1817–1825: The Erie Canal is built, connecting Albany and Buffalo, New York.

1825: The New York Stock Exchange opens its new headquarters at 11 Wall Street.

1826: The first U.S. railway, the Baltimore and Ohio (B & O) is launched.

1831: Cyrus McCormick invents the first workable reaper.

1836: Two thousand women workers go on strike for better wages and conditions at the Lowell textile mills.

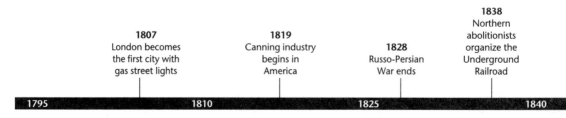

1807
London becomes the first city with gas street lights

1819
Canning industry begins in America

1828
Russo-Persian War ends

1838
Northern abolitionists organize the Underground Railroad

| 1795 | 1810 | 1825 | 1840 |

1837: John Deere invents the steel plow.

1840: The *Lowell Offering,* a journal written by the women workers of the Lowell mills, is launched.

1840s: Immigration to the United States from Europe increases significantly. Between 1840 and 1920 37 million immigrants will arrive in the country.

1844: Samuel F. B. Morse sends the first official telegraph message from Washington, D.C., to Baltimore, Maryland.

1846: Elias Howe patents his sewing machine. Isaac M. Singer will market a more practical sewing machine within four years.

1851: U.S. technology exhibits impress visitors at the Crystal Palace Exhibition of London, the first world's fair.

1852: Samuel Colt opens a large arms manufacturing factory, using advanced mass-production techniques.

1859: The first successful effort to drill for oil gives rise to the oil industry.

1860: Shoemakers in Lynn, Massachusetts, launch a massive strike for better wages and working conditions. The strike will spread to factories over a wide area and include as many as twenty thousand men and women workers.

1862: The Pacific Railroad Act calls for building a transcontinental railroad from Omaha, Nebraska, to Sacramento, California.

1862: Congress enacts the Homestead Act, which provides small pieces of public land to settlers in the West for farming; industry soon expands into the new territories.

1847
Marx and Engels
publish the
Communist Manifesto

1850
Taiping Rebellion begins
in China

1859
John Brown leads a raid on
Harper's Ferry

1845 1850 1855 1860

1864: The first Bessemer converter, a new process for making steel, is introduced in the United States.

1865: **John D. Rockefeller** opens an oil refinery in Cleveland, Ohio.

1866: The National Labor Union (NLU) is formed to promote the eight-hour workday.

1867: In the first cattle drive, organized by James G. McCoy, cattle are driven from Texas to Abilene, Kansas, where they are shipped by railroad to Chicago, Illinois.

1867: The National Grange of the Patrons of Husbandry (usually called the Grange) is founded to advance the interests of farmers.

1867: **Chinese transcontinental railroad workers** represent between 80 and 90 percent of the Central Pacific Railroad workforce building the western portion of the transcontinental railroad.

1867–1868: Cornelius Vanderbilt clashes with Daniel Drew, Jay Gould, and James Fisk for ownership of the Erie Railroad in a competition that became known as the Erie War.

1869: The two railroad companies, the Union Pacific and the Central Pacific, commissioned to build the transcontinental railroad meet at Promontory Point, Utah, marking the completion of the first transcontinental railroad.

1869: The Knights of Labor, one of the early national labor unions, is founded.

1869: On September 24 or "Black Friday," the price of gold fell due to the speculations of James Fisk and Jay Gould, creating a financial panic.

1865
American Civil War ends

1868
Meiji Restoration
begins in Japan

1870
Franco-Prussian
War begins

1865   1867   1869   1871

1869   A fire in the Avondale coal mine in Pennsylvania kills 108 men and boys.

1872:   Hunters and railroad workers have killed millions of buffalo on the Great Plains, reducing their numbers from 15 million to 7 million. The extermination will continue until less than one thousand buffalo remain in the 1890s.

1872:   **Mrs. Astor** meets Ward McAllister, and together they create a New York City institution that will set the tone for high society for years to come: Mrs. Astor's annual ball.

1872:   **Elijah McCoy** patents his invention, a special lubricating cup that can be fitted into the steam cylinders of locomotives, speeding up railroads nationwide. The device will come to be known as "the real McCoy."

1873:   One of the nation's largest banks, owned by Jay Cooke, fails, causing business failures and unemployment. A nationwide depression follows.

1875:   The National Farmers' Alliance is founded. It quickly divides into two groups, the Northern Alliance and the Southern Alliance.

1877:   A large railroad strike begins in West Virginia to protest wage reductions. Within a few weeks, it spreads throughout the nation with about ten thousand participating workers. More than one hundred are killed by federal troops and about one thousand are jailed before the Great Strike is suppressed.

1877:   **Alexander Graham Bell** and Thomas Watson have the first telephone conversation, transmitted over wire from New York City to Boston, Massachusetts.

1875
Civil Rights Act of 1875 is enacted

1876
Battle of Little Bighorn

1881
Clara Barton founds the Red Cross

1873   1876   1879   1882

1881: **Andrew Carnegie** forms Carnegie Steel Company by combining his own successful steel company with several others.

1881: **Booker T. Washington** opens the Tuskegee Normal and Industrial Institute, an industrial school for African American students in Alabama.

1882: **Thomas Edison**'s Pearl Street electrical station supplies power to four hundred incandescent light bulbs owned by eighty-five customers in New York City.

1886: The Haymarket Riots erupt in Chicago, pitting striking workers against police.

1886: The American Federation of Labor (AFL) reorganizes under the leadership of Samuel Gompers as a federation of trade unions formed to improve wages and working conditions, shorten working hours, abolish child labor, and provide for collective bargaining.

1886: The Colored Farmers' Alliance is founded.

1887: Congress passes the Interstate Commerce Act to regulate the railroads. It is the first regulatory act designed to establish government supervision over a major industry.

1888: **Jane Addams** and **Ellen Gate Starr** found Hull House, a settlement house in Chicago.

1889: James Buchanan Duke merges his tobacco company with four others to create the American Tobacco Company, controlling 90 percent of the U.S. tobacco industry.

1890: Congress enacts the Sherman Antitrust Act to prohibit companies from restricting competition or creating monopolies.

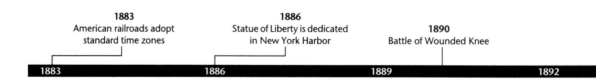

1883
American railroads adopt standard time zones

1886
Statue of Liberty is dedicated in New York Harbor

1890
Battle of Wounded Knee

| 1883 | 1886 | 1889 | 1892 |

1890: The People's Party, better known as the Populists, is formed to combine the interests of farmers in the South and West and laborers nationwide to combat the powers of the Eastern industrialists. **Mary Elizabeth Lease** becomes a stump speaker for the party, giving hundreds of speeches around the country.

1892: In the Homestead Strike, the workers at Andrew Carnegie's steel mills strike to protest low wages and the hiring of nonunion workers. A violent battle ensues, and the union in the steel mills is crushed.

1893: A financial panic, mainly due to the collapse of hundreds of railroad companies, results in a nationwide depression.

1890: **Lewis Lattimer** publishes *Incandescent Electric Lighting: A Practical Description of the Edison System,* a groundbreaking book on electric lighting.

1894: When the workers at the Pullman factory go on strike for better wages, 125,000 railroad workers in the American Railway Union (ARU), under the leadership of **Eugene Debs,** join the strike to support the Pullman workers.

1895: **George Washington Murray,** the only black representative then in Congress, reads into the congressional record a list of 92 patents granted to African-Americans in an attempt to advance African American education.

1899: **Florence Kelley** founds the National Consumers' League, a lobbying agency for protective labor legislation for women and children.

1900: New York City becomes grossly overpopulated, with about 1.2 million people, or about 75 percent of its

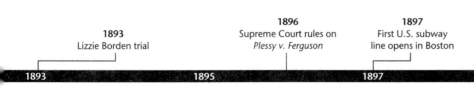

1893
Lizzie Borden trial

1896
Supreme Court rules on
Plessy v. Ferguson

1897
First U.S. subway
line opens in Boston

1893   1895   1897   1899

population living in overcrowded tenement buildings without adequate water, air, sewage, or garbage removal.

1900: About 1.7 million children under the age of sixteen are working in factories.

1900: Industrial accidents kill about 35,000 workers each year and disable 500,000 others.

1900: African Americans begin to migrate from the South to Northern industrial cities. By 1910, 366,880 African Americans will migrate to Northern cities from the South. From 1910 to 1920 between five hundred thousand and one million African Americans will make the trip north.

1900: Several U.S. magazines present a new form of journalism called muckraking, which investigates corruption in big business and government.

1900: **Robert M. La Follette** wins the governorship of Wisconsin by campaigning as a champion of the people, promising to fight big business and political bosses.

1903: President Theodore Roosevelt creates a federal Department of Commerce and Labor to investigate the operations and conduct of corporations.

1903: Frederick Winslow Taylor publishes an essay about making the workplace more efficient that will quickly become the basis of a new movement of scientific business management, or Taylorism.

1904: **Ida M. Tarbell** publishes her classic muckraking work, *History of the Standard Oil Company,* which probes the questionable tactics of the dominant oil-refining company and its owner, John D. Rockefeller.

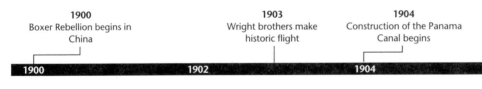

1900
Boxer Rebellion begins in
China

1903
Wright brothers make
historic flight

1904
Construction of the Panama
Canal begins

| 1900 | 1902 | 1904 | 1906 |

1904: The U.S. Supreme Court rules that the Northern Securities Trust, a combination of several railroads owned in a trust under the management of James J. Hill, Edward H. Harriman, and **J. P. Morgan**, is in violation of the Sherman Antitrust Act. It is the first major trust to be dissolved under the act.

1907: A federal law against child labor is introduced to Congress, but it is defeated. Three years later, an estimated 2 million American children are still employed by industries.

1910: In the South, 80 percent of African American farmers and 40 percent of white farmers are either sharecroppers or tenant farmers struggling to survive.

1910: **Henry Ford** opens his Model T automobile factory in Highland Park, Michigan, and begins mass producing affordable cars.

1911: The U.S. Supreme Court rules that the Standard Oil Trust and the American Tobacco Company are in violation of the Sherman Antitrust Act and order them to dissolve.

1911: A fire at the Triangle Shirtwaist Company, a garment factory, kills 146 workers, mostly poor immigrant women and girls.

1912: **Julia C. Lathrop** is appointed chief of the new federal Children's Bureau, which will investigate child labor, infant mortality (death), juvenile courts, and many other aspects of children's well-being.

1913: **Frank and Lillian Gilbreth** open the Summer School of Scientific Management, which trains professionals to teach new ideas about business management, emphasizing the study of motion and psychology.

1908 — 1910 China bans slavery — 1912 The Titanic sinks — 1914 World War I begins

1914: Congress enacts the Clayton Antitrust Act, which updates the Sherman Antitrust Act and includes an important provision allowing workers to unionize and strike.

1920: For the first time in the United States, more people live in the city than in the country.

1925: **A. Philip Randolph** organizes the Brotherhood of Sleeping Car Porters (BSCP), the first African American union in the country to sign a labor contract with a white employer.

1927: Charles A. Lindbergh makes his famous 2,610-mile transatlantic (spanning the Atlantic Ocean) solo flight from Long Island, New York, to Paris, France, launching the aviation industry.

1932 Franklin Delano Roosevelt initiates his New Deal reforms, creating federal jobs, assisting farmers, protecting citizens from losing their homes to mortgage foreclosures, and enacting the Social Security Act to create an old-age pension system and paying benefits to the disabled and widows with children.

1938: Congress passes the Fair Labor Standards Act (FLSA), which sets a minimum wage for all workers, sets a maximum workweek of forty-four hours, and prohibits interstate shipment of goods produced by children under the age of sixteen.

1945: During American participation in World War II, the number of workingwomen rises to 18.6 million, a 50 percent increase from the 11.9 million workingwomen of 1940.

1920
The 19th Amendment grants women the right to vote

1930
First supermarket opens in Long Island, NY

1939–45
World War II

1915   1925   1935   1945

1946: The first real computer, the Electronic Numerical Integrator and Computer (ENIAC), is introduced to the public, starting the computer age.

1969: The first personal computers are introduced.

1980s: Companies begin scale back production and staffs, and American factories begin to deteriorate as investors build factories in other countries to benefit from lower labor costs.

1990s: The U.S. workforce experiences a widespread shift from industrial labor to service labor, marking the start of the postindustrial era.

2000: Multinational corporations account for about 20 percent of the world's production.

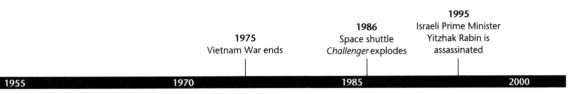

Words to Know

A

anarchist: An individual who advocates the use of force to overthrow all government.

antitrust laws: Laws opposing or regulating trusts or similar business monopolies.

apprentice: Someone who is bound to work for someone else for a specific term in order to learn a trade.

aristocracy: A government controlled by a wealthy, privileged social class.

artisan: A person who is skilled at a particular trade or craft.

assimilation: The social process of being absorbed, or blending into the dominant culture.

aviation: The operation and manufacture of aircraft.

B

bankruptcy: A state of financial ruin in which an individual or corporation cannot pay its debts.

boiler: A tube (or several connected tubes) in which water is heated to steam.

bond: A certificate of debt issued by a government or corporation that guarantees repayment of the original investment with interest by a specified date.

boycott: Consumer refusal to buy a company's goods in order to express disapproval.

bureaucratic structure: An organization with many levels of authority, in which people specialize in their jobs and follow set rules of operation.

C

capital: Accumulated wealth or goods devoted to the production of other goods.

capitalism: An economic system in which the means of production and distribution are privately owned by individuals or groups and competition for business establishes the price of goods and services.

capitalist: A person who invests his or her wealth in business and industry.

compulsory attendance: Mandatory obligation to go to school.

Confederate states: The eleven Southern states that withdrew from the United States in 1860 and 1861.

conservation: Planned management of natural resources to prevent their misuse or loss.

consolidation: A process in which companies purchase other companies and fold them into one large corporation.

conveyor belt: A moving belt that carries materials from one place to another.

corporation: A company, or organization of employers and employees that is permitted by law, usually owned by a group of shareholders and established to carry out a business or industry as a body. Corporations have legal rights usually reserved for individuals, such as the right to sue and be sued and to borrow or loan money.

cylinder: A tube-shaped chamber or tank.

D

depression: A period of drastic decline in the economy.

directorates: Boards of directors of different companies that have at least one director in common.

E

entrepreneur: A person who organizes a new business.

evolution: Evolution is the process by which all plant and animal species of plant and animal change over time because of variations that are passed from one generation to the next. The theory of evolution was first proposed by naturalist Charles Darwin (1809–1882).

F

factory: A building or group of buildings in which manufactured goods are made from raw materials on a large scale.

feudalism: A system in which most people live and work on farms owned by a noble who grants it to them in exchange for their loyalty.

foreclosure: A legal process in which a borrower who does not make payments on a mortgage or loan is deprived of the mortgaged property.

G

gauge: Distance between the rails of a railroad track.

Gilded Age: The era of industrialization from the early 1860s to the turn of the century in which a few wealthy individuals gained tremendous power and influence.

grain elevators: Huge storage bins built next to railroad tracks to hold grain until it is loaded into train cars.

grant: A transfer or property by deed or writing.

Great Plains: An area of grassland that stretches across the central part of North America eastward from the Rocky Mountains, from Canada in the north down to Texas in the south.

gross national product (GNP): The total of all goods and services produced each year.

H

holding company: A company that is formed to own stocks and bonds in other companies, usually for the purpose of controlling them.

horizontal expansion: Growth occurring when a company purchases rival companies in the same industry in an effort to eliminate competition.

hydroelectric power plants: Plants that produce electricity from waterpower.

I

industrialism: The social system that results from an economy based on large-scale industries.

industrialists: People who engage in profit-making enterprises that manufacture a certain product, such as textiles or steel.

industrialization: The development of industry.

Industrial Revolution: A period of rapid industrial growth causing a shift in focus from agriculture to industry beginning in the late eighteenth century and continuing through the nineteenth century. During this time new manufacturing technologies and improved transportation gave rise to the modern factory system and a massive movement of the population from the countryside to the cities. The Industrial Revolution began in England around 1760 and spread to the United States around 1780.

industry: A distinct group of profit-making enterprises that manufacture a certain product, such as the textile or steel industry.

infant mortality: The percentage of babies born in a year that die before they reach the age of one.

intellectual: A person devoted to study, analysis, and reflection, using rational intellect rather than emotions in pursuit of enlightenment.

interchangeable parts: Standardized units of a machine that could be used in any machine of that model.

interstate commerce: Trade that crosses the borders between states.

L

labor union: An organization of workers formed to protect and further their mutual interests by bargaining as a group with their employers over wages, working conditions, and benefits.

laissez-faire: An economic doctrine that opposes government regulation of commerce and industry beyond the minimum necessary.

loom: A frame or machine used to weave thread or yarns into cloth.

M

machine tool: A machine that shapes solid materials.

machinist: A worker skilled in operating machine tools.

magnate: A powerful and influential person in an industry.

manufacture: To make something from raw materials, usually as part of a large-scale system of production using machinery.

mass production: The manufacture of goods in quantity by using machines and standardized designs and parts.

mechanize: To equip with mechanical power.

mediation: Intervention to help two opposing sides of a dispute reach an agreement.

monopoly: The exclusive possession or right to produce a particular good or service.

muckrakers: Journalists who search for and expose corruption in public affairs.

N

New Deal: A set of legislative programs and policies for economic recovery and social reform initiated in the 1930s during the presidency of Franklin Delano Roosevelt.

O

omnibus: A horse-drawn coach for hire.

overhead expenses: The costs of running a business not directly related to producing the goods, such as rent or heating and lighting the workspace.

overproduction: An economic condition that occurs when there are more goods on the market than there are consumers to purchase them, usually leading to lower prices.

P

patent: A legal document issued by a government granting exclusive authority to an inventor for making, using, and selling an invention.

pension: A fixed sum paid regularly, usually as a retirement benefit.

philanthropy: The desire or effort to help humankind, as by making charitable donations.

pools: Agreements among rival companies to share their profits or divide up territories to avoid destructive competition and maintain higher prices.

postindustrial era: A time marked by the lessened importance of manufacturing and increased importance of service industries.

productivity: The amount of work someone can do in a set amount of time.

Progressive Era: The period of the Industrial Revolution that spanned roughly from the 1890s to about 1920, in which reformers worked together in the interest of distributing political power and wealth more equally.

public domain: Land held by the federal government.

pulley: Simple machine consisting of a wheel with a groove through which a rope passes. The pulley is used to move things up, down, or across, such as a flagpole or a curtain rod.

R

refinery: A building in which a raw material is processed to free it from impurities.

reservations: Land set aside by the U.S. government for use by Native Americans.

robots: Machines that automatically perform routine, often complex, tasks.

S

settlement houses: Places established and run by educated, and often wealthy, reformers to provide social and educational services to the residents of poor urban immigrant communities.

sharecropper: A tenant farmer who works the land for an agreed share of the value of the crop, minus the deductions taken out of his share for his rent, supplies, and living costs.

shuttle: A device that carries threads across a loom in the weaving process.

slums: Severely overcrowded urban areas characterized by the most extreme conditions of poverty, run-down housing, and crime.

speculator: A person who takes a business risk in the hope of making a profit, particularly when buying or selling stocks or commodities (economic goods) in order to profit from shifts in the market.

socialism: An economic system in which the means of production and distribution is owned collectively by all the workers and there is no private property or social classes.

solidarity: Unity based on common interests.

steam engine: An engine that burns fuel to heat water into steam, which becomes the power that turns the parts of the engine.

stock: An element of ownership of a corporation that has been divided up into shares that can be bought and sold.

stock market: A system for trade in companies, ventures, and other investments through the buying and selling of stocks, bonds, mutual funds, limited partnerships, and other securities.

strike: A work stoppage by employees to protest conditions or make demands of their employer.

sweatshop: A factory in which workers work long hours in poor conditions for very low wages.

T

tariffs: Government-imposed fees on imported goods.

telegraph: Any system that transmits encoded information by signal across a distance.

tenant farmer: Someone who farms land owned by someone else and pays rent or a share of the crop for the use of the land.

tenement: Urban dwellings rented by impoverished families that barely meet or fail to meet the minimum standards of safety, sanitation, and comfort.

textile: Cloth.

transcontinental: Spanning the continent from one coast to the other.

transcontinental railroad: A railroad that spans a continent, from coast to coast.

trusts: A group of companies, joined for the purpose of reducing competition and controlling prices..

turnover: Employees quitting their jobs and others being hired to take their place.

turnpike: A road which people have to pay to use.

V

ventilation: Air circulation or access to fresh air.

vertical expansion: Growth that occurs when a primary company purchases other companies that provide services or products needed for the company's business, in order to avoid paying competitive prices.

W

wage worker: A person who works for others for pay.

Wall Street: Financial district and home of the nation's major stock exchanges in New York, New York.

warp yarn: The threads that run lengthwise on a loom.

waterwheel: A wheel that rotates due to the force of moving water; the rotation of the wheel is then used to power a factory or machine.

woof: The threads that run crosswise on a loom.

work ethic: A belief in the moral good of work.

workers' compensation: Payments made to an employee who is injured at work.

Y

Yankee: A Southern word for Northerners.

Development of the Industrial U.S.
Biographies

Jane Addams

Born September 6, 1860 (Cedarville, Illinois)
Died May 21, 1935 (Chicago, Illinois)

Social worker

J ane Addams founded the pioneering social settlement of Hull House in Chicago in 1889. It operated by the principle that only through living among the poor could aid workers truly understand their situation and provide help. She and her fellow workers were women from relatively wealthy and educated backgrounds who were determined to improve the dangerous and unhealthy living conditions in the city's poorer neighborhoods. Located in one such area, Addams's Hull House provided a variety of social services to the largely immigrant population, and it went on to become a model for many other settlement houses and community centers around the United States. Addams was widely known and honored during her lifetime, and in 1931 she became the first American woman to win the Nobel Prize for peace.

Addams came from the town of Cedarville, Illinois. Her newlywed parents had arrived there not long after the last local Native American tribe, the Pottawatomies, had sold their lands and left the area. She was born Laura Jane Addams on September 6, 1860, the eighth child in her family but only the fifth to survive—cholera (a disease that affects the stomach

"Nothing so deadens the sympathies and shrivels the power of enjoyment, as the persistent keeping away from the great opportunities for helpfulness and a continual ignoring of the starvation struggle which makes up the life of at least half the race."

Jane Addams. *(Courtesy of The Library of Congress.)*

and intestines) had claimed three previous siblings. When she was two, her pregnant mother collapsed and was taken to bed, but neither mother nor baby survived. Addams later said that this was one of her first memories.

Early life and education

Addams was devoted to her father during her childhood and teens. John Huy Addams (1854–1870) was a prosperous local leader, one of the founders of Cedarville and the owner of the town's sawmill and gristmill (a mill for grinding grain).

A native of Pennsylvania, he was a Quaker and was known for his unshakable honesty. He was already serving in the Illinois state senate by the time Addams was born and was friends with another Illinois political figure, future U.S. president Abraham Lincoln (1809–1865; served 1861–65).

Addams's father encouraged her to read extensively, and she emerged as an excellent student in her teens. She hoped to enroll at Smith College in Massachusetts, one of the new, women-only Eastern schools that featured a challenging academic program, but her father would not permit it because the school was too far away. Instead she entered nearby Rockford Women's Seminary, as her sisters had done. Addams hoped that she might help the less fortunate in society by becoming a doctor—still a relatively rare occurrence for a woman in her time—but her family was opposed to this plan as well, considering it an unseemly profession for a female. She graduated in 1881 as her class valedictorian.

In the years after she finished at Rockford, Addams occupied her time with travel and independent study, and she took courses at the Women's Medical College of Philadelphia for a time. Ill health forced her to quit, and back at home she was frustrated by the lack of choices open to her outside of marriage and motherhood. Her stepmother, Ann Haldeman Addams, urged her to marry a son from her first marriage, George, whom Addams had thought of as a brother for much of her life, but she rejected this idea. Addams suffered from several health issues during these years, including what may have been chronic fatigue syndrome, a condition marked by tiredness, confusion, and sometimes fever. She also underwent spinal surgery and wore a back brace made from leather, steel, and whalebone.

The rise of Hull House

Addams found her direction in life after an 1888 visit to London, England, where she went to see Toynbee Hall, the first so-called settlement house, which was located in an overcrowded, extremely poor section of the city of Whitechapel. Toynbee Hall was a pleasant contrast to the rest of the area, however. It was the work of Reverend Samuel A. Barnett (1844–1913) and was staffed by Oxford University students. The idea was to live among the poor, which was believed to be the best

Hull House, in Chicago, Illinois. *(AP/Wide World Photos. Reproduced by permission.)*

way to improve their living conditions and show a commitment to Christian charity and helping those less fortunate.

Addams decided to move to Chicago with a friend from her Rockford school days, **Ellen Gates Starr** (1859–1940; see entry) and establish her own settlement house. She arrived in the city in early 1889 and went to work finding a suitable property. Due to the widespread railroad network, Chicago had become a national transportation center, and industry in the area was growing rapidly. Although the city was thriving—it was the second largest city in the United States after New York—it was overcrowded and struggling with the arrival of many new residents from the farms of the Midwest and from Europe. The European immigrants lived in the worst neighborhoods. They had come to the city to find work in Chicago's giant meatpacking houses, where cattle and hogs arrived daily by train from the Midwest and were slaughtered for the canned meat products that had become a main part of the American diet. The average laborer worked ten- or twelve-hour shifts, usually for less than $4 a day, and under harsh and often dangerous conditions.

Addams found a property to rent at Halsted and Polk streets, a mansion surrounded by some of the city's worst slums. It had been built three decades earlier by a real estate developer, Charles J. Hull (1820–1889), but with the rise of the nearby meatpacking and shipbuilding industries, shaky wooden houses had sprung up in the area and multiplied. Three or four families often shared small houses that had no indoor plumbing. Outside, sidewalks were made from wooden planks that fell apart quickly, and the streets became rivers of mud during the springtime. Fishing for rats underneath the sidewalks was a popular pastime for children in the neighborhood. The bodies of horses that collapsed on the job were often left to rot.

A divided America

The rapid inflow of immigrants who provided cheap labor for the Industrial Revolution had become one of the defining events of American social history and was a major focus of Addams's newfound mission to serve others. She saw that there had been much wealth created suddenly in the city, thanks to the shift from a farming economy to a manufacturing one, but she also recognized that such prosperity came at a price. The city's housing supply simply could not expand quickly enough to accommodate all those who came looking for low-wage jobs and there were almost no social services to help the poor.

Urban areas like Chicago became severely divided between the rich and the poor. The rich began to fear this new lower class, as some new radical political movements emerged among the poor. Addams and other idealists of the era fought to raise awareness of another radical new idea gaining some popularity at the time: that the poor were not responsible for their troubles—the system was. The poor would remain an underclass, some believed, so long as they were forced to live in conditions that were harmful to the creation of a stable household and safe community. For example, only about one third of the children in the neighborhood where Hull House began were even enrolled in school.

Jane Addams sitting with a group of children at Hull House. *(AP/Wide World Photos. Reproduced by permission.)*

Addams spent nearly $5,000 of her own money to renovate the Hull mansion and raised additional money from local civic leaders. She and Starr moved in, and in September 1889 Hull House opened its doors to their somewhat mismatched new neighbors. There was even the occasional burglar at first, and Addams surprised one in her room one night. The intruder moved to leave by the second-story window, but Addams calmly told him to use the stairs instead and let himself out the front door. Soon, the younger neighborhood children were coming to Hull House to play and take part in crafts activities, and they were followed by older siblings and then parents. Addams, Starr, and the other women who joined them taught classes in sewing, the arts, and even English as a second language. They organized a variety of clubs for children and adults, held a regular lecture series,

Hull House's Historic Firsts

During its years of operation Hull House achieved many historic firsts, some of which are listed below.

- First social settlement that allowed both male and female residents in the United States.
- First citizenship preparation classes for immigrants in the United States.
- First day care and kindergarten in Chicago.
- First public playground in Chicago.
- First public gymnasium and swimming pool in Chicago.
- First college extension courses offered in Chicago.
- Hosted Chicago's first Boy Scout troop.

and ran a community kitchen that served hot, healthy lunches. Hull House soon featured Chicago's first kindergarten and day care center, as well as the city's first playground on a nearby lot. There was a gymnasium, a library, and even an employment agency, and by the second year college-level courses were being offered. Off-site, Addams established affordable cooperative housing for the young working women who worked in the city's shops. She also joined other local leaders in the movement to end child labor in factories and meatpacking houses.

Social reform efforts

Many of the men and women from educated or middle-class backgrounds who came to help out at Hull House and similar institutions were highly influential in the creation of the Progressive political movement in America. The Progressive Era was the period of the Industrial Revolution that spanned roughly from the 1890s to about 1920 during which reformers worked together in the interest of distributing political power and wealth more equally in the United States. The Progressive political party was founded by President Theodore Roosevelt (1858–1919; served 1901–9), who often visited Hull House over the years and supported Addams's mission. In turn she became a delegate to the Progressive Party's first national convention in 1912 and seconded Roosevelt's nomination as the party's presidential candidate. Other prominent visitors to Hull House included American educational reformer John Dewey (1859–1852); English Labour Party leader James Ramsay MacDonald (1866–1937); Sidney and Beatrice Webb (1859–1947 and 1858–1943), also from England and heads of the Fabian Socialist movement, whose ideals appealed to English intellectuals; and feminist writer Charlotte Perkins Gilman (1860–1935).

Because of the reputation it achieved, Hull House and its mission became closely linked to political and social movements that sought reform during the twentieth century. Advocates for the working classes helped secure the passage of federal and state laws that granted workers the right to organize. Activists also urged authorities to regulate a variety of health issues that affected daily life. Such groups vastly improved the standard of living for generations of working men and women.

Addams took an active role in such efforts. In 1894 a typhoid epidemic broke out in the Halsted Street area. The disease passed from person to person, causing headaches, weakness, and intestinal problems. Addams decided that the piles of rotting garbage littering the neighborhood, which caused the illness, needed to be removed. Chicago was divided into wards (districts) run by officials called aldermen, many of whom had been elected through dishonest means. Addams knew that her ward's alderman had given the garbage collection job to a political supporter, who simply took the money without doing the work. She decided to submit a bid to the city council to do the garbage collection herself. Her bid was rejected, but her daring challenge attracted much press coverage, and the mayor appointed her the garbage collection supervisor for the 19th Ward, where Hull House was located. She was the first woman in the city to hold such a job.

Addams was named to many other commissions and investigative panels, including an 1895 one that reported on the terrible conditions at the Cook County poorhouse, and a campaign that regulated the safety of milk. Hull House earned national attention, and many articles were written about Addams's work in magazines and newspapers of the era. By 1892, its third year of operation, Hull House was one of six settlement houses in the United States. Five years later that number had risen to seventy-four, and then to more than one hundred by 1910. Addams was regarded as one of the founding figures in the profession of social work.

Emerged as renowned national figure

Hull House's two-decade anniversary was marked with Addams's 1910 autobiography, *Twenty Years at Hull House*. Addams served as the first woman president of the National Conference of Charities and Corrections, founded the National Foundation of Settlements and Neighborhood Centers, and in 1910 became the first woman to be granted an honorary degree by Yale University. She publicly opposed World War I (1914–18; a war in which Great Britain, France, the United States and their allies defeated Germany, Austria-Hungary, and their allies), campaigned for women's suffrage (the right to vote), and was one of the main figures of the Women's Peace Party, formed in 1915. Later she became president of the International Congress of Women, which evolved into the Women's International Peace League for Peace and Freedom, and she held its presidency until her death.

In 1931 Addams was a co-recipient of the Nobel Prize for peace, sharing it with Nicholas Murray Butler (1862–1947), a noted educator and longtime president of Columbia University. She did not attend the ceremony, however, due to a heart condition, and she died of cancer on May 21, 1935. She was buried at her family's plot in Cedarville, but Hull House continued operation for many years after her death. In the 1960s the original compound became part of the new Chicago campus of the University of Illinois, and Hull House survived there as a museum into the early twenty-first century.

For More Information

Books

Diliberto, Gioia. *A Useful Woman: The Early Life of Jane Addams*. New York: Scribner/A Lisa Drew Book, 1999.

Linn, James Weber. *Jane Addams: A Biography*. Chicago: University of Illinois Press, 2000.

Web Sites

Urban Experience in Chicago: Hull-House and Its Neighborhoods, 1889–1963. http://www.uic.edu/jaddams/hull/urbanexp/contents.htm (accessed on July 7, 2005).

Carolyn Webster Schermerhorn Astor

Born September 22, 1830 (New York, New York)
Died October 30, 1908 (New York, New York)

Socialite

"She was America's substitute for grand duchess and queen."

Milton Rugoff.

Prior to the Gilded Age, the era of industrialization from the early 1860s to the turn of the century in which a few wealthy individuals gained tremendous power and influence, there was a limited number of very rich and privileged families in the United States. The rural nature of the country had long prevented a large wealthy class from rising, since farming did not usually generate huge profits. Similarly, few people could claim an elite ancestry, since most Americans were descended from farmers.

In 1845 there were only ten millionaires living in New York City. They generally kept to themselves and saw little need to show off their wealth. Starting in the late 1860s, however, the soaring profits of new industries created thousands of newly wealthy families, many of whom migrated to the city. The older families called the newcomers the "nouveaux riche," or new rich, an insulting term indicating a lack of tradition and refinement. The newcomers quickly began spending large amounts of their money in highly public ways. They bought huge mansions, fancy carriages pulled by the best horses, and expensive jewelry and clothing. They hired lots of servants and held elaborate balls and

Caroline Webster Schermerhorn Astor.

dinners. The old rich found ways to show off their money as well, while at the same time demonstrating their superior social qualities. Since no real hierarchy (system of ranking in position) existed in the community, the old rich basically created one, and a set of fashionable socialites (socially prominent people) was born. Caroline Webster Schermerhorn Astor, or "Mrs. Astor," as she preferred to be called, was the best-known leader of this movement to redefine the upper crust of New York.

Caroline Astor was born in New York in 1830. Her father was a wealthy merchant with good connections in New York society. Both of her parents' ancestry dated back to the early Dutch settlers of New York. The Schermerhorns claimed to be of Dutch patroon heritage. The patroon system was created in the early seventeenth century by the Dutch West Indies Company, an international trading company based in Holland, to get people to emigrate from Holland to the United States. The company would give a very large grant of land in the United States to any person who would bring over fifty or more colonists at his own expense. In exchange, the patroon owned all the lands in his area and ruled with great authority over his colonists, from whom he collected rent. Some scholars, though, have questioned whether all of the Schermerhorn ancestors were from patroon lineage. In any case, Caroline was considered to be from one of the oldest and most aristocratic New York families and in 1853 she achieved what appeared to be the perfect marriage—the union of her aristocratic background with the immense wealth of William Backhouse Astor Jr. (1830–1892).

The Astor background

Mrs. Astor's new husband was the grandson of merchant John Jacob Astor (1763–1848), whose American Fur Company created the first monopoly (exclusive possession or right to produce a particular good or service) on the fur trade in U.S. territories. John Jacob Astor soon became the wealthiest man in the country. He used his money to buy land in the thinly populated northern sections of Manhattan (a part of New York City) and built commercial buildings and apartments in them. As years went by and real estate values rose, these Manhattan real estate holdings became the basis of the tremendous Astor family fortune.

John Jacob Astor's son, William Backhouse Astor Sr. (1792–1875), inherited about half of his father's wealth and continued to make real estate investments in New York. As large numbers of immigrants began moving into the city in the late 1840s, an urgent need for more living quarters arose. Astor converted many of his buildings into crowded tenements, or urban dwellings rented by impoverished families that barely met minimum standards of safety, sanitation, and comfort. He rented out tiny, airless rooms at high prices. Developing a bad reputation among the less fortunate residents of the city, Astor became known as the "landlord of New York." Many complaints were made about the unhealthy condition of his buildings, but it was years before Astor began to make some improvements. William Astor Sr. left an estate of about $50 million, dividing it up between his two sons, John Jacob III (1822–1890) and the man who later became Mrs. Astor's husband, William Backhouse Jr.

Family life

Caroline and William Backhouse Astor Jr. had five children, the youngest of which was their only son, John Jacob IV (1864–1912). The marriage was never a close or loving union. While Mrs. Astor was socially active, her husband preferred a peaceful evening at his club, long sails on the family yacht, and horseback riding at his estate in the Hudson River Valley. Nonetheless, in 1856, Mrs. Astor convinced him to build the family a home on Fifth Avenue in an area that was becoming popular with the rich. Mrs. Astor's house was an elegant brownstone mansion noted for a large art gallery, which could be converted into a grand ballroom that could accommodate several hundred people.

For most of the 1860s the family lived in the quiet manner of New York's older families, not drawing unnecessary attention to themselves. By the early 1870s, however, Mrs. Astor began pursuing the supreme goal of high society mothers of the time—making good matches (finding romantic partners with money and social standing) for her children. With her daughters frequently accompanying her, she began a busy routine of socializing. She appeared at all the upper-class galas in New York during the winter season; lodged in Newport, Rhode Island, during the summer season; and spent the rest of the year in various elite European settings.

The Patriarchs and the List of 400

In 1872 Mrs. Astor met Ward McAllister (1827–1895), who would become her longtime partner as a society leader and raise her to the status of the queen of New York high society. McAllister decided to become a society man around 1852. His first step was a long trip to Europe where he mixed with the upper class and learned the arts of refined society. When he came back to the United States, he formed an elegant and exclusive social scene in the previously sleepy town of Newport. After his success there, he focused on New York,

Ward McAllister (above) and Caroline Astor created the "List of Four Hundred" fashionable people in New York society. (© Corbis.)

declaring himself the one to ask about foods, wines, dress, and all matters of etiquette (manners). He divided New York society into the Nobs (old money) and Swells (new money). One of his first acts was to form a loose organization of twenty-five of New York's oldest families. The men who headed these families were called Patriarchs, and it was their duty to give an annual ball. Each of the Patriarchs was to invite nine other people—five women and four men—to each ball. This created a select group that included acceptable people from among both Nobs and Swells. In his memoirs, *Society As I Have Found It* (1890), McAllister describes the purpose behind the balls:

> The whole secret of the success of the Patriarch Balls lay in making them select; in making them the most brilliant balls of each winter; in making it extremely difficult to obtain an invitation to them, and to make such invitations of great value; to make them the stepping-stone to the best New York society, that one might be sure that any one repeatedly invited to them had a secure social position, and to make them the best managed, the best looked-after balls given in this city.

McAllister and Mrs. Astor met while she was preparing for the coming out (first appearance as a grown, and therefore eligible for marriage, woman) of her oldest daughter. He wrote in his book that he "at once recognized her ability, and felt that she would become society's leader, and that she was admirably qualified for the position." Together Mrs. Astor and McAllister created a New York institution unlike any other at the time: Mrs. Astor's annual ball. They put together what they referred to as a List of Four Hundred, the number of people invited to the ball. Some say the list was limited to the number of people Mrs. Astor's ballroom could accommodate, but this was generally believed to be a myth. McAllister told a reporter from the *New York Tribune* in 1888 the reason for the number four hundred:

> Why, there are only about 400 people in fashionable New York society. If you go outside that number you strike people who are either not at ease in a ballroom or else make other people not at ease.... Now with the rapid growth of riches millionaires are too common to receive much deference.... So we have to draw social boundaries on another basis; old connections, gentle breeding, perfection in all the requisite accomplishments of a gentleman, elegant leisure and an unstained private reputation count for more than newly gained riches.

Mrs. Astor's balls

Mrs. Astor was a plain woman with little humor and a stern, dignified manner. Her annual balls were not known for witty or interesting conversation and few considered them fun. The ballroom was always beautifully decorated, however, filled with expensive china, silver, crystal, flower arrangements, and art pieces. The servants were dressed in livery (uniforms) that had been copied from that of the royal servants at England's Windsor Castle. The balls were perfectly organized and managed, and, with carefully selected guests and discussion generally limited to the weather and upcoming balls and weddings, there were few embarrassing moments.

The balls began around 11 PM when guests arrived at the brilliantly lit house on Fifth Avenue. They were met by a reception line at the end of which was Mrs. Astor, standing under a large and highly flattering portrait of herself. Along with an elaborate and expensive gown, she wore so many diamonds and other jewels it was said that she could not sit back in her chair comfortably. When the reception period was over, Mrs. Astor would lead her guests into the art gallery that served as the grand ballroom. Mrs. Astor's red silk throne was placed on one side of the room, and many of the female guests hoped to be asked to take the places of honor near it. An orchestra played from a balcony.

Dinners were served on gold-plated china, with silver and crystal utensils. The tables were piled so heavily with serving ware that they sometimes had to be braced in order to hold up the weight. At each place setting there were different forks for salads, fish, vegetables, meats, and desserts. Knowing which fork to use for which food was considered a part of the refinement necessary to belonging to high society.

Thorstein Veblen and *The Theory of the Leisure Class*

One of the outspoken critics of the wealthy and business classes during the Gilded Age was social scientist Thorstein Veblen (1857–1929). The sixth of twelve children born to Norwegian immigrant parents, Veblen grew up in rural Minnesota. He graduated in 1880 from Carleton College, Minnesota, and in 1884 earned a doctorate in philosophy at Yale. After leaving Yale he was forced to spend seven unhappy years on his family's farm in Minnesota after he failed to find an academic job. In 1891 Veblen revived his academic career by enrolling as a graduate student in economics at Cornell University. A year later he became a professor at the University of Chicago, where he remained for the next fourteen years. While at the university he wrote his first and best-known book, *The Theory of the Leisure Class* (1899).

The Theory of the Leisure Class presented a complex economic and social theory as well as a sometimes humorous study of the rich during the last half of the nineteenth century. The book was an unexpected success. Veblen wrote of U.S. economic life as if he were an anthropologist describing the traits of an ancient culture, noting that a leisure class was generally to be found in the higher levels of barbarian societies. Labor in those societies was associated with weakness and lack of power. He argued that the unfavorable view of working for a living continued to present times:

> The . . . distinction between the base and the honourable in the manner of a man's life retains very much of its ancient force even today. So much so that there are few of the better class who are not possessed of an instinctive repugnance [disgust] for the vulgar forms of labour. . . . It is felt by all persons of refined taste that a spiritual contamination [corruption] is inseparable from certain offices [jobs] that are conventionally required of servants. Vulgar surroundings, mean (that is to say, inexpensive) habitations, and vulgarly productive occupations are unhesitatingly condemned and avoided. . . . From the days of the Greek philosophers to the present, a degree of leisure and of exemption [freedom] from contact with such industrial processes as serve the immediate everyday purposes of human life has ever been recognised by thoughtful men as a prerequisite [necessity] to a worthy or beautiful, or even a blameless, human life.

In this book Veblen introduced the term "conspicuous consumption" to describe

Many New Yorkers waited nervously each year for their invitation to Mrs. Astor's ball. Not being invited meant that one was not accepted in New York's high society. For the socially ambitious, the lack of an invitation was devastating and had lasting consequences. That, of course, was the point of the List of 400—to create an exclusive club in the new urban and industrial society. Mrs. Astor did not care for the crude manners of many of the new rich. She developed a particular dislike for the family of the wealthy railroad businessman **Cornelius Vanderbilt** (1794–1877; see entry). Vanderbilt was a rough

Thorstein Veblen. *(© Corbis.)*

compared this to the elite members of ancient tribes, who limited their activities to warring with neighboring tribes, sports, and festivals, and displayed their collections of enemies' goods (or heads) to show their superiority. According to his theory, conspicuous consumption began when the leisure class first learned the art of discrimination: that is, learning to pick out fine wines, the best textiles, and good foods. Conspicuous consumption changes the rich person's "life of leisure into a more or less arduous [difficult] application to the business of learning how to live a life of ostensible [seeming] leisure in a becoming way. Closely related to the requirement that the gentleman must consume freely and of the right kind of goods, there is the requirement that he must know how to consume them in a seemly manner." Conspicuous consumption, Veblen said, led to irrational spending.

Although Veblen's book presented a highly sophisticated economic theory that attacked the mannerisms of the businessmen and middle class of the day, many of his readers were more delighted with the book's exposure of the ridiculous attitudes of the aristocratic families.

the actions of the wealthy. He claimed that the rich felt the urge to buy wildly expensive and often strange things, but that they did not buy these things in order to make themselves happy. Veblen believed they were compelled into this behavior mainly to show others how rich they were, and he

man who chewed tobacco and used vulgar language in mixed company, things of which Mrs. Astor did not approve. Cornelius had never been interested in fashionable society, but his grandson William and William's wife, socialite Alva Vanderbilt, were determined to take their place on Mrs. Astor's List of 400. They built a grand mansion near the Astors on Fifth Avenue, but Mrs. Astor continued to ignore them. Alva then befriended Mrs. Astor's daughter, Carrie, and made certain that she was around during the planning of a very large costume ball at the Vanderbilt home—one of the biggest social events of the year. Then she let it be known that she could not invite Carrie to the party since Mrs. Astor had never paid a visit to the Vanderbilts. In order to ensure an invitation for her daughter, Mrs. Astor included the Vanderbilts in her invitations from that time on.

"The" Mrs. Astor and the Waldorf-Astoria Hotel

Mrs. Astor had insisted from the time of her marriage on being called simply "Mrs. Astor," to show that she was "the" Mrs. Astor, queen of the Astor family as well as of New York society. This did not please her husband's nephew, William Waldorf Astor. Upon the death of his father, John Jacob Astor III (William Backhouse Astor Jr.'s older brother), William claimed that his wife, Mary, was entitled to be "the" Mrs. Astor. Mrs. Astor, however, would not under any circumstances give up her title. Hostilities grew, continuing well beyond the death of William Backhouse Astor Jr. in 1892. In 1893 William Waldorf Astor and his wife moved to England in disgust, but Mrs. Astor's nephew took a final parting shot at her. He had his father's house, which was right next door to hers, torn down, and on the property he built the original Waldorf Hotel. With a busy hotel right next door, Mrs. Astor and her family were forced to move.

In the end, however, the Astors profited from the move. Mrs. Astor's son, John Jacob IV, had his mother's old house destroyed and built the Astoria Hotel in its place. The Astoria was sixteen stories high, five floors higher than its neighbor, the Waldorf. The two elegant hotels were connected by an indoor bridge. In 1897 they merged to become the famous Waldorf-Astoria Hotel, the largest hotel in the world, and for a couple of decades it drew the rich and famous from all over the world.

The decline of an era and its queen

In 1893 Mrs. Astor moved to a large and beautiful double mansion on Fifth Avenue at 65th Street. It had a private living area for her and another for her son and his family, but they shared entertaining halls. There she continued to give her annual balls, but they were no longer the important social events they had once been. She also still spent the summers at Beechwood, her mansion in Newport, where she entertained her distinguished, but aging, guests. She no longer relied on the advice of McAllister, who died in 1895, a few years after he became a subject of public ridicule for his outdated snobbery. Times and attitudes toward society were changing.

In 1893 the United States experienced a severe economic depression (a period of drastic decline in the economy). The depression began with the failure of several railroads, and soon hundreds of banks and businesses collapsed in the Northeast. Thousands of farmers lost their farms, and unemployed industrial workers could not pay rent and many became homeless. Poor families could be seen walking the streets in search of food or work. Large labor union strikes resulted in violent conflicts between workers and the powerful industrialists.

The economy started to recover in 1897. Along with new industries came many fresh job opportunities, increases in educational and leisure activities, and a growing middle class. But the public was more aware than ever that American wealth and income remained unevenly distributed. For the first time since the beginning of U.S. industrialization, people from all social classes joined together to demand political reforms. This was the beginning of the Progressive Era, the period of the Industrial Revolution that spanned roughly from the 1890s to about 1920, in which reformers worked together in the interest of distributing political power and wealth more equally. It was a time when many journalists chose to write about the huge gap between the poor and the rich. Articles ridiculing the upper class's waste of money and energy on unnecessary pursuits became popular reading material. The showy displays of riches on Fifth Avenue did not end, but they received scornful attention from many people.

By the late 1890s, wealthy New Yorkers were paying much less attention to the strict social rituals that had ruled the city in the previous decades. They saw Mrs. Astor as an amusing representative of another time. Although recognized as the queen of a former culture, she would never hold a place of authority in her city again. In 1905 Mrs. Astor suffered a stroke. She lived an invalid until her death in 1908. With her passing, one of the last visible and memorable personalities of the Gilded Age was gone.

For More Information

Books

Homberger, Eric. *Mrs. Astor's New York: Money and Social Power in a Gilded Age*. New Haven, CT: Yale University Press, 2004.

McAllister, Ward. *Society As I Have Found It*. New York: Cassell, 1890.

Ruggoff, Milton. *America's Gilded Age: Intimate Portraits from an Era of Extravagance and Change, 1850–1890*. New York: Henry Holt and Company, 1989.

Smith, Page. *The Rise of Industrial America: A People's History of the Post-Reconstruction Era*. New York: McGraw-Hill, 1984.

Periodicals

"A Chat with Ward McAllister: How He Came to Be a Famous Ball Organizer." *New York Tribune* (March 25, 1888): p. 11.

Web Sites

"A Classification of American Wealth: History and Genealogy of the Wealthy Families of America. Part 2: America in the Gilded Age." http://www.raken.com/american_wealth/encyclopedia/comment_1891.asp (accessed on July 7, 2005).

Micheletti, Ellen. "The Gilded Age." *All About Romance*. http://www.likesbooks.com/gildedage.html (accessed on July 7, 2005).

Veblen, Thorstein. *The Theory of the Leisure Class*. Text available online at American Studies at the University of Virginia. http://xroads. virginia.edu/~HYPER/VEBLEN/veblenhp.html (accessed on July 7, 2005).

Alexander Graham Bell

Born March 3, 1847 (Edinburgh, Scotland)
Died August 2, 1922 (Nova Scotia, Canada)

Inventor
Teacher

A lexander Graham Bell's most famous invention, the telephone, was the result of his primary career focus: teaching the deaf to speak. Bell had been successful in his work with the hearing-impaired and had instructed a generation of teachers in his methods. He sought to reproduce human speech by creating a machine with a wire that could be vibrated by the voice. Backed by a team of eager financial supporters, Bell and his assistant, Thomas Watson (1854–1934), perfected their speech-transmission device in March 1876. Their invention revolutionized communication and created an entirely new industry.

"Business is hateful to me at all times."

Bell family background

Bell was born on March 3, 1847, in Edinburgh, Scotland, and was the middle child of three sons. He shared the same given name as his well-known grandfather, who was a professor of elocution (the art of public speaking in which gesture, vocal production, and delivery were emphasized) in London, England, and the author of several books on speech impediments and pronunciation. Bell's father, Alexander Melville

Alexander Graham Bell. *(AT&T Bell Laboratories. Reproduced by permission.)*

Bell, carried out similar research on human speech and elocution and devised a system he called visible speech. This was a set of symbols that indicated the proper position of the lips, throat, and tongue for each of the sounds produced by the human voice. It was the first universal phonetic alphabet, and was originally created by Bell's father as a learning tool for foreign languages. He realized that it could also be used to teach the sounds of speech to the deaf, an important discovery in his own household, for his wife and Bell's mother, Eliza Grace Symonds, began to lose her hearing in the late 1850s.

Bell was taught at home by his mother when he was very young, but at the age of ten he entered McLauren's Academy in Edinburgh. He finished at the city's Royal High School at the age of thirteen. He spent several months with his grandfather in London and then took a student teaching position at the Weston House Academy in Elgin, Scotland. He was already conducting experiments in speech with his brother, once building a skull that spoke the word "ma-ma" when air was blown through it. He became particularly fascinated by the work of a German scientist, Hermann von Helmholtz (1821–1894), which involved reproducing vowel sounds with the help of tuning forks that had been wired with a basic electrical current.

When Alexander Bell, the grandfather, died in 1865, Bell's father relocated to London in order to continue his work. The twenty-year-old Bell joined him there in 1867, the same year his younger brother, Edward, died of tuberculosis, an infectious disease of the lungs. In 1868 Bell enrolled at University College in London, where he studied anatomy and physiology. He also carried on his father's research work on visible speech while his father visited the United States on an extended lecture tour in 1868. Melville Bell's book, *Visible Speech: The Science of Universal Alphabets* had failed to attract much attention in European scientific circles, and when Melly, the eldest of the three Bell sons, also died of tuberculosis, the family decided to move to Canada for its better climate. They settled in Brantford, Ontario, in August 1870.

Bell in Boston

Bell continued to experiment with various means of reproducing sound and began working on his version of a harmonic telegraph, which could tell the difference between various musical notes. It had a potentially profitable use in the field of telegraphy, the first electronic form of communication. A working transmitter that used this principle would allow the transmission of several messages across a single telegraph wire, thereby reducing costs significantly.

Bell's main focus during these years, however, was teaching the deaf, which grew out of his work with visible speech. He devised a method to notate his father's work and was invited to come to Boston, Massachusetts, to train teachers of the deaf there. By late 1872 he had founded his own school in the city, and the following year he became a professor of vocal physiology and the mechanics of speech at Boston University's School of Oratory. He became well known for his methods and was a leading advocate in his time for teaching the deaf to communicate orally. Sign language was another means of communication for the hearing-impaired, but Bell recognized that there were varying degrees of deafness. Some students, he discovered, could be taught the phonetic sounds of the alphabet, and how to use them to communicate orally.

Bell took private pupils occasionally, and in 1873 he moved in with a wealthy family in Haverhill, Massachusetts, to teach their son, who had been deaf since birth. The boy's progress under Bell's education so impressed the father, Thomas Sanders, that the prosperous leather merchant offered to finance Bell's scientific experiments in the harmonic telegraph and the phonautograph, another invention he was working on at the time. The phonautograph, based on an earlier version created by a French inventor, Leon Scott (1817–1879), would help deaf students correct their tone. Both of these research projects led Bell to the creation of the telephone.

Teamed with Watson

By 1874 Bell learned that Elisha Gray (1835–1901), an employee of the Chicago-based Western Electric Company, which supplied the relays and other equipment to the telegraph industry, was also working on a project similar to the harmonic telegraph for the transmission of sounds through electrical current. Thomas Sanders and another backer, a well-connected Bostonian named Gardiner G. Hubbard who was also president of a school for the deaf, urged Bell to file the paperwork for a patent. A patent is a legal document giving an inventor the exclusive right to make, use, or sell an invention for a certain term of years. In early 1875 Bell began working out of an electrical shop on Court Street in Boston, and teamed there with a young assistant to perfect his harmonic telegraph. Thomas Watson was a skilled machinist from Salem, Massachusetts, who had a particular expertise in electrical engineering, which Bell lacked.

The first of Bell's two important patents, No. 161,739, for an "Improvement in Transmitters and Receivers for Electrical Telegraphs," was filed on April 6, 1875. Two months later Bell

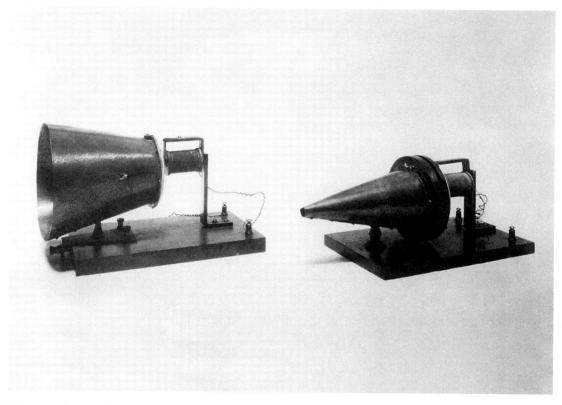

The transmitter and receiver of Bell's first telephone. *(© Bettmann/Corbis.)*

realized when tuning the reeds of his harmonic telegraph model that a steel spring could reproduce both the tone and the overtones (higher notes) that gave the sound the necessary complexity similar to human speech, and therefore made it understandable to the listener. He instructed Watson to develop a new device, and the next day they tested it. Watson could hear Bell's voice but could not understand all of the words. They kept making improvements, and finally, on March 10, 1876, Watson brought over a new transmitter to the Boston rooming house where Bell was then living and working. They went into separate rooms, and Bell said the famous words, "Mr. Watson, come here; I want you," the first words ever spoken by telephone.

No. 178,399, the second significant patent of Bell's career, was filed on June 6, 1876, for a Telephonic Telegraph Receiver. A few weeks later, Bell demonstrated it before a well-respected

Milestones in Telephone History

1878: First local telephone exchange in the United States established in New Haven, Connecticut.

1885: First long distance line installed between New York and Philadelphia.

1892: New York to Chicago long-distance service begins; rate is $9 for the first five minutes.

1915: First transcontinental telephone runs between New York and San Francisco, California; rate is $20.70 for the first three minutes.

1919: AT&T introduces the first dial telephones in Norfolk, Virginia.

1927: Transatlantic service begins from New York to London; rate is $75 for the first three minutes.

1934: Transpacific telephone service begins between the United States and Japan.

1946: AT&T introduces early mobile telephone service using antennas.

1951: Direct-dialing for long-distance telephone calls begins in New Jersey.

1958: First commercial modem introduced by AT&T.

1963: Touch-tone telephones introduced in Pennsylvania.

1974: Direct-dialing for international long-distance calls begins.

1983: Chicago area is site of first commercial cellular telephone system.

panel at the International Centennial Exhibition at Philadelphia, Pennsylvania. He then spent the next several months working with Watson on perfecting a transmitter. On April 3, 1877, they conducted the first telephone conversation, which occurred over telegraph wires between Boston and New York. By the end of May of that same year, they had installed a working telephone line in Boston that ran between the offices of two bankers, as well as another that ran from the banker's office to his home in nearby Somerville. In July 1877, Bell and Watson, along with Thomas Sanders and Gardiner Hubbard, became partners in the newly formed Bell Telephone Company.

Two days after the company was formed Bell married Mabel G. Hubbard, the deaf daughter of his financial backer. In August the couple sailed for Europe, where they spent their honeymoon month demonstrating the telephone to excited audiences across England and France.

Achieved world fame with his invention

The success of Bell's invention, and of the company named after him, was not without some accompanying drama. The Western Union Telegraph Company filed a patent-infringement lawsuit, based on a caveat (a legal warning to stop proceedings) Elisha Gray had filed with the U.S. Patent Office in February 1876, and that and other legal battles went on for a number of years. In total there were nearly six hundred lawsuits filed against Bell and the company, but the U.S. Supreme Court eventually ruled in his favor. In another settlement, Western Union agreed to not venture into telephone service, and in return Bell's company agreed to stay out of the telegraph business.

Bell's telephone business remained his secondary career. He considered himself primarily an inventor and remained actively involved in teaching deaf students. In 1880, when he received the Volta Prize for scientific achievement from the French government, he established the Volta Laboratory with the prize money to further his research efforts in both fields. He constructed a photophone, which could transmit speech through a ray of light, and the first working metal detector, which was tested on President James A. Garfield (1831–1881; served March–September 1881). He improved on the early phonograph invented by **Thomas Edison** (1847–1931; see entry) by creating a wax cylinder that vastly improved the quality of the recorded sound, and sold his 1886 patents for this.

With the money he earned from those patents, Bell established the Laboratory Volta Bureau for the Increase and Diffusion of Knowledge Relating to the Deaf, which was associated with the American Association for the Promotion of the Teaching of Speech to the Deaf. He served as president of the organization and wrote books about the hearing-impaired, including his 1884 work *The Formation of a Deaf Variety of the Human Race*. Although he was married to a deaf woman, Bell advocated enforced sterilization (a medical process by which a person was rendered unable to produce children) for deaf women and the criminalization of marriage between two deaf people. Such attitudes were not unusual in his era, and Bell believed such measures would help eliminate congenital (existing from birth) deafness in following generations.

Other inventions and achievements

Bell's list of other scientific projects was impressive. He invented a tetrahedral kite, which demonstrated to aviation skeptics that an object with a large surface area could still be light enough to achieve flight; an early air conditioning system; a device that used sonar waves to locate icebergs under water; and one of the first working iron lungs, a machine used for artificial respiration. He was fascinated by flight and founded the Aerial Experiment Association in 1907. From 1914 to 1918 he worked on a motorboat that reached a speed of seventy-one miles per hour. He also cofounded the magazine *Science,* which later became the periodical of the American Association for the Advancement of Science, and served as president of the National Geographic Society from 1896 to 1904. He was a member of the governing board of the Smithsonian Institution after 1898 and earned numerous honors during his lifetime.

The Bell Telephone Company went through numerous changes, even in its early years, but was a success from its formation and continued to be an innovator in its field. By 1878 Bell had sold his part of the business, and seven years later it became the American Telephone and Telegraph Company (AT&T). In 1913, with government approval, AT&T became a monopoly (a company holding the exclusive right to produce or sell a particular good or service). Telephone service became a necessary element in commerce and in daily life after 1945, and by 1960 only 21 percent of U.S. households were without a telephone. That rate fell sharply to 2.4 percent by 2000, according to U.S. Census data. AT&T retained its monopoly until 1984, when it agreed to break up its local regional operating companies into the so-called Baby Bells, among them Nynex in New England and SBC, which was formerly known as Southwestern Bell of Texas.

Bell became a naturalized U.S. citizen in 1882. He spent his summers on an estate in Nova Scotia, called Beinn Bhreagh, and died there on August 2, 1922. During his burial at nearby Bras d'Or Lakes, all telephones in North America went silent in honor of his achievement.

For More Information

Books

Brooks, John. *Telephone: The First Hundred Years.* New York: Harper & Row, 1975.

Bruce, Robert V. *Bell: Alexander Graham Bell and the Conquest of Solitude.* Boston, MA: Little, Brown, 1973.

Web Sites

Milestones in AT&T History. http://www.att.com/history/inventing.html (accessed on July 7, 2005).

Andrew Carnegie

Born November 25, 1835 (Dunfermline, Scotland)
Died August 11, 1919 (Lenox, Massachusetts)

Industrialist
Philanthropist

"There is no class so pitiably wretched as that which possesses money and nothing else."

During his lifetime Andrew Carnegie's name immediately brought forth thoughts of the immense wealth he made through the steel empire he created almost single-handedly. The Scottish-born businessman possessed tremendous foresight and sharp managerial skills, and the innovations he brought to American industry revolutionized it and helped make the country a global economic power in the years following his death. Carnegie's legacy, however, involved more than making money. Carnegie came from a humble background and gave generously in his lifetime. After nearly thirty years in the steel industry, Carnegie sold his company to Wall Street financial backer **J. P. Morgan** (1837–1913; see entry) in 1901, and the deal made him the richest man in the world. He used it to fund his philanthropic efforts (aid given to promote human welfare), which centered on public libraries and schools in the United States and England. At the time of his death in 1919, Carnegie had given away nearly 90 percent of his fortune.

Andrew Carnegie. *(AP/Wide World Photos. Reproduced by permission.)*

Carnegie background

The story of Carnegie's rise from his poor beginnings became a symbolic success story of the American dream for generations of new immigrants. He was born on November 25, 1835, in Dunfermline, Scotland. Dunfermline was a noted textile center, and Carnegie's father was a handloom weaver by trade. In the late 1840s, however, steam-powered looms became standard in the mills, and many in Dunfermline found themselves out of a job. Carnegie's father, William, was among the unemployed. Weavers in

Scotland attempted to organize and demand some economic reforms that would protect their livelihoods, but they were unsuccessful. The hardship of these years made a tremendous impression on young Carnegie, and though his own industry was guided by the same principles as those of the mills—favoring productivity over job protection—he would later attempt to improve the lives of the working class through other means.

Margaret Carnegie, his mother, believed that a better life could be made in America, and she convinced her husband to relocate the family there. The family, which also included Andrew's younger brother, Thomas, left in 1848 and settled in Allegheny, Pennsylvania, near Pittsburgh. They lived in poor quarters, and William Carnegie had a difficult time finding a job that could support the household. Although he was just thirteen, Andrew soon went to work to help out, finding a job as a bobbin boy in a textile mill. His duty was to collect the used spindles of yarn from the looms. He progressed from that to a better job as a messenger in a telegraph office, and from there to being a telegraph operator. The year he turned eighteen he was chosen by the superintendent of the Pennsylvania Railroad company's western division, Thomas Scott, to become his personal telegraph operator and office assistant.

Carnegie spent the next twelve years with the Penn Railroad, which was one of the major transportation lines in its day. Two years into the job, in 1855, his father died, and Carnegie became the sole supporter of his mother and brother. Because he had entered the working world at such a young age, he had little formal education, but he spent his free time reading about a variety of subjects. He was a frequent visitor to the local free library, where anyone could come in to read. He also took night school courses in bookkeeping and advanced to other positions within the railroad company. In 1859, when Scott became a vice president, he made Carnegie the supervisor of the Penn Railroad's western lines. The division prospered under Carnegie's shrewd management, and he even invented a military telegraph system for Union Army communications during the American Civil War (1861–65; a war between the Union [the North], who were opposed to slavery, and the Confederacy [the South], who were in favor of slavery).

The Age of Steel

During his years as a railroad executive, Carnegie also began making investments in other businesses. After meeting George Pullman (1831–1897), inventor of the sleeping car for trains, he bought a stake in the Woodruff Sleeping Car Company for $217. Within two years that investment was yielding an annual return of nearly $5,000. Carnegie also began buying partnerships in iron mills and factories, and in 1865 he decided to retire from the Penn Railroad and start his own firm. His Keystone Bridge Company constructed bridges from iron, which was quickly replacing wood as the standard material, and, like nearly everything that Carnegie established, the business prospered. During this time he also sold bonds in both the United States and England for railroad and bridge company enterprises and reportedly earned $1 million in commissions in a five-year period.

By 1870 Carnegie was convinced that steel would soon become the building material of choice for the growing United States. Steel was produced by combining iron with carbon, but in its early days the process was difficult. On a visit to England, Carnegie saw huge Bessemer furnaces, in which impurities were removed from molten iron by compressed air. The process had been patented by Henry Bessemer (1813–1898) in 1855. It was an inexpensive way to make steel, which lasted longer than iron and was lighter in weight. Prior to the Bessemer method, steel was made from iron, and about three tons of coke, a fuel made from coal, were needed to fire the furnaces for each ton of steel produced.

The extensive Bessemer factories in Sheffield, England, were producing steel using the new method, and Carnegie quickly realized the advantages of it. By 1872 he had two Bessemer-type furnaces in operation at mills he owned in Pennsylvania, and soon he founded his first business devoted fully to the manufacture of steel, Carnegie, McCandless, and Company, which later became simply Carnegie Steel. The company opened its first completely operational plant in 1875 in Braddock, Pennsylvania. It was named the J. Edgar Thomson Works, after the president of the Pennsylvania Railroad. The two companies were linked in another way as well, for the first major order at Carnegie's new plant came from the railroad for two thousand steel rails. Railroads were

Henry Clay Frick (above) and Andrew Carnegie were business partners for many years. *(Courtesy of The Library of Congress.)*

the main form of transportation at the time, with hundreds of miles of new tracks being laid down every year as Americans moved westward.

Steel for the nation

Carnegie had been correct: steel was cheaper than iron to produce, and the price of rails fell sharply from $160 per ton in 1875 to $17 per ton in 1900. Open-hearth steel production, another innovation he introduced, also lowered the manufacturing costs, and his firm prospered. The open-hearth method allowed for greatly increased temperatures which normal furnaces and fuels had been unable to reach, to remove impurities from pig iron. By 1878 Carnegie Steel was worth $1.3 million and was the leading steel manufacturer in the United States. In 1881 Carnegie bought a stake in a thriving Pennsylvania coke company owned by Henry Clay Frick (1849–1919). Coke was in plentiful supply thanks to Pennsylvania's coal mines, and soon the Carnegie plants were producing two thousand tons of steel daily.

The partnership between the two industrial leaders was a successful one for many years. Frick oversaw day-to-day operations, while Carnegie was responsible for expansion and cost-cutting measures at the plants. He made a wise purchase of a rival in 1883 when he bought the Homestead Works, whose mills churned out the steel structural elements for elevated railways in New York City and Boston, Massachusetts. Homestead also provided the steel beams used in the new skyscrapers rising in American cities, including the first skyscraper, the Home Insurance Company Building in Chicago, Illinois. Carnegie's company made large profits over the next two decades, providing steel for thousands of miles of rail and a great number of buildings. The company was also instrumental in the creation of landmarks, with both the Washington Monument in the District of Columbia and New York City's Brooklyn Bridge built using steel from Carnegie's plants.

Even during a serious economic downturn, the Depression of 1893–96, Carnegie's company remained successful because of his sound management. He was earning a salary of nearly $25 million annually by 1890 and was regarded as one of the country's most impressive business minds. One major setback came in 1892, however, when workers at the Homestead facility went on strike. Initially Carnegie was not opposed to labor unions, unlike many of his fellow industrialists—in fact, in one of the many articles he authored, he argued in an 1886 issue of *Forum Magazine* that workers should have the right to form a union. But Carnegie's view changed and he opposed the unionization of the workers in his plants, believing that unions interfered with good company management. Frick, on the other hand, had always been strongly opposed to organized labor.

Strike at Carnegie's company

When the Homestead workers went on strike in mid-1892, Carnegie was in Scotland on his annual summer vacation. Frick, left in charge, was determined to break the hold of the union, the Amalgamated Association of Iron and Steel Workers, at the company's mills. He enlisted guards of the Pinkerton Detective Agency, who had gained a reputation as dedicated strike-busters, and the Homestead picket line erupted into violence. In the end five workers and three Pinkerton agents died, and many more were left injured. The incident captured national attention, and the Pennsylvania governor sent in the state militia to maintain order. It was a bitter end, and Frick became one of the main enemies of the labor movement, even being targeted for an assassination attempt. The Homestead workers remained locked out, however, and no other union attempted to organize at a Carnegie plant until the 1930s.

Carnegie and Frick parted ways in 1899, and the following year a dispute over the market value of the coke that Frick's plants sold to Carnegie's had to be settled by lawyers after a lawsuit was filed. Carnegie had already begun his extensive philanthropic efforts by this time, and as the new century drew near, he hoped to retire and devote himself more fully to his charitable projects.

By the late nineteenth century, Wall Street financial backer J. P. Morgan was interested in setting up a steel cartel, a combination of independent business organizations formed to regulate production, pricing, and the marketing of goods. Though Carnegie was initially opposed to cartels, considering them against free-market principles, he was ready to retire, and so in 1901 he sold his interest in his company to Morgan for a sum of $480 million. It was the most significant takeover in American business until then, and the amount was also the most profitable personal commercial transaction at that time. Carnegie alone personally made $225 million from it, which made him the richest man in the world. Morgan combined the former Carnegie properties with his own Federal Steel to form the United States Steel Corporation, the first billion-dollar corporation in the world. Over the next few decades, it served as a leading producer of steel and was a powerful player in the economic and industrial might of twentieth-century America. The company even built the city of Gary, Indiana, and, because of its immense size and power, was referred to simply as "the Corporation" by a generation of investment bankers and traders on Wall Street.

Established pension fund

There was another, sometimes overlooked, achievement of Carnegie's company in 1901: the creation of the first funded pension system for workers. After establishing a fund to pay workers when they were injured on the job or to provide a financial allowance to their families if they were killed at work, Carnegie also set aside another portion of money. According to a 1999 article in *Pensions & Investments* magazine, Carnegie wrote a letter saying the second portion was to be used "to provide small pensions or aids to such employees as, after long and creditable service, through exceptional circumstances, need such help in their old age and who make good use of it."

The retirement plan Carnegie devised was based on one used by his former employer, the Pennsylvania Railroad, but the railroad funded its plan through worker contributions, which then went into a general pool that was invested in stocks

Andrew Carnegie and spelling reform

Andrew Carnegie was known for his commitment to education, but one of the steel businessman's more unusual philanthropic efforts came out of his hope for world peace. In the early years of the twentieth century, he donated generously to a spelling reform movement promoted by the National Simplified Spelling Board. After its formation in 1903, the board urged the adoption of a simplified spelling system that was the work of Melvil Dewey (1851–1931), creator of the Dewey Decimal System that was used by libraries to catalog books. Dewey's suggestions included the elimination of unpronounced vowels, like "ue" at the end of *dialogue*, and the abolishment of unnecessary double consonants, like the second "l" in *spelling*.

Carnegie believed that a simplified spelling system in the English language had many potential benefits. It would make the language easier to learn for new immigrants, reduce teachers' classroom instruction hours, and save time and money in the publishing world. Carnegie also hoped that a simplified universal language might be adopted by diplomats and other representatives of nations. A common tongue, he believed, would reduce differences among peoples and promote world peace, and he felt that English was ideally suited for such a task. Its spelling rules were frustrating and confusing, however, and the new system would be the first step in making the language easier to use.

The plan of the National Simplified Spelling Board was to recruit famous writers who would commit to using the new spelling of a dozen words in their works. These first twelve words were *program, catalog, decalog, prolog, demogog, pedogog, tho, altho, thoro, thoro fare, thru,* and *thruout.* The list of revised words would grow as the movement caught on. Author Mark Twain was an early supporter of the system, and the Board's work was also endorsed by President Theodore Roosevelt (1858–1919; served 1901–9). The *Worcester Telegram* of Massachusetts was the first newspaper to adopt the style.

Carnegie gave a total of nearly $300,000 to the spelling reform movement, but it failed to catch on with the public. Major newspapers poked fun at his "Bored of Speling," and he finally abandoned the cause in 1915 with the onset of World War I (1914–18; a war in which Great Britain, France, the United States and their allies defeated Germany, Austria-Hungary, and their allies) and more pressing concerns. In his own correspondence, however, Carnegie continued to use it, even in his last will and testament. Some of the simplified spellings advocated by the board did eventually become standard. For example *program* replaced the more old-fashioned *programme,* and *labor* became the preferred American version of the British word *labour.*

and bonds. Carnegie's, by contrast, was funded from the great profits of Carnegie Steel before he sold it to Morgan. He also set up a similar fund to provide for college professors who had become too old to teach any longer. He donated $10 million to

Skibo Castle, the Scottish estate of Andrew Carnegie. *(© AP/Wide World Photos. Reproduced by permission.)*

establish the Carnegie Teachers' Pension Fund, which eventually evolved into the Teachers Insurance and Annuity Association-College Retirement Equities Fund, also known as TIAA-CREF.

Carnegie did not marry until 1887, when he was fifty-one years old. His spare time was spent at Skibo Castle in Scotland, which he bought in 1897 as a vacation retreat for his wife, Louise, and their daughter, Margaret, born that same year. He spent the next twenty years of his life as one of history's most generous philanthropists. The arts, education, and public libraries were his passions, and he built Carnegie Hall, the famed concert hall in New York City. He donated $5.2 million to the New York public library system so that it could build its branch libraries, and a foundation he created provided funds for any city or town in the United States that wished to establish a free library. His generosity was responsible for the building and stocking of some 2,800 public libraries in the United States and Great Britain. He established the Carnegie Institute of Technology, later known as Carnegie-Mellon University, in Pittsburgh, and the Carnegie Foundation for the Advancement of Teaching. The Carnegie Corporation of New York, established by Carnegie in 1911, was still making financial grants to worthy people and causes in the early twenty-first century.

Carnegie died on August 11, 1919, at his Lenox, Massachusetts, estate known as Shadowbrook. He was survived by his wife Louise and daughter Margaret. By the time of his death, he had given away some $350 million of his fortune, estimated to be about 90 percent of his total wealth.

For More Information

Books

Krass, Peter. *Carnegie*. Hoboken, NJ: John Wiley & Sons, 2002.

Periodicals

Chernow, Ron. "Blessed Barons." *Time* (December 7, 1998): p. 74.

"The Making of the Modern Company." *Business Week* (August 28, 2000): p. 98.

"Steel Baron Andrew Carnegie Pioneered Pension Funding." *Pensions & Investments* (December 27, 1999): p. 34.

Wren, Daniel A. and Ronald G. Greenwood. "Business Leaders: A Historical Sketch of Andrew Carnegie." *Journal of Leadership Studies* (Fall 1998): p. 106.

Web Sites

"Rags to Riches Timeline." *PBS*. http://www.pbs.org/wgbh/amex/carnegie/timeline/timeline2.html (accessed on July 7, 2005).

Chinese Transcontinental Railroad Workers

In the mid-nineteenth century, large numbers of Chinese men immigrated to the United States in search of better futures for themselves and the families they left behind. From 1864 to 1869, somewhere between ten thousand and twenty thousand of these immigrants were responsible for a major part of the western construction of the transcontinental railroad, which spanned the country from the Atlantic coast to the Pacific coast. These workers gained the respect of many who worked with them, but strong anti-Asian sentiments in the United States, due mainly to uninformed opinions, kept most of the Chinese on the outskirts of American society. Few records remained of the individual men who accomplished this overwhelming task through courage and discipline, and there were no known first-person accounts, such as memoirs or letters, left by the railroad workers.

Troubles in China: Why they came

China is one of the world's oldest cultures. For thousands of years, under a series of long-term ruling families, the Chinese developed a highly advanced culture in which the arts, philosophy, science, commerce, and the military flourished. After initial contacts with other nations were made in the sixteenth and seventeenth centuries, China tried to isolate itself from foreigners, viewing Europeans in particular as barbarians and inferiors. In the early nineteenth century, the English became aggressive in their pursuit of trade with China, and this eventually led to two devastating wars. The Chinese lost the wars and were forced to open their ports to Europeans.

War was only one of the problems the Chinese people faced in the early- to mid-nineteenth century. China's population had soared from about 150 million people in 1700 to 400 million in 1850. Over the same period of time China had experienced major floods and droughts (shortages of rain), and its farms were unable to feed the rapidly growing population. Life for the huge peasant class (people who worked the soil for a living as renters, small landowners, or laborers) in China had always been difficult, but at this time it became particularly grim and many people had no food to feed their families. Rebel groups arose around the country, and in the Taiping Rebellion (1851–64), a violent conflict between the peasants and the Chinese rulers, an estimated twenty million to thirty million people were killed.

For many Chinese the situation in their homeland was unbearable. Some families in the Kuangtung Province, where the capital city and port of Canton was located, began to prepare their sons to travel to other lands to find work. Though the Chinese government banned all emigration, it was not difficult for a young man to get from Canton to the island of Hong Kong, where his long voyage would begin. These young men promised to make their fortune and return with desperately needed money for their families. Until 1850 very few of them went to the United States, but when news reached China of the 1848 discovery of gold in California, thousands of Chinese men set out on the seven-thousand-mile voyage to the state, which they called *Gum Sam,* or "Gold Mountain."

The sojourners

Almost all of the immigrants from China arriving in California between 1850 and 1900 planned to return to their native country. They were called sojourners (people who stayed as temporary residents) because they had no intention

The Trip to the United States

Most of the young Chinese males traveling to the United States around 1850 were from poor peasant families who did not have enough money to pay for the trip. Tickets on a ship from Hong Kong to San Francisco, California, usually cost more than a Chinese family's income for a full year. To pay to send a son overseas, Chinese families sold precious property or livestock and usually had to borrow money as well. The young men knew that if they did not make their fortunes and return to repay the loans, their families would face terrible consequences. Trying to pay back the loans on their own, many would be forced to sell their meager homes and belongings, and some would starve. Soon Chinese companies were established for the sole purpose of lending money for passage to emigrants, which was to be paid back later with interest (a percentage of the sum borrowed). These companies became very powerful, and some forced the new arrivals in the United States into gang labor to pay their debt. In later decades recruiters from American businesses, particularly the railroads, came to China in search of laborers and offered to pay the young men's passage in exchange for their agreement to work for a set amount of time.

The eight-week journey from China to California was dangerous, and conditions aboard the ships were unhealthy and cramped. Unable to pay for more comfortable quarters, the young Chinese immigrants were crammed into overcrowded spaces below the ship's deck, often wedged in between machinery that emitted dirty smoke. There were not enough toilet facilities for all the passengers and there was no place to clean up. People became sick and the smell was often unbearable. Epidemics of infectious diseases often spread in the close quarters.

of remaining in the United States, though many did. Almost all Chinese immigrants were male because most Chinese did not believe women should act independently of their families. In Chinese society, when a woman married she went to live with her husband and his parents. If the husband left to go to the United States, she was expected to remain under the control of her mother-in-law.

The young Chinese men who came to California were likely to practice one of the primary Chinese religions: ancestor worship, Confucianism, Taoism, and Buddhism. Confucianism was based on the idea that one's role in life was set at birth and must be carried out. It stressed respect for elders and people of higher rank. Taoism and Buddhism were ways of thinking and living to help one find inner peace and a spiritual path. Chinese spiritual beliefs were strong and profoundly influenced the young men who arrived in the United States. Most were extremely loyal to their ancestors, villages, and families and were highly disciplined. They were less likely to complain about their workload and more likely to perform difficult and dangerous jobs quietly. They usually did not drink alcohol. These traits made Chinese immigrants desirable to employers, but they also made them seem threatening to other workers who feared the Chinese might take their jobs.

The Chinese immigrants had a difficult time fitting into American society. They practiced unfamiliar religions, spoke an unknown language, and looked, dressed, and acted different than the rest of the population. In China at the time, all males were required to wear their hair in a long braid called a queue, in honor of Chinese tradition. For Chinese sojourners the queue was important because without it they could not go home. Because they were treated with suspicion and hostility in the new country, they tended to stick together, living in small Chinese communities and keeping to their own customs.

Arriving in California

As soon as word of the California gold rush reached China, thousands of young men set off for the United States. By 1850 there were an estimated 4,000 Chinese people in the country, and ten years later there were nearly 35,000. In 1890 the census recorded more than 100,000 Chinese in America. Ninety-five percent of this population was male.

The earliest immigrants arrived in San Francisco and quickly headed for the goldfields. At first they were welcomed. Because most did not have much money with which to purchase a claim (the right to mine for gold in a small area), they frequently worked as cooks or servants in the gold camps. Some Chinese miners pooled their funds and bought claims that other miners had abandoned, and they were often able to find gold where others had not. Not long after the early immigrants arrived, however, public sentiment turned against the Chinese. Miners who were not finding gold resented the success of some of the Chinese. There was almost no law and order in the camps, and some of the miners began to attack the Chinese. In 1850 the California government passed a foreign miners' tax, demanding $20 a month from Chinese and Mexican miners. By the 1860s the gold rush was over. Like so many gold seekers in California, most of the Chinese miners had not made large amounts of money. About half of the early Chinese sojourners returned to China. Some who longed to go home could not bear the disgrace of returning without the fortune they had been sent to America to find, so they stayed in the United States and sought work elsewhere.

An opportunity to work: the transcontinental railroad

In 1862 Congress passed the Pacific Railroad Act, in which the government committed federal funds toward the creation of a transcontinental railroad. Two companies, the Central Pacific and the Union Pacific, were selected to build the railroad. Construction on the Central Pacific lines was to begin in Sacramento, California, and work its way east, while the Union Pacific construction would begin in Omaha, Nebraska, and work its way west. At some point the two companies and the tracks they were laying would meet. Because there was government money for the company that laid the most tracks, the two railroads viewed the huge project as a race.

The Central Pacific Railroad began construction in 1863, but two years later only about fifty miles of tracks had been laid. The construction was under the direction of Central Pacific partner Charles Crocker (1822–1888) and his project supervisor, James Strobridge (1827–1921). Their biggest problem was a lack of willing workers. Their crew barely amounted to eight hundred men, and the managers of the project figured they needed about five thousand to complete the job. Most of their laborers were Irish immigrants, and many worked only long enough to get passage west so they could go to work in the Nevada silver mines. Only about one in ten of the men that were hired stayed on the job longer than a week.

At the time there were about forty-two thousand young Chinese males living in California, and some had worked on the construction of smaller railroads in the state. The Chinese faced harsh anti-Asian prejudice that excluded them from many jobs, so many were anxiously seeking work. Strobridge did not want to hire a Chinese crew, but at Crocker's urging he hired a group of fifty Chinese workers in 1865 and he found them to be quick, dedicated, reliable workers able to successfully complete all the various tasks of construction. Soon the

Central Pacific was seeking Chinese laborers throughout California and even in China. By 1867 Chinese workers represented between 80 and 90 percent of the Central Pacific Railroad workforce.

Working conditions

The Chinese workers received from $26 to $35 a month, from which they had to buy their own food. The Irish laborers received more than the Chinese: about $35 a month with food provided. The workweek was exhausting, consisting of six twelve-hour days. The Chinese workers on the railroad lived separately from the other laborers. They were organized into groups of about twenty men. Each group had a leader who collected their wages from the railroad, took out a portion for their food and supplies, and then gave the workers their fair share of what was left. Each group also had a cook, who obtained their food and prepared their meals. The Irish workers viewed the food the Chinese ate with disgust. Their diet, which was actually very healthy, included dried oysters and cuttlefish (a squid-like marine animal), vegetables, dried fruit, chicken, mushrooms, and dried seaweed. The cooks worked with railroad management to special order these foods at the Chinese workers' expense. The Chinese workers never drank plain water; instead they drank warm tea. The cook would carry it to them at their work site throughout the day. Since the water in the tea had been boiled, the Chinese did not get the illnesses caused by unsanitary water that affected many other workers. When the work crews finished for the day, the cook had a large tub of hot water to distribute to them so that each could bathe using a sponge, which was also considered odd by the other workers.

The rough road ahead

Just west of Sacramento the foothills of the rugged Sierra Nevada Mountains began their ascent. In the fall of 1865 the Central Pacific crew faced the task of laying tracks over ground that rose in a rocky wall from sea level to an elevation of seven thousand feet in just one hundred miles. Their job had to be done mainly by hand, with picks and axes and occasionally explosives. Blasting a ledge for the roadbed one thousand feet above the American River at Cape Horn took six months of dangerous and physically exhausting work.

When the crew finally reached the summit of the mountains they faced an even tougher challenge: digging and blasting many tunnels through the granite walls. The workers used only handheld drills, explosives, and shovels to dig and hand carts to carry the loose rock from the tunnels. Some of the granite was so hard even blasting would not make it give way. The workers persisted, chipping away at the rock even when they were only making eight to ten inches of progress a day. The overseers assigned crews to shifts so that work could continue day and night. Soon everyone was weary and run-down. The longest summit tunnel was nearly 1,700 feet long and took more than two years to finish. There were fifteen summit tunnels, totaling about 6,213 feet, when the project was finished. Work on the tunnels became much easier when the railroad began manufacturing nitroglycerin (a heavy, explosive liquid) at the worksite that was capable of blasting through even the toughest granite.

The winter of 1866–67 featured some of the most severe weather on record. More than forty feet of snow fell as the Central Pacific crew worked. The laborers slept in the tunnels they were digging or in rough shacks that were completely buried in snow. They cleared the areas around the chimneys of the shacks to create air vents and then lived in the dark. Long tunnels ran from their camps to the work sites. Avalanches (snow slides) killed entire gangs of workers.

In 1867 two thousand Chinese workers in the Sierra Nevadas walked off their jobs, going on strike for better pay and shorter working hours. The strikers were peaceful, simply stating their demands and quietly awaiting a decision. Crocker cut off their pay and stopped supplies from reaching them, leaving them alone at the work site for one week. The Chinese had little choice but to agree to Crocker's conditions. The conditions did include a small raise, but no relief from the long workdays.

By the summer of 1868 the construction crew had broken through the mountains and was heading to the desert regions of Nevada and Utah. There the tired Chinese workers, most of whom had now been on the job for three years, faced very different weather, with the temperature dropping well below freezing at night and then rising above 120 degrees Fahrenheit during the day. Fortunately, an end was in sight. The Central

Pacific Railroad met the Union Pacific at Promontory Point in Utah on May 10, 1869. Chinese workers were not invited to many of the festivities marking the completion of the nation's first transcontinental railroad, but several tributes were made to them. Many of the country's railroad managers, journalists, and politicians had come to appreciate the essential role the Chinese workers had played in American history.

No one knows how many Chinese workers died building the Central Pacific Railroad. Most accounts suggested there were more than one thousand Chinese deaths and estimates range up to two thousand. Some historians, however, believed these numbers were greatly exaggerated and that as few as one hundred Chinese workers died during the construction of the railroad.

The bachelor society

After the transcontinental railroad was done, Chinese workers took up factory, handicraft, and retail work in cities. Many opened small businesses such as laundries, restaurants, and grocery stores. Three-fourths of all Chinese immigrants in the United States in 1870 lived in California, with a large number concentrated in San Francisco. Chinatowns of all sizes appeared along the West Coast. Most began with a temple and a cluster of stores. These immigrants formed what became known to Chinese and Americans alike as the "bachelor society" because they had no wives and children with them and remained isolated from the rest of American society. Since they had no family obligations, the men often passed the time by gathering in gambling rooms to play games and bet on the outcomes.

Anti-Asian feelings increased in the 1870s. As the U.S. economy took a turn for the worse and many workers were out of jobs, politicians spoke out against what they called the "Yellow Peril," claiming that Asian workers were invading the country and taking work away from white men. In truth the number of Chinese workers remained relatively small. Nevertheless, mobs in Los Angeles, San Francisco, and other cities in the West attacked Chinese communities, often killing or severely beating the residents. In 1882 the federal government passed the Chinese Exclusion Act, which prevented Chinese workers from entering the country. It was the first time the nation had restricted immigration. The Chinese population of the country dropped significantly after that. Many of the Chinese workers who had been instrumental in building the transcontinental railroad went back to China. Those who opted to stay, perhaps hoping that they could make their fortune or that the 1882 immigration law would be overturned, lived out their lives in the bachelor societies of U.S. Chinatowns.

For More Information

Books

Ambrose, Stephen. *Nothing Like It in the World: The Men Who Built the Transcontinental Railroad, 1863–1869*. New York: Simon & Schuster, 2001.

Chew, William F. *Nameless Builders of the Transcontinental Railroad*. Victoria, British Columbia, Canada: Trafford Publishing, 2004.

Perl, Lila. *To the Gold Mountain: The Story of the Chinese Who Built the Transcontinental Railroad*. New York: Benchmark Books, 2002.

Periodicals

Chugg, Robert. "The Chinese and the Transcontinental Railroad." *The Brown Quarterly* (Spring 1997). This article can also be found online at http://brownvboard.org/brwnqurt/01-3/01-3f.htm (accessed on July 7, 2005).

Web Sites

"Chinese Contribution to the Transcontinental Railroad." *Central Pacific Railroad Photographic History Museum*. http://cprr.org/Museum/Chinese.html (accessed on July 7, 2005).

"Transcontinental Railroad." *American Experience: PBS*. http://www.pbs.org/wgbh/amex/tcrr/index.html (accessed on July 7, 2005).

Eugene Victor Debs

Born November 5, 1855 (Terre Haute, Indiana)
Died October 20, 1926 (Elmhurst, Illinois)

Labor activist
Presidential candidate

B y the late nineteenth century the industrial workforce in the United States had grown very large. Factory workers labored long hours at dull, repetitive, often dangerous jobs, yet many did not make enough money to provide food, clothing, and shelter for their families. The fear of losing their jobs prevented most people from speaking out against the unfair working conditions in the country's big industries, and there were few organizations or reformers willing to help. Labor leader Eugene Victor Debs was one man who devoted his life to providing a strong voice for the workers. He struggled tirelessly for twenty years to promote the labor union movement, which sought to protect the common interests of workers, particularly with respect to wages and working conditions. Debs believed that if they united, laborers could have more control over the workplace. When he felt the labor movement had failed, he attempted to lead an independent political party that would support American workers. Although in the early years of his fight for reform he was viewed as a radical and even a criminal by many Americans, by the end of his life Debs was almost universally

"While there is a lower class, I am in it; while there is a criminal element I am of it; and while there is a soul in prison, I am not free."

49

Eugene V. Debs. *(Courtesy of The Library of Congress.)*

known as someone who had selflessly committed himself to helping others.

Childhood in Terre Haute

Debs's parents, Daniel and Marguerite Debs, emigrated from Alsace, France, in 1849. Daniel's parents were wealthy mill owners in Alsace, and when Daniel announced his intention to marry Marguerite, one of the workers in the family mills, his parents refused to give him any financial support.

Daniel and Marguerite arrived in New York City with little money and were quickly married. They spent the next five years moving about the country looking for work. When Eugene was born in 1855, they were penniless and living in Terre Haute, Indiana. However, their fortune soon changed for the better when Marguerite began operating a store out of the front room of the family home. The business prospered, providing modest comfort for the family. Though not rich, the Debs were a happy family that grew to include ten children.

Debs was taught at home by his father before entering school. He was a good student who loved classic French literature. He quit at age fourteen to take a job as a painter in the local railroad yards, although he did continue to attend night classes at a local business school when possible. In 1870 Debs became a fireman (the person who feeds the coal into the fire to fuel the engine) for the railroad. Three years later he lost his job due to a severe economic downturn. In search of work, he traveled to St. Louis, Missouri. The extreme poverty of the city's working class made a strong impression on him and was one of the factors that led him to become an advocate for the rights of the nation's laborers.

Early union work

Back in Terre Haute a year later, Debs obtained a job as a billing clerk for a grocery firm, but he maintained a strong association with railway workers. In 1874 he attended the first meeting of a local division of the Brotherhood of Locomotive Firemen (BLF), a benevolent association (a society formed to aid others) that sought to supply health insurance to its members. Debs was elected secretary. He began to devote all his extra time to the cause of labor organizations, traveling around the country to support strikes and encourage railway workers to join their respective unions. He also edited the BLF's magazine and acquired a following among the workers for his well-spoken defense of their rights.

In 1885 Debs married Kate Metzel. It was a loving union that was to last until Debs's death. That same year he was nominated as the Democratic candidate for the Indiana House of Representatives, a position he won easily. Debs always voted according to his convictions and beliefs. He supported bills calling for women's suffrage (the right to vote) and an end to racial discrimination (treating groups of people differently due to the color of their skin or other racial characteristics). He also introduced a bill to hold the railways responsible for job-related injuries. By the end of his term, however, Debs knew that he did not want a career in politics. He had learned that most political actions were achieved by buying or trading favors and making deals with one's opponents. It was not in his nature to compromise on the principles he believed in or to enter into the kind of political maneuvering necessary to pass legislation.

Establishing the American Railway Union

Debs was also losing faith in the BLF. He had come to the conclusion that, in order to have more power to negotiate with employers, railway workers should be organized in one big union rather than spread out in various organizations according to different jobs. Whether fireman, conductor, or engineer, railway workers needed to unite and support each other to obtain better pay and working conditions from the railroad owners. Debs announced his retirement from the BLF in 1891, and in 1893 he formed the American Railway Union (ARU), which was open to any and all railway workers. As soon as it was created the ARU began to grow at an unexpectedly fast pace. In the first twenty days of organizing, thirty-four locals (branches) were established and two hundred to four hundred men signed up daily. The men were attracted to the principle behind the ARU and the cheap membership fees, which allowed many to join who previously could not afford it. There is little doubt, however, that a major reason for the success of the ARU was the importance and reputation among workers of the ARU president—Eugene Debs.

The Pullman strike

The ARU had existed less than a year when it became involved in one of the major union conflicts of the times, the Pullman workers' strike. Pullman, Illinois, was an unusual factory town. Between 1861 and 1865, George Pullman (1831–1897) had created a thriving industry with his line of luxury sleeper and dining cars for trains. In the 1880s he decided to build a technologically advanced factory about fifteen miles outside of Chicago. Next to the factory he built the town of Pullman for the factory workers to live in. Pullman envisioned his town as a model of efficiency and good health in which workers and their families could lead comfortable, safe lives. Workers began moving into the row house rentals in 1884, but life in Pullman was not the ideal that George Pullman had promoted, since he allowed the residents of his town almost no say in the running of their community. For most, however, it was still better than living among the filth and crime in the poor neighborhoods of the large cities. Then, in 1893, an economic downturn hit the U.S. economy, causing a drop in orders of Pullman cars. The company fired more than half the workers in Pullman and cut the wages of the remaining workers by more than 25 percent. The company did not, however, reduce the high rent on the laborers' houses or lessen charges in other facilities of the town. The workers could not afford to feed themselves and continue to pay their rent. On May 11, 1894, the Pullman employees went on strike.

The recently formed ARU executive board took a vote and decided in favor of supporting the Pullman workers' strike. Debs believed in the Pullman cause, but he was worried about involving the ARU in a major strike. The union did not yet have sufficient financial reserves to fund a long conflict. Also, most of the members and their leaders were new to the union movement and thus lacked the experience necessary to sustain a prolonged strike. Nonetheless, once the decision was made, Debs devoted all his skill to the cause. He helped organize a boycott (an organized refusal to deal with a company in order to protest policy or force action) in which all ARU members would refuse to work on any trains carrying Pullman cars. Since most trains had at least one Pullman car, the boycott would effectively halt the railroads. The response to the boycott was overwhelming. By the fourth day, 125,000 men were off the job, and twenty railroad lines had been stopped. Debs insisted there was to be no violence, no stopping of trains, and no destruction of railway property. For the first two weeks, the strike was orderly and nonviolent.

Railway owners sided with the Pullman Company, hoping they could take advantage of the strike to destroy the ARU, which threatened to become too powerful for their comfort. All twenty-six railroad companies were represented against the unions by the powerful General Managers' Association (GMA).

Ray Stannard Baker

Despite having strong initial misgivings about the workers' movement, Ray Stannard Baker (1870–1946) of the *Chicago Record* was one of the few journalists who ended up supporting Debs and the Pullman strikers.

Baker had become a reporter and editor for the newspaper when he left his graduate studies in 1892. His work introduced him to the miserable scenes in Chicago's soup kitchens and charity wards, and he witnessed daily the thousands of homeless, starving men crowding the city streets. Conditions in Chicago became even more desperate in 1893 when an economic slump left millions unemployed. At first Baker felt contempt for the poor, wondering why they didn't help themselves and do something about their poverty. Once he decided to help a needy young man find work, however, he was surprised to find that, even with every possible effort being made, there was not a job to be found.

In the winter of 1893–94, groups of unemployed workers across the country organized to march on Washington, D.C., to try to persuade the federal government to provide them with economic relief. These groups, or "armies," as they were called, ranged in size from several dozen to a few thousand men. Baker was assigned to go with Coxey's Army, a group of about one hundred men led by Jacob Sechler Coxey (1854–1951), a successful manufacturer and a reformer who worked to help the unemployed. Coxey's Army left Massillon, Ohio, on March 25, 1894, hoping to attract one hundred thousand supporters on the way to Washington. When Baker set out with the army, he was highly skeptical of the group's method of seeking reform. But after marching with them into the nation's capital he got to know the men and their stories and became convinced of the worthiness of their cause. In Washington, the leaders of the march were arrested and the rest were stopped by police. Though Coxey's Army failed in its mission, it received nationwide publicity for its cause,

The GMA took several well-planned actions, including urging the federal government to attach mail cars to trains carrying Pullman cars. This allowed President Grover Cleveland (1837–1908; served 1893–97) to call out the U.S. Army by arguing that the strike was interfering with the federal mail system. When troops marched into ARU headquarters in Chicago on July 4, rioting began. The conflict turned violent and resulted in thirteen deaths. Resistance spread outward from Chicago, and minor battles between strikers and federal troops and state militia broke out in twenty-six states from Maine to California. Thirty-four people were killed.

and Baker was one of the chief journalists responsible for that.

Soon after Baker returned to Chicago from the march, the Pullman strike began. Baker held conflicted views about the strike. He knew that the workers were barely able to survive on the wages they were receiving from their employers and had no power to negotiate. But, like many Americans, he watched the strikers as they began to riot and worried that they posed a threat to the law and order of the nation. Then, on July 8, 1894, Baker observed an angry mob trying to turn over a Pullman car in Indiana. A train full of soldiers pulled into the station and they began randomly firing their guns into the crowd. In horror, Baker saw people drop as bullets pierced them. Baker's sympathies were drawn to the strikers and their cause after that. He wrote many stories about their suffering and their heroic battle to win a decent life for their hard work. His stories were so effective that his readers began to send in contributions to help the strikers, which he distributed. During this time Baker came to greatly admire Eugene Debs, referring to the Pullman strike as Debs' rebellion.

Baker had, without meaning to, established himself as a muckraker. The muckrakers were a group of journalists who sought to expose dishonesty in business and government. In 1898 he went to work for *McClure's Magazine* along with fellow muckrakers **Ida Tarbell** (1857–1944; see entry), Lincoln Steffens (1866–1936), and Frank Norris (1870–1902). The foursome wrote about conditions in industry and took up many reform issues. By 1906 they became unhappy with *McClure's* and took over another journal, *American Magazine*.

During the 1910s Baker became the first prominent journalist to focus on America's racial divisions. He wrote philosophical essays under the pen name of David Grayson that were collected in nine popular books. Baker also spent fourteen years researching and writing a biography of President Woodrow Wilson (1856–1924; served 1913–21). He died in 1946.

Debs realized that the ARU could not win against the railroads. The American Federation of Labor (AFL) and the various railroad brotherhoods refused to help. Samuel Gompers (1850–1924), the head of the AFL, spoke against the Pullman Company but acknowledged that since the federal government had taken the side of the railroads there was no hope of winning a general strike. The public as a whole had little sympathy for the striking workers, particularly since the country was still recovering from the economic slump. No one wanted to see the rail business halted. Newspapers attacked the strikers, calling them criminals and traitors and demanding their arrest. On the other hand, those who bothered to learn the reasons behind the strikers' protests, notably the Chicago newspapers, farmers in the West, and workers' organizations worldwide, often sided with the Pullman laborers.

Finally the government secured an injunction (court order or formal command) against the strike leaders that forbade them from organizing and leading the strike. Debs and the other leaders ignored it and were arrested on July 17. With Debs in jail, the Pullman strike quickly collapsed. After the strike the ARU disbanded and the employees at Pullman were persuaded to sign pledges that they would never form or participate in another union.

Turn to socialism

Debs was sentenced to six months in prison for his part in the strike. Debs had been a fairly well-known public figure, at least among union circles, prior to the Pullman strike. His articles appeared frequently in widely read union papers and he was a skilled speaker who often drew huge crowds. Even people who disagreed with his ideas often enjoyed listening to him. His imprisonment after the Pullman strike elevated Debs to the position of national celebrity. From that point on he was recognized as a prominent labor leader throughout the country.

Reflecting on the events that had led to his imprisonment, he concluded that the nation's two-party political system was failing U.S. workers. Debs had long supported the Democratic Party and had even campaigned on behalf of President Grover Cleveland (1837–1908; served 1885–89, 1893–97). During the ARU boycott, however, Cleveland had sided with the railroads and had sent armed troops to battle the strikers. Debs decided that the working class needed its own party since both of the mainstream ones were allied with the employers, and he turned toward socialism, an economic system in which production and distribution of goods was owned collectively by all the workers and there was no private property or social classes. His reasoning was reflected in a later speech, "The Issue," given on May 23, 1908:

> As long as a relatively few men own the railroads, the telegraph, the telephone, own the oil fields and the gas fields and the steel mills and the sugar refineries and the leather tanneries—own, in short, the sources and means of life—they will corrupt our politics, they will enslave the working class, they will impoverish and debase society, they will do all things that are needful to perpetuate [cause to continue indefinitely] their power as the economic masters and the political rulers of the people. Not until these

Eugene V. Debs delivering an antiwar speech. *(© Bettmann/Corbis. Reproduced by permission.)*

great agencies are owned and operated by the people can the people hope for any material improvement in their social condition.

After his release from prison, Debs helped create the Social Democratic Party (later the Socialist Party) in 1898. The party's missions included a strong commitment to the country's working people. Debs advocated the development of industrial unions, the formation of a socialist economic system, and opposition to capitalism (an economic system characterized by private or corporate ownership of goods and free market competition). These ideals affected the way he reacted to events over the next twenty-five years.

Running for president—five times

As America's most prominent socialist, Debs was nominated as the party's candidate for president in the elections of

Eugene V. Debs, shortly before his release from prison in 1920. *(© Bettmann/Corbis. Reproduced by permission.)*

1900, 1904, 1908, 1912, and 1920. In 1900 and 1904 he led the Socialists to a fourfold increase in national voting strength, raising the number of votes the party received from about ninety-seven thousand to more than four hundred thousand. In 1912 Debs won 897,011 votes, 6 percent of the total and a major triumph for an independent party. Between campaigns Debs was a tireless speaker and organizer for the party, and he traveled the nation defending workers in their strikes and industrial disputes.

Debs fought his last presidential campaign from within the walls of the federal prison in Atlanta, Georgia, where he was serving a ten-year sentence for speaking out against U.S. involvement in World War I (1914–18; a war in which Great Britain, France, the United States and their allies defeated Germany, Austria-Hungary, and their allies). Such an action had not previously been a crime, but in 1917 Congress passed the Espionage Act, which made it illegal to make false reports that might aid an enemy, to incite rebellion within the armed forces, or to obstruct military recruitment. Debs believed that the working people were being forced to die in a war that would only benefit the capitalist class. In a speech on June 16, 1918, to the Socialist Party in Canton, Ohio, Debs stated: "... the working class who fight all the battles, the working class who make the supreme sacrifices, the working class who freely shed their blood and furnish the corpses, have never yet had a voice in either declaring war or making peace. It is the ruling class that invariably do both." Thirteen days later a federal grand jury indicted (formally charged) Debs for violation of the Espionage Act. His conviction for obstructing recruitment and inciting rebellion was upheld by a unanimous Supreme Court decision. On April 12, 1919, at sixty-four years of age, Debs was sent to prison. Two years later, as the war memories faded and another president took office, Debs was released by order of President Warren G. Harding (1865–1923; served 1921–23). During his captivity he had won almost a million votes in his 1920 presidential campaign. He was also greatly admired among the prisoners, who gathered to say farewell when he was released.

Debs returned to Terre Haute exhausted and ill. Two and a half years in prison had gravely affected his health. Debs was also confronted with bitter conflicts within the Socialist Party. The Socialist Party brought together people with sharply differing views and goals as one party—farmers, immigrants, laborers, idealists and intellectuals, and the unemployed—and its history was characterized by internal fighting among interest groups and inconsistent policies. In 1920 continuous fighting in the party had resulted in a split into three separate organizations. Debs stood by his party, hoping he could once again unite all its elements. His failing health prevented him from accomplishing this goal. Debs died on October 20, 1926.

For More Information

Books

Debs, Eugene. "The Issue." Speech, May 23, 1908. In *Debs: His Life, Writings and Speeches*. Edited by Eugene Debs and Bruce Rogers. Girard, KS: The Appeal to Reason, 1908.

Debs, Eugene. "Statement to the Court." Speech, 1918. In *American Voices: Significant Speeches in American History, 1640–1945*. Edited by James Andrews and David Zarefsky. New York: Longman, 1989.

Schlesinger, Arthur M., ed. *Writings and Speeches of Eugene Debs*. New York: Hermitage Press, 1948.

Smith, Page. *The Rise of Industrial America: A People's History of the Post-Reconstruction Era*. New York: McGraw-Hill, 1984.

Periodicals

Zinn, Howard. "Eugene Debs and the Idea of Socialism." *Progressive Magazine,* January 1999. This article can also be found online at http://www.thirdworldtraveler.com/Heroes/ EugeneDebsSocialism.html (accessed on July 7, 2005).

Web Sites

Official Site of the Eugene Debs Foundation. http://www.eugenevdebs.com/ (accessed on July 7, 2005).

Thomas Edison

Born February 11, 1847 (Milan, Ohio)
Died October 18, 1931 (West Orange, New Jersey)

Inventor
Entrepreneur

"I never did anything worth doing by accident, nor did any of my inventions come by accident; they came by work."

Thomas Edison was a legendary figure in his lifetime, and even decades after his death in 1931 he is considered one of history's most significant inventors. Edison's enduring achievement in this realm was tied to the incandescent light bulb, but he also came up with a safe, efficient way to deliver the power that lit those bulbs. It ushered in a new era, changing the way the modern world lived, worked, and played. He also made improvements to the telephone invented by **Alexander Graham Bell** (1847–1922; see entry), devised the first working phonograph, and made important scientific contributions to the early motion-picture industry. His accomplishments in the final two decades of the nineteenth century were so valuable that the period was once commonly called the "Age of Edison" in school history books for many years.

Thomas Alva Edison was born on February 11, 1847, in Milan, Ohio. His father, Samuel, was Canadian, but had fled Ontario after taking part in a rebellion against the province's British-appointed governor. In Ohio, Samuel Edison established himself in a lucrative shingle business, and he and his

Thomas Edison. *(AP/Wide World Photos. Reproduced by permission.)*

wife, Nancy, a former teacher, added three more children to the four they had brought with them from Canada. Thomas was the youngest of them. When he was seven years old, the family relocated to Port Huron, Michigan, where his father ran another prosperous business, this one dealing in grain and lumber.

Schooled at home

Edison began his formal schooling in Port Huron, but he was a sickly child and did poorly. Not long after the family's arrival in Port Huron, he came down with scarlet fever (a severe contagious bacterial disease), which likely led to a loss of hearing that worsened with age. His first teachers were frustrated by what seemed to be his lack of ability and ridiculed him as a daydreamer and possibly even developmentally disabled. After just three months, Nancy Edison decided to remove him from school and teach him at home. Though some historians believe Edison may have suffered from dyslexia, or a learning disorder that interferes with the ability to comprehend written words, he emerged as an enthusiastic reader in his youth, a hobby that would continue for the rest of his life.

Curious about the world, "Al," as Edison was known as a child, studied a variety of subjects but became particularly intrigued by chemistry. At the age of ten, he set up a laboratory in the basement of the family home and carried out his first experiments there. He began working at the age of twelve in order to buy more materials for his lab, becoming a newspaper and candy seller on the Grand Trunk Railway line. He embarked on a train that ran daily between Port Huron and Detroit, selling candy to the passengers. On his layovers in Detroit he spent hours reading at the public library. His railroad bosses even gave him permission to set up a small chemistry lab on board the train. In time, he even ventured into journalism, publishing his own newspaper, the *Weekly Herald,* using a printing press he set up in the baggage car.

One story about young Edison was given, for many years, as the reason for his loss of hearing. He claimed that he was running to make the train one day, and a brakeman swooped him up by his ears and pulled him aboard. Edison recounted that he felt something snap in his head, and later attributed his hearing loss to that event. Scholars believe, however, that it was more likely the result of the scarlet fever. No matter the cause, the young inventor became increasingly withdrawn as his hearing worsened in his teens and spent long hours in his lab.

Worked as telegraph operator

The telegraph was one of the new areas of scientific innovation that fascinated Edison at an early age. He had close contact with it because the transmitting stations were often located in railway stations. This was the first form of electronic communication, and it revolutionized American business in the mid-nineteenth century. In another well-told episode from Edison's biographers and newspaper accounts about his early life, the teenager swooped the stationmaster's young son out of the way of an oncoming train one day in 1862, and in gratitude the stationmaster offered to teach him how to operate a telegraph machine. A telegraph transmitted encoded information by signal across a distance. The device relied on electric current, controlled by electromagnets (a type of magnet in which the magnetic field is created by a flow of electric current; when the current ceases the magnetic field disappears). When the telegraph operator pressed down on the key, or small switch, electricity flowed out of the machine and traveled through external electrical wires to waiting receivers in other parts of the world. The electrical current flowed through the receiver's electromagnet, creating a magnetic field, which in turn caused the receiver's key to be attracted to the plate beneath it. As the key came into contact with the plate, it made a click. Using a code developed by American scientist Samuel F. B. Morse (1791–1872), the sender could vary the sound of the click by holding the key down for a shorter or a longer period of time. The shorter clicks (dots) and longer clicks (dashes) represented the different letters of the alphabet. Edison proved adept at the machine, partly because his hearing loss made him oblivious to other noises and distractions in the telegraph office. He heard only the clicking of the Morse code.

Over the next five years, Edison held a number of telegraph-operator jobs throughout the Midwest, but he continued to read extensively. He was particularly devoted to *Experimental Researches in Electricity and Magnetism,* a multivolume book from British physicist and chemist Michael Faraday (1791–1867). Faraday's work in the 1830s in electromagnetism (the study of electricity and magnetism) was crucial to the development of electricity, but reading about Faraday's methodology was also crucial to Edison for another reason: Edison disliked math, and much of the scientific experimentation of the era had urged its mastery. Faraday believed otherwise, and Edison decided to pursue a career as an inventor, despite his lack of formal education.

Edison settled in Boston in 1867, taking a job at a Western Union Telegraph Company office. By then he was testing different ways to improve the telegraph machine, which led to other experiments in electronic communication. He received

Edison's universal stock ticker. *(AP/Wide World Photos. Reproduced by permission.)*

the first patent (a legal document issued by a government granting exclusive authority to an inventor for making, using, and selling an invention) of the 1,300 patents in all of his career—more than any other American—for an electrographic vote recorder in 1869. His device recorded the voice votes in the state legislative assembly, but it failed to ignite much interest. Edison vowed from then on that he would not make something he could not sell, or that did not have commercial application.

Potential financial backers were impressed by Edison's incredible work habits. He regularly boasted of sleeping just a few hours a night, relying on brief naps to refresh his mind and body. Established business leaders provided the capital (accumulated wealth or goods devoted to the production of other goods) for his first ventures, and with that he began to perfect the earliest electric-transmission devices. He made one vast improvement to the telegraph machine, creating a method for transmitting two messages at the same time across a single wire. Another early invention was a device that kept stock tickers (telegraphic receiving devices that automatically print off stock quotations) in unison; when the Gold and Stock Telegraphic Company bought it in 1870, he was paid the enormous sum of $40,000 for the patent rights.

Edison moved on to the New York City area, and by the end of 1870 had set up a laboratory in nearby Newark, New Jersey. On Christmas Day 1871 he married a young woman named Mary Stilwell who had been hired as a telegraph clerk in a subsidiary company of his, the News Reporting Telegraph Company. By then Edison was prospering, both as an inventor and entrepreneur, and young electrical engineers came from across the United States and even Europe to work with him— often at an extremely rapid pace. This was the first enterprise dedicated solely to making new discoveries that would have potentially lucrative applications in the consumer and industrial sectors. The atmosphere at Edison's lab was driven by the belief that the world could be changed overnight by sheer determination and hard work in pursuit of innovation. Edison took the concept of mass production, in which one worker was devoted to a specific task, and applied it to the process of scientific invention. The setting was later replicated in many other industries, and is the foundation of the research and development (R&D) divisions of major corporations.

Moved invention factory to Menlo Park

In 1876 Edison was able to move his invention factory facility into larger quarters in Menlo Park, New Jersey, and from it a record number of innovations were created over the next decade. He became world-famous and was dubbed the "Wizard of Menlo Park" in the press. One of his first significant patents was again tied to the work of Alexander Graham Bell. A Canadian of Scottish birth, Bell had patented a device for the transmission of voice over telephone wires in 1876, but Edison designed a part that made a vast improvement in sound quality. His carbon-button transmitter was a type of miniature battery. A pair of carbon buttons were connected to one another by a wire. One of them was also attached to the telephone receiver. When the receiver picked up human speech,

Thomas Edison in his laboratory in Menlo Park, New Jersey. *(© Bettmann/Corbis.)*

the buttons would be pressed closer together, reducing electrical resistance so that the transmitted sound was clearer. The carbon-button transmitter that Edison devised remained the standard in telephone speakers and microphones for more than a century.

The telephone-receiver work that Edison carried out led to what historians deem the most innovative and imaginative creation of Edison's impressive career: the phonograph. In his research, he recognized some principles governing the steel stylus, or pen-type device, that attached to a diaphragm, the disk that vibrates to generate sound waves. He imagined that the stylus could imprint vibrations onto a piece of moving tinfoil, and so he designed a tinfoil-covered cylinder (a tube-shaped part with an attached lever) that, when cranked by hand, was imprinted with grooves from the stylus. The device could then be rewound, and the brief recording—about ten seconds long for the first version—would be repeated. Edison first demonstrated this in December 1877, reciting the beginning lines of a well-known poem for children, "Mary Had a Little Lamb." His first phonograph was instantly dubbed the "talking machine," and it stunned those who witnessed it. Though it took several further improvements to make it ideal for recorded music, within a decade the phonograph had caught on with the public, and went on to revolutionize popular culture by providing a cheap, easy way to reproduce music.

The most significant invention of Edison's career, however, was the fiber element inside the incandescent light bulb. He did not invent the light bulb, which actually dated back to the work of English chemist Joseph Wilson Swan (1828–1914) in the late 1840s. Swan's efforts were tied to the idea that an electrical current can pass through a filament, or a thin wire. When it met with resistance, the wire heated up and gave off a steady light. However, Swan and other experimenters had a difficult time coming up with a way to keep the filament from burning up altogether. Encasing the wire inside a vacuum tube, a glass cylinder from which all air had been removed, seemed to be one way, but the filament still burned out too quickly to have any practical use. After trying nearly six thousand types of vegetable fibers, Edison and his team of researchers developed a charred cotton thread for the filament inside the bulb in October 1879. He had his assistants help him watch it for the next two days, and the bulb gave off a glow for forty hours straight.

News of Edison's light bulb was announced in the *New York Herald* newspaper on December 21, 1879. A year earlier, Edison had formed the Edison Electric Light Company with a group of wealthy investors that included Wall Street financier **J. P. Morgan** (1837–1913; see entry). The news of the world's first long-burning light bulb caused concern in the gas market, and share prices for gas companies dropped immediately. The streets of major cities, beginning with London, England, in the 1820s, were lit by gas lamps, but these needed to be tended to nightly. Their successor, arc lights, used a primitive form of electrical current but were dangerous and gave off strong fumes, making them impractical for household use. Various types of oil and gas lamps were the only widespread method of household lighting before Edison's incandescent bulb.

Edison applied for a patent on his electric incandescent lamp bulb on January 27, 1880, but a court ruled he must share the patent with Swan. Light bulbs went on sale that same year, but the problem of delivering an electrical current to them remained. Back at the lab, Edison devoted himself to creating a series of switches, devices, and transmitters that could conduct electricity to homes and businesses. The system was first tried out in London at the Holburn Viaduct in early 1882. A more integrated version went into operation on September 4, 1882, inside the New York City branch of Edison's company. He threw the switch himself for what became the world's first power station. It generated electricity that powered about 59 residences in a one-square-mile radius surrounding the Pearl Street office.

Formed the Edison General Electric Company

From there, Edison's company expanded rapidly in the manufacture and installation of freestanding power plants that lit businesses, hotels, and theaters. The Pearl Street grid system was replicated across the cities and suburbs of America. In January 1883, the first electricity-delivery system that used overhead wires began lighting homes in Roselle, New Jersey. A modified version began lighting cities around the world. No other invention of the modern age altered daily life so immediately. Businesses stayed open later, students could study longer hours, and an array of electricity-powered consumer goods came onto the market. Edison's own company made one of the first electric appliances, a tabletop fan produced at its Fort Wayne, Indiana, factory. His various business ventures were consolidated, or folded together, to form the Edison General Electric Company in 1890. Two years later, this became the General Electric Company, one of the most successful companies in American business history.

Edison also made several advances in the earliest years of the motion-picture industry. He even produced a famous film, *The Great Train Robbery*, in 1903 but lost interest when he could not figure out how to master the problem of synchronizing sound with the film. He did, however, form the Motion Picture Patents Company (MPPC), also known as the Edison Trust, which held many of the first significant patents for the new technology. All the major film studios at the time belonged to it, and the MPPC vigorously pursued violations from outside filmmakers. This was one of the main reasons that some renegade film studios relocated to California; crews filming there could flee across the border to Mexico if they learned that MPPC agents were coming to investigate possible infringements against the Edison Trust. A 1915 U.S. Supreme Court decision cancelled all the patents held by the MPPC, however, on the basis that the cinema industry was a business and could not be run as a monopoly.

In the realm of pure scientific achievement, Edison's most important finding would come to be known as the "Edison effect." This has to do with how electrical current is directed, and he first observed the phenomenon on the carbon that stuck to the inside of the glass bulb. It seemed that the carbon was carrying an electrical charge as well, but because he did not see any commercial applications for it, he abandoned this field of inquiry as well. A few years later, however, English electrical engineer J. Ambrose Fleming (1848–1945) studied it further and realized it could be used to change the oscillating, or fluctuating, currents from radio waves. Despite his numerous and profoundly impacting inventions, Edison never won the Nobel Prize, but in 1912 he and Serbian-born physicist Nikola Tesla (1856–1943) were considered as joint nominees for it. Tesla had been a colleague of Edison's at the New Jersey lab in the late 1880s, but the two disagreed over electricity delivery methods. Tesla believed that alternating current (AC) was better, while Edison was an adherent of direct current (DC). In the end, the AC standard prevailed, but Edison remained obstinate, and Tesla was adamantly opposed to the idea of sharing the Nobel Prize with his professional rival.

Edison worked well into his senior years. His wife, Mary, with whom he had three children, died in 1884. In 1886 he wed Mina Miller, with whom he had another three children. Celebrated around the world, he was one of the most respected and legendary figures of his era. He had a summer home near Fort Myers, Florida, close to the residence of his friend, auto pioneer **Henry Ford** (1863–1947; see entry). In the Detroit area, Ford had established an extensive museum of technology, and with it a re-created historical village in which Edison's Menlo Park laboratory had been reconstructed. In 1929, to mark the fiftieth anniversary of the invention of his incandescent light bulb, Edison traveled to Dearborn, Michigan, the site of the Greenfield Village museum, to take part in an official ceremony to honor him. He collapsed during the festivities, and though he recovered, his health declined, and he was bedridden in his final months. He died on October 18, 1931, in West Orange, New Jersey. In tribute, President Herbert Hoover (1874–1964; served 1929–33) asked Americans to turn off their lights momentarily to honor Edison's lifetime of achievement and the most significant gift of his genius to the world.

Many people believe that Edison's legacy is unmatched in American history. From his early improvements to telegraph transmission, to his design of the light bulb and then the world's first power station for the safe delivery of electricity to homes, Edison was a visionary whose commitment to inventing the impossible ushered in an era of unprecedented consumer convenience. In 1928 Edison was awarded the Congressional Medal of Honor. At the award ceremony U.S. Treasury Secretary Andrew W. Mellon (1855–1937) noted, according to *Edison: Inventing the Century,* that Edison was a figure "set apart as one of the few men who have changed the current of modern life and set it flowing in new channels."

For More Information

Books

Baldwin, Neil. *Edison: Inventing the Century.* New York: Hyperion, 1995.

Periodicals

Gray, Paul. "Thomas Edison (1847–1931): His Inventions Not Only Reshaped Modernity but also Promised a Future Bounded Only by Creativity." *Time* (December 31, 1999): p. 184.

Hoar, William P. "The Man Who Lit Up the World: Thomas Edison Changed the World Through His Ability, Persistence—and Hard Work." *The New American* (June 30, 2003): p. 33.

Web Sites

Edison's Miracle of Light. http://www.pbs.org/wgbh/amex/edison/filmmore/index.html (accessed on July 7, 2005).

"History of Light." *General Electric.* http://www.gelighting.com/na/business_lighting/education_resources/learn_about_light/history_of_light/index.htm (accessed on July 7, 2005).

John Fitch

Born January 21, 1743 (Windsor Township, Connecticut)
Died July 2, 1798 (Kentucky)

Inventor
Entrepreneur

In 1787 American inventor John Fitch built the world's first working steamboat. He demonstrated the vessel on the Delaware River in Philadelphia, Pennsylvania, for a panel of prominent politicians who were meeting in the city to take part in the Constitutional Convention, the meeting of delegates to draft the U.S. Constitution. Fitch's boat was moved by steam-powered oars, and he became involved in a bitter rivalry with an inventor from Virginia who had also constructed a steam-propelled vessel around the same time. Neither boat was a financial success, however, and Fitch died in poverty. It took twenty years and the achievement of Robert Fulton (1765–1815) to launch the age of steam travel in America.

"I know of nothing so perplexing and Vexatious to a man of feelings, as a turbulant Wife and Steam Boat building. . . . [F]or one man to be [faced] with Both, he must be looked upon as the most unfortunate man in this World."

Early life and work

Fitch was born on January 21, 1743, in Windsor Township, Connecticut. He was descended from an old but unexceptional colonial family. His paternal ancestors had left Essex, England, and settled in the Windsor area in the early 1600s. Fitch was the last of five children in the family, and his mother died

John Fitch. *(© Bettmann/Corbis.)*

when he was four years old. His father, a farmer who was also a devout Presbyterian, was strict with him, and the two had an unhappy relationship. Fitch attended a local dame school, an informal classroom run by a woman in her home, until he was nine, but his father took him out of school in order to put him to work on the farm. Fitch eagerly read any book he could find when he was done with his chores, however, and was particularly fascinated by geography, astronomy, and mathematics.

Fitch first tried to leave the family farm by signing on as a sailor on a vessel whose route was along the Atlantic Ocean.

The ship endured terrible weather during his five-week tryout, and he gratefully returned to land. At the age of fifteen, he became an apprentice clockmaker but was not allowed to actually learn the trade. Instead he was given household chores, and complained so much about his duties that finally he was transferred to the shop of the man's brother, who was also a clockmaker. There, too, he was never allowed to even see a watch or clock being made or repaired. The brothers were probably not eager to train a future competitor in the area, and had simply wanted an extra hand for lowly jobs. Fitch did manage to learn some brass-making skills during his three years as an apprentice, and at the age of twenty-one he opened his own brass-smith business in East Windsor, Connecticut. He did well but lost a great deal of money on an investment in potash, a compound of potassium carbonate that was used in brass-making.

By this time Fitch had married Lucy Roberts of Simsbury, Connecticut, and was the father of a young son. Displeased with both his business and his marriage, he left in 1769, recounting in his autobiography that Lucy followed him out the door and far down the road pleading with him to stay. He did not know at the time that she was expecting a second child. He settled some distance away, in Trenton, New Jersey, where he again established a brass-making business that included some silversmith trade as well. With the onset of the American Revolution (1775–83), when the American colonists fought England to win their independence, Fitch enlisted in the Continental Army. He served briefly as a lieutenant but walked away when he was denied a promotion. Upon returning to Trenton, he found that his business had been looted and destroyed by English troops.

Settling around Bucks County, Pennsylvania, in late 1777, Fitch ran two successful businesses. He fixed guns for the Continental Army, and secretly sold tobacco and beer to the troops. In 1780 he headed west as a surveyor of lands. At the time the American West consisted of the areas past Pittsburgh, Pennsylvania, and the start of the Ohio River there. In Kentucky he put in a claim for 1,600 acres, a common practice at the time in the unsettled territory. In 1782 he went west again but was taken hostage by Delaware Indians, a Native American tribe that was allied with the English. He was handed over to English military authorities, taken to Canada, and held there until late 1782. Fitch later said that dreams he had of being chased by Delaware Indians in their canoes inspired his idea for a much faster watercraft.

Fitch made one final trip out west in 1785 and gained a bit of fame for a map he made of the Northwest Territory, as the area surrounding the Great Lakes was called during this period. He settled in Philadelphia and began work on his steamboat project. He claimed to have come up with the idea from a book that included an illustration of a steam engine. Steam had been first mentioned by the ancient Greeks as a possible source of power, but only in 1681 did a French inventor, Denis Papin (1647–1712), manage to harness its power. Papin built the first pressure cooker, and by 1712 an English inventor named Thomas Newcomen (1664–1729) had created a steam-driven water pump that became widely used in England's mining industry. In 1784 a Scot named James Watt (1736–1819) teamed with an English metalsmith and engineer, Matthew Boulton (1728–1809), to build the first successful steam engine. The Boulton & Watt engines were used extensively during the Industrial Revolution in England, but their export to the former colonies was banned by English law because of the war.

Steamboat demonstrated in Philadelphia

Initially Fitch dreamed of building a steam-powered wagon, which might have been the first successful automobile. But he switched to building boats instead, perhaps recognizing that the new American nation had few roads connecting its major Atlantic seaboard cities with the new lands of the Northwest Territory. However, there was a rich network of rivers and large streams from Pittsburgh's rivers to the Great Lakes, and further south to the port of New Orleans. Ships sailed by using wind power, which was effective for east-west journeys by ocean but extremely inefficient for river travel. Trade in the newly independent colonies was increasing, but river transportation was almost impossible. To take goods from Pittsburgh to New Orleans, for example, a barge had to be hauled down the Ohio and Mississippi Rivers by the laborers on board, pushing the boat with poles for almost the entire distance, and it took six weeks. The crew then had to walk back.

Fitch's first steamboat. *(© Bettmann/Corbis.)*

Fitch hoped to receive money from the Continental Congress, the early American legislature, to pursue his idea but could only secure the exclusive right to operate steamboats from a few states. He was granted a contract for New Jersey in 1786, and by 1787 he had won similar rights for vessels that would operate in Pennsylvania, New York, Delaware, and Virginia. Each of these gave him a fourteen-year monopoly (the exclusive possession or right to produce a particular good or service) on steamboat travel, which state governments granted in order to encourage inventors at a time when they had little extra money to help finance such projects themselves.

Fitch convinced a group of Philadelphia investors to fund his project. He teamed with Henry Voight, a Philadelphia clockmaker and master mechanic, to build a steam engine, since he was unable to buy a Boulton & Watt one. In August 1787 a panel of state and federal officials, meeting in Philadelphia for the Constitutional Convention, gathered to witness the steamboat's maiden voyage on the Delaware River. Fitch's method of moving the boat forward involved six steam-powered oars on either side of it, which made it look somewhat awkward, but it did move. Later steamboats that Fitch built employed a paddle wheel instead. This was a large wheel on the rear of a boat, part of which rested in the water. A steam engine made the wheel turn, and as it churned the water around, the boat went forward. This was a vast improvement over the oars.

Rival steamboat builder

Fitch's efforts were complicated by the arrival of James Rumsey (1743–1792) of Virginia, who was also working on a steamboat project. Rumsey had met George Washington (1732–1799) in 1784 and told him about his work. Washington was enthusiastic about Rumsey's idea for a boat and endorsed it publicly. Fitch went to see Washington in November 1785 at Washington's Virginia plantation and home, Mount Vernon. Fitch inquired about Rumsey's work, but Washington was hesitant to give answers. Fitch asked Washington for a letter of introduction to the Virginia Assembly, but Washington refused to write one. The former Continental Army commander may have remembered Fitch as a seller of beer and rum to his troops during the war. Furthermore, Fitch was the physical opposite of Rumsey. The Virginian was a handsome, well-dressed, gentleman farmer, while Fitch was scruffy in appearance, with shabby clothes and shoulder-length hair. In a February 1786 letter, Washington informed Rumsey of Fitch's steamboat work in Philadelphia, and Rumsey went to Philadelphia at one point to investigate. Both sides issued pamphlets defending their claims on the steamboat, a common form of public relations at the time. Fitch even wrote a lengthier work, *The Original Steamboat Supported,* in 1788.

In July 1788 Fitch launched a sixty-foot vessel with a paddle wheel that carried passengers between Burlington, New Jersey, and Philadelphia. A third boat, christened in 1790, traversed another section of the Delaware River, but public acceptance of the new form of travel was slow. Because of this Fitch's business failed to earn much return money for its investors. He was, however, granted a patent (a legal document giving an inventor the exclusive right to make, use, or sell an invention for a certain term of years) for his steamboat in August 1791, but Rumsey was awarded one that same day as well. This seemed to be a compromise decided on by future U.S. president Thomas Jefferson (1843–1826; served 1801–9), who was secretary of state at the time, but it meant that neither Fitch nor Rumsey earned money for their work.

Fitch began building a fourth boat, the *Perseverance,* but it was damaged in a bad storm while still under construction, and his weary investors finally pulled out of the project. He turned to Europe as a potential new source for funding and traveled to France, as Rumsey also had before he died in 1792. Fitch was granted a French patent for his steamboat in 1795, but he was also there during the unrest that followed the beheading of King Louis XVI (1754–1793; reigned 1774–92). The news of the king's death and the violence that followed had not yet reached America when Fitch sailed for France, and so he arrived in the Atlantic seaport of La Rochelle in April 1793 during a bloody civil war that brought business in the country to a standstill. He spent time in Nantes, then went on to London to look for investors there.

Settled in Kentucky

Out of money, Fitch returned to the United States by bargaining with a ship's captain for passage back to Boston, Massachusetts. In return, he had to spend several months as a dockworker in Boston. He then spent a year or so near his Windsor, Connecticut, hometown, probably at the home of his sister. Around 1796 he made one final attempt to find financial backers, stopping in New York City and demonstrating a small steam-powered vessel on a pond that then stood in Lower Manhattan, but his effort was unsuccessful. Fitch auctioned off his remaining business property, which included a boiler, cast-iron wheels, a lead pump, and his steam engine.

Fitch went to Kentucky to live on the land he had surveyed and claimed some fifteen years before. In the intervening years the area had been settled by many others, and he made a deal with a tavern keeper in the Bardstown area for room, board, and a pint of whiskey a day. In return he gave the bar owner the title to a tenth of his land. His biographers are in disagreement over whether he died by his own hand in July 1798, or from heart or liver failure, but he had written letters to friends stating his intention to drink himself to death.

Other inventors continued to work on the steamboat project, and a wealthy New York lawyer and politician, Robert Livingston (1746–1813), knew about Fitch's work from the time he had served in the Continental Congress. Livingston used his political connections to have Fitch's fourteen-year monopoly on steamboat travel in New York State taken away in March 1798. He then teamed with investors but their first boats were unsuccessful. In 1801 President Thomas Jefferson appointed Livingston to serve as minister to France, and there he met American engineer Robert Fulton, who was working on several projects for the French government, including one of the first working submarines.

Nine years after Fitch's death, in August 1807, Fulton and Livingston's boat, the *North River,* made its first trip from New York to Albany on the Hudson River. The vessel set a record time of thirty-two hours for a trip that usually took four days. Four years later a new boat from Fulton, the *New Orleans,* made its first trip from Pittsburgh to New Orleans, but the journey was slowed by one of the largest series of earthquakes ever to hit the continental United States. At one point just before the tremors began, the steamship passed just twenty miles from Fitch's grave in Bardstown, Kentucky. The era of steamboat travel had begun, and it helped a rapidly growing new nation expand with similar speed. Steam-engine locomotives followed, and even the steam-powered wagon that Fitch had once envisioned came to pass by the turn of the twentieth century.

For More Information

Books

Prager, Frank D. *The Autobiography of John Fitch.* Philadelphia, PA: American Philosophical Society, 1976.

Sutcliffe, Andrea. *Steam: The Untold Story of America's First Great Invention.* New York: Palgrave Macmillan, 2004.

Web Sites

"John Fitch: First Steamboat." *PBS.* http://www.pbs.org/wgbh/theymadeamerica/whomade/fitch_hi.html (accessed on July 7, 2005).

Henry Ford

Born July 30, 1863 (Dearborn, Michigan)
Died April 7, 1947 (Dearborn, Michigan)

Industrialist
Automotive executive

American automotive pioneer Henry Ford was one of twentieth-century industry's greatest innovators, and even during his lifetime he was proclaimed as the man who ushered in the modern age. Though he did not invent the gasoline-powered "horseless carriage," as the car was initially called, his inventive ideas about accelerating the manufacturing process made him one of the most important visionaries of the industrial age. Over a twenty-year period, his Ford Motor Company churned out some eleven million Model T cars, the first automobile to be mass-produced. The quick-moving assembly line at Ford's Detroit-area plant, where each worker was responsible for completing a single task, was a model of efficiency and became the standard for the modern factory floor. The concepts Ford first tested there would be widely copied by his competitors and applied to countless other manufacturing processes.

Ford often claimed that his ideas about efficient work habits were the result of his dislike of the farm chores he was forced to do as a child. "My earliest recollection is that, considering the results, there was too much work on the place," he

> "Paying good wages is not charity at all—it is the best kind of business."

Henry Ford.

wrote in his memoirs, according to Douglas Brinkley's *Wheels for the World: Henry Ford, His Company, and a Century of Progress*. Ford was born on July 30, 1863, at home on the family farm in Greenfield Township, Michigan. The area later became part of the city of Dearborn, a suburb of Detroit. Henry was the second of eight children in the family, and a third-generation Irish immigrant of Protestant stock. His education was basic and lasted just eight years, from 1871 to 1879. He lost his mother the year he turned thirteen, of complications from childbirth, and the teenager then became eager to escape the backbreaking life of the farm. He learned watch repair, and left the farm in

December 1879, when he was hired as an apprentice, or someone who is bound to work for someone else for a specific term in order to learn a trade, at a Detroit firm, James Flower and Brothers Machine Shop.

The Detroit job paid little, however, and his living expenses in the city were high, so Ford took a second job at a jewelry shop fixing watches in the evening hours. By the following summer, he was working at the Detroit Drydock Company, a thriving local shipbuilder, in its engine shop. When his apprenticeship period was completed in 1882, he found a job with the Westinghouse Engine Company repairing steam traction engines, wheeled engines used to move heavy loads or to provide power at various locations, on farms across southeastern Michigan. He occasionally returned to his father's farm to help out with chores but was still determined to forge his own career. Near the time of his 1888 marriage to Clara Bryant, who came from a nearby farm family, his father gave him a plot of land. The elder Ford strongly advised his son to set up his own farm, and the newlyweds did live on the property for a time. There Ford built a little shed to serve as his own machine shop, where he experimented with different types of engines. He had become increasingly fascinated with the emerging automobile industry.

Two German inventors, Gottlieb Daimler (1834–1900) and Karl Benz (1844–1929), had separately made important discoveries for a gasoline-powered engine and a four-wheeled vehicle in the 1880s. Their efforts launched an automobile-manufacturing industry in Europe, which then migrated to the United States and joined the push to build a self-propelled vehicle already underway there. In 1893 Massachusetts brothers Charles E. Duryea (1861–1938) and J. Frank Duryea (1869–1967) built the first American-made, gasoline-powered automobile and started their own company to manufacture more. Ford, because of later legal difficulties and possibly as an attempt to secure his place in history, would claim that he had also designed and built a self-propelled gasoline vehicle—or, in other versions of the story, a working motor for one—in the period between 1888 and 1892, but such claims have been disproved as early company lore.

Invents the quadricycle

Ford quit farm life forever in mid-1891 when he took a job as a night engineer with the Edison Illuminating Company in Detroit. Within a short time he was promoted to chief engineer, at a salary of $100 a month, but he continued to work on a prototype vehicle inside the small brick workshop behind his two-family Detroit house. He saw the debut outing of Detroit's first car, built by Charles B. King and Oliver E. Barthel in 1896, and that same year achieved his true manufacturing first: a four-cycle, air-cooled engine that operated on two cylinders and had a four-horsepower (h.p.) capacity. He named it the quadricycle, and it made its first run on June 4, 1896.

Ford had gained a reputation as one of the city's new generation of technological innovators, and Detroit's mayor and other business leaders provided the start-up money for his first automobile-manufacturing venture, called the Detroit Automobile Company. The first model was a two-passenger car, which featured an inventive electric-spark ignition and chain-and-sprocket transmission. The Detroit Automobile Company was incorporated on August 5, 1899, the first in the city established solely for the purpose of making gasoline-powered vehicles, but it went under late in 1900 after producing just twenty vehicles. Many of the other early car-manufacturing ventures in Detroit also had rough starts, and few of them survived their first decade in business.

Deeply committed to the possibilities of the internal-combustion engine, Ford was uninterested in making a car that was powered by any other method. The internal-combustion engine burned fuel (gasoline) within the engine rather than in an external furnace, as in a steam engine. Some of the early automobiles were driven by steam power, and for a few years there was a tremendous industry debate over which was better— gasoline or steam. Steam engines could be lit with a match and did not require the driver to manually hand-crank the engine to start it. There was also a small but growing electric car market, which were especially well-suited to women drivers because they were also simple to start. Neither steam nor electric vehicles could attain anything but a rather leisurely speed, and Ford knew that the internal-combustion

The Rise of the Motor City

Detroit's rise to become the center of the automotive industry did not happen entirely by accident. When bicycles became the newest craze in the 1880s, Michigan and neighboring Ohio emerged as manufacturing centers. Detroit also boasted many carriage-making shops, and there were numerous producers of marine engines as well. In short, the city had many small light-industrial shops and a large skilled-labor force who staffed them, both of which easily made the transition to automotive manufacturing. Furthermore, the engine-building process required iron ore, and there were vast mines of it in Michigan's Upper Peninsula, and a highly developed water-transportation system that brought it to Detroit. Finally, Detroit had a good number of wealthy citizens—Midwest tycoons who had made quick fortunes in timber or shipping—who were eager to fund new ventures. All of these factors earned Detroit its reputation as the "Motor City." Although the automobile industry declined in the late twentieth century, the country's top three auto manufacturers, Ford, General Motors, and Chrysler still have their headquarters in Detroit.

engine might be perfected enough to be able to reach a much more advanced horsepower. He was encouraged to further develop the gas-powered engine by world-famous inventor **Thomas Edison** (1847–1931; see entry), whom Ford met on a trip to New York when he was still the chief engineer at the Edison plant. Edison asked Ford about his side project, and Ford sketched it out for him. Edison agreed that a car with an internal-combustion engine was the ideal, for electric-car batteries were far too heavy, and needed to be near a recharging station.

Ford tinkered with engines and aerodynamics, or how air flows around an object, on prototype cars that he raced himself on a track in Grosse Pointe, a posh resort community north of the city. This was a shrewd marketing strategy that attracted influential crowds and boosted his reputation as an innovator. A new group of investors recapitalized the Detroit Automobile Company, but Ford disagreed with their strategies and resigned in March 1902. He found a more like-minded partner in Alexander Y. Malcomson, a successful Detroit coal dealer, and once again was made a principal in a company in which he had invested not a cent of his own money. On June 16, 1903, the Ford Motor Company was formally incorporated.

The Model A is introduced

The Model A was Ford's first vehicle, and it sold for $850. It had a two-cylinder, eight h.p. engine and began selling at a rate of over one hundred each month. The cars were made at a new Ford factory on Piquette Avenue and Beaubien Street, but Ford ran into problems with Malcomson, who wanted to concentrate on top-of-the-line models, like the Model B of 1905, which sold for $2,000. Nearly all the automobile manufacturers in this era focused on producing luxury vehicles. The costs of manufacturing a single car were still quite high and most companies believed that the initial start-up costs could be more easily recovered by selling high-end cars, which had higher profit margins. Ford believed otherwise and bought out Malcomson's share in the company.

Ford's next big project was the Model N, introduced in 1906 with a base price of $700. His plan was to make 10,000 of them in one year, and he teamed with Walter E. Flanders, an expert in the machine-tool industry, to refine the manufacturing process. Flanders's ideas formed the basis of Ford's new arrangement for the factory floor to reach maximum efficiency, and the company thrived. The legendary Ford Model T was introduced on October 1, 1908. It was the reliable, affordable car that permanently shifted the automotive industry focus from the luxury consumer to the mass market. It featured a four-cylinder, twenty h.p. water-cooled engine and an innovative magneto starter, which was a self-contained starter unit that provided power to the spark plugs. It originally sold for $850, but Ford managed to reduce the costs of production and offer three different versions by 1916, the cheapest of which was the Runabout, which sold for $345.

Ford was able to reduce costs because of his company's production methods. The maximum-efficiency concept became a reality with the design of an even larger new Ford plant, this one located on sixty acres in Highland Park, just outside the Detroit city limits. It was a state-of-the-art facility, designed by noted architect Albert Kahn (1869–1942), and was the largest industrial plant in the state when Ford models began rolling off its new assembly line on December 1, 1913. It cut the average assembly time for one vehicle from 728 minutes to an astonishing 93 minutes. The idea was based upon a continuously moving assembly process, helped along by overhead conveyors; materials were also brought to the worker by gravity, with items coming down chutes. The work came to the worker, not the worker to the work, with everything located at waist level to reduce wasted movement.

The Highland Park factory produced cars at a fast pace that attracted attention from around the world, and its methods were soon widely copied in the production of countless other consumer goods. But Ford's company built no other cars except for the Model T for nearly twenty years. Since black paint dried the fastest, the other colors in which it was first offered were eventually dropped, giving rise to Ford's famous pronouncement, "Any customer can have a car painted any color that he wants so long as it is black," according to Brinkley. The Model T sold well in rural America, at a time when farms still dominated the landscape and agriculture was a mainstay of the economy. It was ideally suited to bad roads because of its sturdy construction, and farmers were enthusiastic about the way it had transformed their lives. Rural areas were no longer isolated because now people could easily travel back and forth between the city and the country.

The $5-a-day wage

Ford and his team of engineers continued to perfect the manufacturing process, but the emphasis on efficiency alienated workers at the plant. The company seemed to view them as if they were part of the factory itself, not human beings. To soothe growing discontent, Ford announced a new $5 a day wage in January 1914; he also reduced the day's work hours at his plant from nine to eight. At the time, the rate in Detroit for unskilled labor was about $1.80 a day; skilled workers earned $2.50 a day. The American business community was outraged and predicted that Ford's headline-grabbing strategy would be the death of his company. Wall Street was also contemptuous, but in other quarters Ford was hailed as the new breed of company president, one who was both progressive-minded and a humanitarian.

Ford's influence and innovation seemed to peak around this time, however. During World War I (1914–18; a war in which Great Britain, France, the United States and their allies defeated Germany, Austria-Hungary, and their allies) he provided heavy financial support to a foundation that attempted to negotiate an end to the European conflict on board a "Peace Ship." The press criticized Ford heavily for this. At the office, he had battles with longtime trusted associates and investors, many of whom left. There were nasty legal fights as well; eventually a court ordered his company to pay its minority shareholders millions of dollars. Ford used this 1919–20 crisis as an opportunity to retake control of his company by buying up all outstanding shares and turned the Ford Motor Company into a privately held one. It remained a predominantly family-run business until 1956, when it became a publicly traded company, but Ford's descendants still hold a majority stake.

Ford did not like books and was dismissive of art; he was a poor public speaker, and his business rivals mocked his limited education. In 1919 he was called upon to give testimony in a libel case he had instigated against the *Chicago Tribune,* which had described him as an "anarchist," linking him to radical political groups of the era who believed in the overthrow of organized government, in a 1916 editorial because of his anti-war views. The automotive tycoon was repeatedly asked by defense lawyers during cross-examination to read documents they set before him, but he evaded the challenges. The trial judge supported the newspaper's right to freedom of the press, and that decision was upheld by the Illinois Supreme Court on appeal. Ford also became involved in politics, losing a 1918 bid for one of Michigan's two U.S. Senate seats. He invested some $4 million into a newspaper called the *Dearborn Independent,* which published offensive editorials and promoted the idea of a worldwide "Jewish conspiracy," the claim that European and North American Jews had an unusual amount of influence in the corporate world and the media. The paper had a nine-year run, but Ford was finally forced to close it in 1927 when a Chicago lawyer sued him for defamation of character, or unfairly attacking his reputation.

The Rouge plant

In the end, Ford had one final and grand idea that secured his place in American manufacturing history: the Rouge plant, located on the banks of the Rouge River that ran near his boyhood home in Dearborn. The massive facility opened in stages just after World War I. It was soon the largest industrial complex in the world. Visitors came from every country to

Ford's Rouge plant. *(© Rykoff Collection/Corbis.)*

study its methods and marvel at its efficiency. Raw materials arrived at one end of the plant by ship or train, and a car came out on the other end. The Rouge had everything necessary in the automotive manufacturing process right on site, from blast furnaces to foundries, where metal was cast, to glass-making kilns (high-temperature ovens), all arranged in the most efficient way possible.

Ford and his wife had only one child, a son named Edsel (1893–1943), who took over as company president in 1918. The father, however, remained a commanding presence. The family had a lavish estate, called Fair Lane, also on the banks of the Rouge, but in a more rural spot. In his senior years, Ford seemed to retreat into the past and was keen to preserve a vanishing rural America—the same one he had been so eager to escape in his youth. He established a historical museum and village in Dearborn, called Greenfield Village, that became a model for modern-day historic preservation.

Ford's nostalgic ideas of his earlier years did not seem to keep pace with the times. As one of the leading industrialists of his era, he was strongly opposed to labor unions, and the Ford Motor Company had an internal security department whose union-busting hired hands were among the most notoriously brutal thugs inside an already-violent anti-union movement. They were supervised by Harry H. Bennett (1892–1979), the company's director of personnel and plant security. The company was the last of the major Detroit automakers to sign a contract with the United Automobile Workers union, and Ford allegedly did so only after his wife threatened to leave him. Clara Ford had taken the side of their son, Edsel, who believed that Bennett exerted undue influence over his aging father.

By 1941 Ford suffered the second of two strokes, and his health declined. Edsel died of stomach cancer in May 1943. Bennett used the opportunity to move toward taking over but was quickly ousted by Edsel's son, Henry Ford II (1917–1987), who joined the company in August 1943. The youngest Ford led the company through its impressive postwar boom years, and though it later became a publicly traded one, descendants of the founder still held vital positions in the company leadership ranks a century later.

Ford died on April 7, 1947, of a cerebral hemorrhage at his Fair Lane estate. Years before, a younger man had been discussing educational issues with him and pointed out, "These are different times: this is the modern-age," to support his argument. "Young man," Ford retorted, according to Brinkley, "I invented the modern age."

For More Information

Books

Bak, Richard. *Henry and Edsel: The Creation of the Ford Empire.* Hoboken, NJ: Wiley, 2003.

Brinkley, Douglas. *Wheels for the World: Henry Ford, His Company, and a Century of Progress.* New York: Viking, 2003.

Periodicals

Iacocca, Lee. "Driving Force—Henry Ford." *Time* (December 7, 1998): 76.

Web Sites

The Model T. http://www.hfmgv.org/exhibits/showroom/1908/model.t.html (accessed on July 7, 2005).

Frank and Lillian Gilbreth

Frank B.Gilbreth
Born July 7, 1868 (Fairfield, Maine)
Died June 14, 1924 (New Jersey)

Lillian M.Gilbreth
Born May 24, 1878 (Oakland, California)
Died January 2, 1972 (Scottsdale, Arizona)

Industrial engineers
Management consultants
Authors

Industrial engineers Frank and Lillian Gilbreth were one of the most well-known working couples in the United States during the early years of the twentieth century. Corporations hired them for their pioneering work in scientific industrial management, while magazines profiled their smoothly run household and large family of eleven children. The Gilbreths were efficiency experts at both home and work, and they conducted motion studies, or the analysis of a specific job to determine the most efficient way to accomplish the task, and analyzed workforce behavior for dozens of industrial companies in the United States and Europe. By mid-century many of their ideas for streamlining work processes had been incorporated into the daily operations of the nation's factories. The Gilbreths authored numerous books and articles, both together and separately, and Lillian's works introduced psychology into the field of modern industrial management. Yet no title of

> "It was a fifty-fifty proposition throughout. Any woman can do it with that sort of husband."
>
> *Lillian M. Gilbreth.*

Frank and Lillian Gilbreth. *(Underwood & Underwood/Corbis. Reproduced by permission.)*

theirs ever sold as well as the 1948 book written by a son and daughter, *Cheaper by the Dozen*. The amusing memoir documented the Gilbreths' attempts to apply their time-management theories to their household.

The Gilbreths became nationally known around 1915, but Frank had achieved some measure of fame before their 1904 marriage. He was born in July 1868, in Fairfield, Maine, into an old New England family. His father, a local hardware businessman, died when Frank was three years old. His mother left the area to find better schools for Frank and his siblings, and they eventually settled in Boston, Massachusetts. Frank finished at the city's English High School in 1885, but his mother was disappointed when he decided against college. He had qualified to enter the well-respected Massachusetts Institute of Technology but chose to become a bricklayer's apprentice instead.

The "one best way"

Gilbreth had larger ambitions and had taken the job merely as training for a career in construction management. He found his true calling, however, on his first day on the job. He realized that the bricklayer who was instructing him used three different methods—one to demonstrate, another when he was talking with colleagues while working, and a third when he was falling behind. Other laborers also seemed to vary in their work styles, and Frank became determined to discover what he called the "one best way" to lay brick, or to do any task. He gained hands-on experience in several building trades and took courses in mechanical drawing at night school. By 1895 he had established his own contracting firm in Boston, Frank Gilbreth and Company, whose slogan was "Speed Work."

Gilbreth made sure his employees knew the "one best way" to carry out their jobs, but he was open to suggestions from them and looked for innovative ideas or products that would make their jobs easier. When he could not find something he needed for the business, he invented it himself, and one of his earliest patents (legal documents giving an inventor the exclusive right to make, use, or sell an invention for a certain term of years) was for a vertical scaffold for working on the sides of buildings. When his firm became skilled at pouring concrete, a new construction material that had begun to replace brick, he devised a new type of concrete mixer. Another of his patents was for an early waterproofing product for concrete basements.

When Gilbreth's firm won the bid to construct the Lowell Laboratory at the Massachusetts Institute of Technology, the building was finished in only eleven weeks. It made newspaper headlines on the East Coast and led to larger and more profitable jobs. The company built dams, canals, and residential and factory buildings.

The Gilbreth family

Gilbreth met Lillian Moller of Oakland, California, in 1903. She came from a wealthy family of real estate developers and was planning to go to Europe after having earned a master's degree in English from the University of California at Berkeley. Brilliant and determined, she planned on pursuing a doctorate, although at that time women who held graduate degrees were still quite rare.

It would take Lillian some time to earn that last degree, for not long after she and Gilbreth wed in October 1904 she found herself expecting their first child. Anne was born in September 1905, followed by eleven siblings, one of whom died at the age of five from diphtheria, a deadly childhood disease that affected the heart and nervous system. In the first years of their marriage, the Gilbreths lived in New York City. Frank's mother lived with them for many years and provided much-needed help in caring for the growing clan. The last Gilbreth child, Jane, was born in 1922.

Lillian had already started to use her writing skills even before their marriage, revising a booklet Frank had written entitled *Field System*. He had interviewed his workers at length, finding out how their day progressed and incorporating their suggestions for improvement. The work, not published until 1908, was written to be read specifically by laborers, which was an unusual notion at the time.

Became followers of Taylorism

Still fascinated by the "one best way" theory, Frank discovered the ideas of Frederick Winslow Taylor (1856–1915). Frank first met Taylor in 1907, and he and Lillian became members of Taylor's growing circle of professional followers. Considered the founder of the field of scientific management, Taylor believed that managing an industrial workplace could be a professional field of study all by itself, on the same level as engineering or law. Overseeing a large crew of workers and helping the workplace run smoothly was no easy task in the increasingly complex industrial age, and Taylor believed that there were a number of principles and concepts that should be mastered by a professional manager.

Taylor's theory of scientific management was based on his extensive research on the factory floor. He believed that an employee whose job involved a dull or unchallenging task would work at the slowest pace he could without attracting the attention of his supervisors. Taylor called this "soldiering," and some of the ideas he devised, such as rest breaks for workers, were attempts to eliminate the behavior. However, Taylorism, as his philosophy was known, also made him the enemy of organized labor. Taylor's views about factory efficiency seemed to view employees as part of the machinery itself, and he was known to be sharply critical towards them. Some workers even staged walkouts when the management expert, with his ever-present stopwatch, was brought in to reorganize a work site.

The Gilbreths' philosophy of scientific management treated the workers more fairly, and some of this was because of Lillian's interest in industrial psychology. Lillian decided to return to school to work on her doctorate, this time in psychology. She was unable to receive her degree from Berkeley because of residency requirements, but her dissertation (a written treatment of a subject, usually submitted to earn a doctorate) was published as *The Psychology of Industrial Management*. The publisher, however, insisted it appear under the name L. M. Gilbreth, so that it would not be automatically rejected by its intended male readership because the author was a woman.

Frank Gilbreth eventually abandoned his construction business to concentrate on industrial management full time. He wrote more books with Lillian, and both were active in the American Society of Mechanical Engineers. In 1910 Frank testified before the Interstate Commerce Commission (ICC) in Washington, D.C. This was a federal agency established to monitor the rates that railroads charged their freight customers. He explained to lawmakers the principles behind his motion studies of workers on the job. At one point he even demonstrated his point by stacking up law books to show how a brick wall was built. He argued that the railroads, which had asked the ICC for permission to raise their tariffs, or rates, could be run more efficiently by using some of the ideas behind scientific management. In the end the commission members voted against the proposed tariff increase, and

Gilbreth's new management consulting business earned a lot of free publicity.

The year 1912 was one of great change for the Gilbreths. They had five children by then, but their second daughter, five-year-old Mary, died at home of diphtheria in January. They also had a professional disagreement with Taylor, who even claimed that he had given Frank Gilbreth the idea for the adjustable scaffold back in the 1890s, long before the two had ever met. Taylor was under a great deal of criticism at the time, and his ideas were called authoritarian (favoring blind submission to authority) and insulting to the workers. He was forced to defend them before lawmakers who sat on the Labor Committee of the U.S. House, and that led to a forty-year ban on the use of the stopwatch on any federal project.

The Gilbreths moved to Providence, Rhode Island, in May 1912 so that Lillian could enter Brown University and finally earn her doctorate. Their new consulting firm had also won its first major client, the New England Butt Company, which made the braiding machines that were used to manufacture shoelaces and other consumer goods at its vast Providence headquarters. The Gilbreths installed the factory organization scheme known as the Taylor system there but also put some of their own theories into practice. One of these was a suggestion box, and the company gave a monthly cash prize to the worker with the best new idea.

Lillian was a strong advocate of the rest break, which was considered an unusual concept at the time. She presented studies proving that it actually increased productivity in workers. She also designed a number of motion study experiments, which Frank carried out at the Butt Company. The motion studies would become the Gilbreths' most significant professional achievement, and they spent hours perfecting their ideas. At their home Frank set up a special desk with a grid pattern on it. He filmed Lillian doing various small tasks over the squares of the grid while she wore a ring with a small electric light attached to it. They then studied the film footage and plotted out, with the help of the grid, how to reduce wasted motion. Their system, which they named the stereo-cyclegraph, was first used at their next consulting job, this time for a New Jersey handkerchief factory.

Pioneering work with war veterans

In 1913 the Gilbreths founded the Summer School of Scientific Management, which offered courses on their motion study and psychology research. The school was well attended by management professionals from across the United States and helped boost their reputation as innovative industrial engineers. During the early part of World War I (1914–18; a war in which Great Britain, France, the United States and their allies defeated Germany, Austria-Hungary, and their allies), Frank was hired by Allgemeine Elektriziäts Gesellschaft (AEG), a huge German company that was similar to General Electric in the United States. He spent two months touring AEG factories and suggesting improvements, and during this time he saw the permanently injured soldiers returning from the battlefield. He began to think about applying some of the motion study ideas to try to help the suddenly disabled recover physically.

Frank began working with veterans in military hospitals who had lost a limb or part of one. Out of this effort came his study of the seventeen fundamental motions used to perform physical tasks. These included search, find, select, grasp, and position, and each of these he called a "therblig," which was Gilbreth spelled backwards. He devised a chart that showed diagrams for each, which was used to help the disabled relearn certain tasks.

Lillian, meanwhile, was granted her doctorate from Brown in 1915. She was the first among the founders of scientific management to earn one in the field of industrial psychology. One of the few women of her generation to accept a Ph.D. at a commencement ceremony, six of her children were there to cheer for her.

In the years following World War I, the Gilbreths' consulting business thrived. Frank was determined to avoid the bad reputation that Taylor had earned among ordinary workers and labor unions, and he would only take clients who were progressive in their attitudes. These included Eastman Kodak, U.S. Rubber, and Pierce Arrow, an automobile manufacturer. They were also hired by the Remington Typewriter Company to come up with the ideal method for teaching beginners how to type. By then the Gilbreths had discovered that their growing family could be used to help them carry out their research, and they practiced typing methods with the younger children

Cheaper by the Dozen

Frank Gilbreth Jr., the first of the Gilbreths' six sons, teamed with his sister Ernestine Gilbreth Carey, the second-oldest daughter, to write a comic memoir of their family life that was published in 1948. *Cheaper by the Dozen* spent months on the best-seller lists and was still in print fifty years later. Lillian approved of the manuscript, but was reportedly unhappy with her portrayal in a 1950 film version in which actress Myrna Loy (1905–1993) was cast to play her. The role of the fictional Gilbreth mother was further decreased in a 2003 remake that had little to do with the original book's plot and centered on the often comic daily life inside a household of twelve children. As Frank Jr. and Ernestine wrote in their book, newspaper photographers were regular visitors at their home, which would prompt their father to "whistle assembly, take out his stopwatch, and demonstrate how quickly we could gather. Then he would show the visitors how we could type, send the Morse code, multiply numbers, and speak some French, German, and Italian. Sometimes he'd holler '*fire*' and we'd drop to the floor and roll up in rugs."

on Remingtons with color-coded keys. Once the younger ones were put to bed, the older children sat down at typewriters with blanked-out keys.

Frank's interests in medicine and recorded motion studies led to his filming of operations in hospitals. He was the first person to do so, though it later became a common practice in medical schools. He also hired a camera operator when several of the Gilbreth children underwent surgery to have their tonsils removed. This was done at their home, but the footage was never released, perhaps because of technical problems. This multiple-surgery event appeared in the first film version of *Cheaper by the Dozen*, the 1948 best seller written by two of the Gilbreth children.

The Gilbreth system perfected—at home

In 1919 the Gilbreths moved to Montclair, New Jersey, where much of the household management system detailed in the book by Frank Jr. and Ernestine was perfected. All the Gilbreth children had chores and were expected to deliver written reports to their parents on various household efficiency topics. A weekly Sunday night council was held in order to discuss plans, special tasks, and goals for

Frank and Lillian Gibreth with their eleven children. *(© Bettmann/Corbis.)*

the coming week. Lillian was frequently profiled in newspapers and magazines as one of a new kind of American woman: the working mother. In the interviews she often pointed out that an efficiently managed household allowed a woman to pursue a career outside the home with a minimum of stress.

However, Frank's sudden death from a heart attack in June 1924 nearly ended Lillian's professional career. She quickly found that despite her impressive qualifications, corporate executives were unwilling to hire a woman consultant. With her typical ability to adapt, she instead turned herself into an expert on women's work. She founded the Motion Study Institute out of her home and wrote numerous articles for women's magazines about household management. Her book *The Home-Maker and Her Job* appeared in

1927. She was a consultant to appliance manufacturers and college home economics departments for many years and in 1935 was hired by Purdue University as a professor of management.

Lillian Gilbreth carried on some of her late husband's work with the disabled. She authored an early title in the field of modern occupational therapy, *Normal Lives for the Disabled,* with Edna Yost in 1944 and designed a kitchen for patients of New York University Medical Center's Institute of Rehabilitation that was widely copied. She remained active well into her senior years and was still lecturing at the age of ninety. She died in Scottsdale, Arizona, in January 1972.

The Gilbreths' work laid the foundation for industrial management of the twentieth century. One of their most important achievements came out of a presentation they made at the 1921 convention of the American Society of Mechanical Engineers. It was titled "Process Charts - First Steps in Finding the One Best Way" and showed a detailed method for organizing the flow of work in a manufacturing facility. The chart relied on simple symbols, with an arrow standing for a transportation step in the process (for example, when a product or part was moved from one station to another) and a square symbol standing for a quality inspection stage. The process chart was widely used during the American manufacturing boom of the 1940s and 1950s. But it was the more human-focused ideas that the Gilbreths championed—that the worker's input, physical well-being, and psychological health were all important to the ultimate financial success of a company—that made them pioneers in their field.

For More Information

Books

Gilbreth, Frank B. Jr. and Ernestine Gilbreth Carey. *Cheaper by the Dozen.* New York: Thomas Y. Crowell Company, 1948. Exp. Ed. 1963.

Lancaster, Jane. *Making Time: Lillian Moller Gilbreth—A Life beyond "Cheaper by the Dozen."* Boston, MA: Northeastern University Press, 2004.

Periodicals

"Assisting the Handicapped: The Pioneering Efforts of Frank and Lillian Gilbreth." *Journal of Management* (March 1992): p. 5.

"Frank and Lillian Gilbreth: Motion Study Pioneers." *Thinkers*. (December 2000).

Web Sites

The Gilbreth Network. http://gilbrethnetwork.tripod.com/front.html (accessed on July 7, 2005).

Florence Kelley

Born September 12, 1859 (Philadelphia, Pennsylvania)
Died February 17, 1932 (Philadelphia, Pennsylvania)

Social worker

"She galvanized us all into more intelligent interest in the industrial conditions about us."

Jane Addams.

Florence Kelley was a passionate crusader for workers' rights in an era when there was almost no federal or state regulation to protect them. She carried out much of her most important work in Chicago, Illinois, and lived at the famous Hull House settlement founded by **Jane Addams** (1860–1935; see entry). Kelley was tireless in her efforts to end child labor and improve working conditions for the women who were employed in the light-industry factories that produced consumer goods before the rise of organized labor. She was the first official inspector of factories in the state of Illinois, and she fought for the establishment of the Children's Bureau to protect the health and safety of the underage.

Background and education

Kelley was born on September 12, 1859, into a prominent Philadelphia family. Her father, William Darrah Kelley, was a local judge. One of the founders of the Republican Party in Pennsylvania, he was elected to Congress in 1860 and served in Washington, D.C., for thirty years. Kelley's mother, Caroline

Florence Kelley. *(UPI/Corbis-Bettmann. Reproduced by permission.)*

Bartram Bonsall, hailed from an old Philadelphia family of Quaker faith. Quakers are members of the Religious Society of Friends, a Christian group noted for its opposition to war, oath taking, and rituals. An ancestor, John Bartram (1699–1777), was known as the father of American botany and, in the 1720s, established the first botanical garden in the North American colonies.

Kelley was one of eight children in her family, but half died in infancy or childhood, and she was the sole daughter to survive. Her parents kept her out of school when she was young due to concerns for her health, but she was taught at home. By her teens she had become an eager reader with a sharp interest in politics and social reform movements. She entered Cornell University in 1876 as a member of its first coeducational class. Like her companions at Hull House, she was part of a new generation of college-educated American women who used their talents and energies to help the under-privileged and immigrant classes.

Continuing poor health forced Kelley to take time off from Cornell, but she eventually earned her undergraduate degree in literature in 1882. She hoped to enter the University of Pennsylvania law school, but even her family connections could not help her overcome the prejudices of the day against women professionals, and her application was rejected. For a time she taught night school courses for women in Philadelphia and then entered the University of Zurich in Switzerland, which was one of the few institutions at the time that would grant a doctorate degree to a woman. In Zurich she came to know a number of young Russians and Poles who had been forced to leave their native countries because of their radical political views, and she married one of them, Lazare Wischnewetzky, in 1884. He was a Polish-Russian physician, and they had three children together: Margaret, Nicholas, and John Bartram.

Translated famous book

Kelley's first major career achievement came thanks to that Zurich circle of political outcasts. She met Friedrich Engels (1820–1895), the German-born political philosopher who, with Karl Marx (1818–1883), co-authored the landmark 1848 work *The Communist Manifesto*. Engels asked her to translate an earlier book of his, *The Conditions of the Working-class in England in 1844*, into its first English edition in 1887. The nonfiction work described in horrific detail the living and working condi-tions of the Industrial Revolution's labor class and raised public awareness that some government regulation of business was needed.

By the time that work was published, Kelley and her hus-band had moved to America and settled in New York City. They were active in social circles there, but the marriage was an unhappy one, for Kelley's husband was physically abusive.

Friedrich Engels

Friedrich Engels was born into a wealthy German family that had earned its fortune from textile manufacturing. When he entered the family business as a young man, he was sent to Manchester, England, to run a cotton-producing plant there. Manchester had quickly become one of Europe's leading textile centers, and many Irish immigrants, fleeing a terrible potato famine on their home isle, came to find work in its factories. Engels was horrified by the conditions he saw in Manchester's slums and began recording his informal investigations on paper. The first edition of *The Conditions of the Working-class in England in 1844* was published in the original German in 1845. In his book Engels observed:

Friedrich Engels.

> *All conceivable evils are heaped upon the heads of the poor. If the population of great cities is too dense in general, it is they in particular who are packed into the least space. As though the vitiated [morally impure] atmosphere of the streets were not enough, they are penned in dozens into single rooms, so that the air which they breathe at night is enough in itself to stifle them. They are given damp dwellings, cellar dens that are not waterproof from below or garrets [rooms on the top floor of a house, usually under a sloped roof] that leak from above. Their houses are so built that the clammy air cannot escape. They are supplied bad, tattered, or rotten clothing, adulterated [contaminated because of inferior ingredients] and indigestible food. They are exposed to the most exciting changes of mental condition, the most violent vibrations between hope and fear; they are hunted like game, and not permitted to attain peace of mind and quiet enjoyment of life. They are deprived of all enjoyments except that of sexual indulgence and drunkenness, are worked every day to the point of complete exhaustion of their mental and physical energies, and are thus constantly spurred on to the maddest excess in the only two enjoyments at their command.*

Soon after the publication of his groundbreaking book, Engels joined with Karl Marx to produce their 1848 *Communist Manifesto*. It urged industrial workers to organize and overturn capitalism (an economic system characterized by private or corporate ownership of goods and free market competition). The communist world envisioned by Marx and Engels would do away with land ownership and inheritance. All industry, public transportation, and utilities would be run by the government; citizens would enjoy equal access to free housing, health care, and education; and eventually a classless society would arise.

In 1891 she left him, taking the children with her, and moved to Chicago, where a divorce was easier to obtain than it was in New York. She arrived without a job or a place to stay, but she knew of the work of Jane Addams and Hull House. One of the first settlement houses in the United States, Hull House operated by the principle that only through living among the poor could a Christian aid worker or social reformer truly understand their situation and provide help. Addams introduced Kelley to a local journalist, Henry Demarest Lloyd (1847–1903), whose 1894 work *Wealth Against Commonwealth* helped arouse public sentiment against the huge monopolies (companies that had exclusive rights to sell or produce a product) of American business during this era. Lloyd worked for the *Chicago Tribune,* the newspaper started by his father-in-law, and he and his wife took in Kelley and her children. She later lived at Hull House for a time.

In New York City Kelley had been active in a group that called for regular factory inspections by government agents to help stop child labor. The practice of employing underage workers, some as young as eight years old, was legal at the time, but there was a movement underway to force its end. Because of her previous experience, in 1892 Kelley was hired as a special agent for the Illinois Bureau of Labor Statistics. Her duty was to visit tenements (rundown apartments that barely meet minimum standards of safety, sanitation, and comfort) that also doubled as manufacturing sites. This arrangement occurred most commonly in the garment business. Clothing manufacturing was sometimes assigned on a piece-by-piece basis to the workers, and in some of the poorest immigrant neighborhoods of the city entire families sewed for fifteen hours a day.

Reform in Chicago

Kelley and her fellow inspectors launched a public awareness campaign, bringing in newspaper reporters to see the conditions in these garment shops for themselves. Chicago's dailies began publishing alarming accounts of toddlers infected with smallpox—a deadly contagious disease that caused high fever and a widespread rash—crawling near coats destined for the upscale Chicago department store Marshall Field's. Soon Kelley was called to testify before Illinois lawmakers in Springfield, where, reading from her notebook, she described conditions further, as quoted in *Report and Findings of the Joint Committee to Investigate the "Sweat Shop" System*:

> The first Saturday afternoon in June I found this scarlet fever case at 98 Ewing street. The mother was working alone, and employed no one else, in her own bedroom. At 65 Ewing street, the following week, I found a case, in a Sicilian family, where four children were just recovering from scarlet fever, and cloak making had been carried on continuously throughout the illness. On the second Sunday afternoon in July I found, at 145 Bunker street, a Bohemian customs' tailor, sewing a fine, customs cloak, not more than six feet from the bed; and on this bed his little boy lay dying of typhoid fever, and I ascertained that the child died of typhoid fever the following week. At 128 Ewing street I found a diphtheria notice posted, and the patient suffering on the ground floor, in a rear room, with cloaks being finished in the room in front, and knee pants in the room overhead.

The state legislature passed the Illinois Factory Act of 1893, partly due to Kelley's efforts. It was modeled after a piece of draft legislation that Kelley had written herself. It limited women to an eight-hour workday, restricted child labor, and called for the establishment of an office of factory inspector. That same year she was named to head that office by a newly elected, reform-minded Illinois governor, John P. Altgeld (1847–1902). Kelley wrote a number of reports during her four years on the job, giving simple, factual descriptions of the slums where the poor lived and the unhealthy conditions under which they labored. She also worked towards her law degree during this period and graduated from Northwestern University in 1895.

Kelley's next major project was inspired by the 1889 work of English philanthropist and sociologist Charles Booth (1840–1916). His *Life and Labour of the People of London* surveyed that city's districts and examined living conditions in much detail. Booth's work was the first to use the term "poverty line," which was the minimum income needed by a household to live decently. Kelley conducted similar research by going door-to-door in some of Chicago's worst neighborhoods, aided by a team of women she gathered from Addams's settlement house. The findings, published in 1895 as *Hull-House Maps and Papers,* became a valuable historic source for data on Chicago's ethnic communities.

Altgeld did not win his 1897 reelection bid, and Chicago's reform period came to an end for a time. Kelley lost her position as the state's factory inspector, and the groundbreaking Illinois Factory Act of 1893 was challenged and eventually declared unconstitutional by the Illinois Supreme Court. Remembering the impact of the newspaper campaign regarding the tenement garment factories had made on shoppers at Chicago's best stores, Kelley turned to consumer action as a method of spurring change. In 1899 she became executive secretary of the National Consumers' League and was the group's dedicated leader for many years. Its goal was to raise public awareness of the terrible conditions in which some of the finest American luxury goods were made. One of her first significant achievements as the league's head was the White Label, a federally approved mark on goods that assured shoppers the product had been manufactured under fair working conditions and without using child labor.

Champion of maternity care

Kelley had a long career even after she left Chicago in the early 1900s. She returned to New York City and was active in another well-known settlement house, Henry Street, until the mid-1920s. With its founder, Lillian D. Wald (1867–1940), she spent a decade advocating the establishment of the United States Children's Bureau. It was created by an act of President William Howard Taft (1857–1930; served 1909–13) in 1912. Kelley also worked toward the passage of a federal bill that would guarantee a minimum wage for working women and campaigned for passage of the Nineteenth Amendment that gave American women full voting rights. She was active in the National Conference of Charities and Corrections, which later became the Conference on Social Work, and in the final year of World War I (1914–18; a war in which Great Britain, France, the United States and their allies defeated Germany, Austria-Hungary, and their allies) she served as secretary of the United States board of control of labor standards for army clothing.

Among her extensive list of accomplishments, however, Kelley claimed she was proudest of the 1921 Sheppard-Towner Act. This bill authorized the establishment of partnership programs between the federal government and states' public health departments to reduce maternal and infant mortality (death) rates. Kelley spoke in support of the bill before Congress in 1920, telling lawmakers that she could still recall the grief in her own household when each of her siblings had died. She challenged them to demonstrate concern that an average of 680 infants and toddlers died every day in the United States that year.

Kelley was an excellent public speaker and was known for her energetic personality and quick wit. In 1905, with novelists Upton Sinclair (1878–1968) and Jack London (1876–1916), she became a cofounder of the Intercollegiate Socialist Society. (Socialism is an economic system in which the means of production and distribution is owned collectively by all the workers and there is no private property or social classes.) This group fostered the establishment of socialist political clubs on the campuses of American colleges and universities, and Kelley was one of its featured guest lecturers for a number of years. One student she impressed and became a mentor to was a 1910 Columbia University graduate, Frances Perkins (1807–1965). Upon receiving her degree, Perkins joined the New York Consumers' League and became the first woman ever appointed to a cabinet post when U.S. president Franklin D. Roosevelt (1882–1945; served 1933–45) made her labor secretary in 1933.

Kelley did not live to witness Perkins's achievement, nor many of the workplace changes that she herself had spent her career working to enact. She died in Philadelphia in 1932 at the age of seventy-three and was laid to rest on the grounds of a summer home she had in Brooklin, Maine. Several months later Roosevelt was elected to the White House, and among the sweeping changes that came during his historic New Deal period of labor and economic reform was a 1937 minimum-wage law for women and children. A year later Congress also passed the Federal Fair Labor Standards Act. This bill guaranteed all workers a minimum wage and specified a time-and-a-half rate of that wage for any hour worked above forty a week.

For More Information

Books

Diliberto, Gioia. *A Useful Woman: The Early Life of Jane Addams*. New York: Scribner/A Lisa Drew Book, 1999.

Linn, James Weber. *Jane Addams: A Biography*. Chicago: University of Illinois Press, 2000.

Periodicals

Frank, Dana. "Florence Kelley and the Nation's Work: The Rise of Women's Political Culture, 1830-1900" (book review). *Nation* (June 5, 1995): p. 797.

Web Sites

Document 10: "Florence Kelley's Testimony on the Sweating System," Report and Findings of the Joint Committee to Investigate the "Sweat Shop" System (Springfield, Illinois: H.W. Rokker, 1893), pp. 135-39. http://womhist.binghamton.edu/factory/doc10.htm (accessed on July 7, 2005).

Robert M. La Follette

Born June 14, 1855 (Primrose, Wisconsin)
Died June 18, 1925 (Washington, D.C.)

Politician
Lawyer

R obert M. La Follette served in the United States Senate for nearly twenty years, and was a key figure in the Progressive Era (the period of the Industrial Revolution that spanned roughly from the 1890s to about 1920, in which reformers worked together in the interest of distributing political power and wealth more equally). Before heading to Washington, La Follette spent five years as governor of his home state, Wisconsin. In both offices he championed some of the first laws in the country that placed government regulations on business and supported others that were aimed at helping average wage earners and farmers. La Follette was a well-known figure in his time and enjoyed immense popular support. When he ran for president as a third-party candidate in 1924, he won an impressive five million votes. That year he was the front-runner of the Progressive Party, which he had founded.

> "Free men of every generation must combat renewed efforts of organized force and greed to destroy liberty."

Background and early career

La Follette was born in June 1855, in his family's log cabin on a farm near Primrose, in Wisconsin's Dane County. His father, Josiah, was originally from Kentucky,

Robert Marion La Follette. *(© Corbis.)*

where La Follette's grandfather farmed land that was next to the property belonging to the father of U.S. president Abraham Lincoln (1809–1865; served 1861–65). Josiah died when La Follette was still an infant, and his mother remarried a much older man. He was a stubborn child and teen, and sometimes his stepfather disciplined him with beatings.

La Follette studied at the University of Wisconsin in Madison and emerged as an impressive public speaker. After graduation he took law classes at Madison and worked in the office of a local attorney before taking the bar examination. Admitted to the Wisconsin bar in February 1880, he opened his own practice in the city, which was also the state capital, and became active in Republican Party politics. He quickly became a noted figure in Madison, known for his compelling speeches, and for the fact that his thick hair seemed to stand straight up and add some inches to his below-average height. In 1882 he married Belle Case (1859–1931), whom he had met in college. She went on to become a lawyer as well, and would take an active role in his political career.

La Follette's first experience with politics came when he ran for the Dane County district attorney job in 1880, though he did not have the local Republican Party support to do so, who favored another candidate. He won the job and was reelected two years later. In 1884 he ran for a seat in the U.S. House of Representatives, once more defying his party bosses, and won that election as well. He went on to win two more two-year terms, but failed to win reelection in 1890. Other Republican Party members in the House also lost seats that year. One of the reasons for this was the Tariff Act of 1890, which called for a 50 percent tax on all goods coming into the United States from foreign producers. The act was designed to protect American farmers, but it was deeply unpopular. It had succeeded because of a closed-door congressional pact to pass the Sherman Silver Purchase Act along with it. That bill resulted in higher prices for many consumers because it put much more American currency into circulation, and Americans expressed their disapproval at the polls that year.

Once out of office La Follette returned to his Madison law practice, but in late 1891 the state Republican Party leader asked him to take a case defending some Republican officials— caretakers of the state treasury—who were accused of financial wrongdoing. La Follette claimed that he was offered a bribe to sway the case, which was going to be heard in the courtroom of a Democratic judge who also happened to be his brother-in-law. Disgusted by this and other acts of political dishonesty he had witnessed over the past decade, La Follette turned against the party and its Wisconsin leadership. He decided to shape his political career around his own ideals, not the party line.

Belle Case La Follette

When Belle Case accepted Robert La Follette's proposal of marriage, she asked that the word *obey* be removed from their wedding vows for the 1882 ceremony. Like her husband, La Follette was an independent thinker who had also been born in a Wisconsin log cabin. They met while students at the University of Wisconsin, and he encouraged her to pursue a law degree at the school after their marriage. This was an unusual choice of profession for her gender, for at that time few women worked outside of the home. In 1885 she became the University of Wisconsin's first female law graduate.

La Follette had returned to school after the birth of her first child, a daughter named Fola. The couple went on to have three more children: Bob Jr., Philip, and Mary. She was known as an efficient manager of the La Follette household, but she was also active in many other projects during her long career. Committed to women's suffrage (right to vote), she spoke at county fairs, urging women to become more politically active. In Washington she was shocked by the segregation of the Jim Crow era, as the laws were known that gave local communities the right to maintain separate public facilities for blacks and whites. She thought it shameful that the nation's capital was the site where African Americans from northern cities on their way to visit relatives in the South were forced to change trains and board segregated trains. She wrote several articles on the matter for *La Follette's Magazine,* the weekly she founded with her husband in 1909.

La Follette's husband often said that his wife was his best political adviser, and she played an essential role in writing many of his most important political speeches. He described her as "altogether the brainiest member of my family," according to the *Milwaukee Journal Sentinel,* and claimed that his wife's "grasp of the great problems, sociological and economic, is unsurpassed [not exceeded] by any of the strong men who have been associated with me in my work." After her husband's 1925 death, La Follette carried on his work at the magazine, which became *The Progressive.* She turned down an offer to serve out the remainder of his Senate term in favor of one of her sons and died in 1931, just after completing a biography of her husband.

La Follette's Progressive agenda

Some of La Follette's beliefs came from other political movements of the era, such as the Grange movement and Populism. The Grange movement arose in the late nineteenth century when American farmers banded together in local organizations to fight the excessive fees the railroads charged for transporting their goods. The Populist Party emerged out of an economic crisis for farmers in 1873, when the entire

U.S. economic system collapsed briefly because of the bankruptcy (a state of financial ruin in which an individual or corporation cannot pay its debts) of a well-known Philadelphia banking house that had extensive ties to the railroad industry. The price of agricultural goods fell sharply, and dozens of railroads went out of business in the subsequent panic. The Populist Party had widespread support in the relatively new western U.S. states, where farmers resented the influence of the East Coast financial establishment; the Populists believed that there should be more local control of prices and goods, not those dictated by Wall Street.

La Follette believed that the problem of political dishonesty could not be solved unless the caucus system was abolished. A caucus is a meeting of party members during which they choose who will become the party's next candidates. La Follette had been shut out of the process himself more than once and believed that the caucus system kept political power in the hands of a few. Direct primaries, in which voters went to the polls to choose candidates from a list of Republican or Democratic contenders, would become one of the main goals of his political career. He argued so forcefully for the change that he won over many Wisconsin voters, and the primary system would later become the standard in most American states. This was one of the Progressive movement's most lasting achievements.

La Follette's Progressive platform also supported a relatively new idea during the era: regulatory laws. These were regulations designed to keep businesses from operating without regard to the health and safety of their workers, the surrounding environment, and in some cases even the nation's overall financial stability. He found increasing support for his political views during two races he entered for the governor's office in 1896 and 1898. Struggling farmers in the western part of Wisconsin came to hear him speak at country fairs and were influenced by his ideas. He also found sympathetic audiences when he campaigned in the northern part of the state, where there was much resentment of the powerful lumber industry. During these campaigns La Follette was unable to win the Republican Party nomination as a candidate, but he finally did so in 1900 when the party bosses realized that he had tremendous popular support. He won the governor's race later that year.

Popular support

When La Follette became governor at the turn of the twentieth century, Wisconsin was deeply divided between rich and poor. Nearly half of all farms were mortgaged, meaning their owners owed money to banks for their land. The railroads charged high rates to transport crops, which cut into any small profit the farmer might earn for his labor. While many people were barely managing to cover their bills, railroads and other businesses were required to pay few taxes. The cities of the eastern part of Wisconsin—Milwaukee and Green Bay—were industrialized, but urban factory workers lived in terrible poverty.

La Follette's solution, which came to be known as the Wisconsin Idea, involved reform on several levels. The first was the passage of a law that ended the caucus system in favor of direct primaries. There would also be direct election of U.S. senators, who had previously been chosen by state legislatures. La Follette also called for a progressive tax, or one in which the wealthier citizens and corporations would pay a higher tax rate based on their income. Workers' compensation laws were another important issue he focused on once he entered the governor's office. At the time if a worker was permanently injured on the job, they were simply out of a job, even if the injury was the result of a dangerous workplace or improperly maintained machinery. Their only way to obtain compensation for the loss of income was to sue the employer, and the burden fell on the factory worker to prove that the employer was at fault for the injury. La Follette's workers' compensation law, a radical one in its day, called for automatic payments to the disabled who could no longer work and whose injuries were the result of their employers' disregard for workplace safety. Wisconsin was the first state to pass such a law.

La Follette battled to win support for these ideas during his first two terms, but they were blocked in the legislature by more conservative members of his own party. One fellow Republican even bought the *Milwaukee Sentinel* and regularly attacked La Follette in its editorial pages. Supporters established the *Milwaukee Free Press* and the *Capital Times* in Madison to counter the challenge. The fight served to split the state Republican Party in half, with the anti-La Follette side behaving so badly that in 1904, Wisconsin voters elected him to a third term and also replaced many Republicans in the state house with new Progressive lawmakers. A year later nearly all of La Follette's Wisconsin Idea bills were passed by the legislature and signed into law by him. He remained, if in name only, a member of the Republican Party.

La Follette in the Senate

La Follette then moved on to national politics, winning an election to become Wisconsin's U.S. senator in 1905. He took office the following year and served for the next nineteen years. By then Progressivism was gaining national recognition and had been adopted by President Theodore Roosevelt (1858–1919; served 1901–9). Roosevelt had been vice president under William McKinley (1843–1901; served 1897–1901) and took office when McKinley was assassinated. He immediately announced his intention to eliminate the mighty trusts that dominated the American economy. A trust is a group of companies joined for the purpose of reducing competition and controlling prices. There were oil trusts, railroad trusts, and even beef and sugar trusts. Roosevelt ran a 1904 reelection campaign on promises to break up the trusts and ensure fair market competition in the marketplace.

La Follette believed that Roosevelt was not truly committed to the Progressive platform but had merely recognized its appeal to a broad spectrum of voters in the Midwest and joined it as a political strategy. His battles with the president, and with Roosevelt's Republican and Democratic successors in the White House, were legendary. There was a rise in popular support for Progressive ideas in the years before 1914, however, and many of La Follette's Wisconsin Ideas began spreading to other states and were passed into law.

Unlike many in the U.S. Senate—which was known as the "millionaires' club" at the time because of the vast personal wealth of its members—La Follette was a supporter of labor unions. Organized labor, he believed, was one way that businesses could be restrained from taking advantage of their workers in order to make higher profits. Curbing corporate greed was important, he believed, because if workers continued to suffer they might turn to socialism, a political and economic theory that advocated collective or government ownership and administration of the production and distribution of goods. He wrote about many of his ideas in *La Follette's Magazine,* a weekly that he and his wife launched in 1909.

In 1911 La Follette's Washington home was the site of the first meeting of the National Progressive Republican League. The new political organization championed direct primaries and the direct election of senators. La Follette seemed to be the logical choice for its 1912 presidential ticket, but Roosevelt stepped in and won the nomination as the Progressive Party's candidate instead. A three-way race occurred, and Roosevelt and current president William Howard Taft (1857–1930; served 1909–13) were defeated by the Democratic candidate, Woodrow Wilson (1856–1924; served 1913–21).

World War I

La Follette supported many of Wilson's domestic programs, which borrowed heavily from his own Progressive platform. These included the creation of a Federal Reserve System, which was charged with regulating banks, and the Federal Farm Loan Act, which granted low-interest loans to struggling farmers. The Keating-Owen Act outlawed child labor, and the Kern-McGillicuddy Act of 1916 established a national workers' compensation system. La Follette's most lasting legacy of this period in his political career was the Seaman's Act of 1915, which regulated working conditions and hours for merchant seamen aboard any American-owned ship above a certain tonnage, or weight. It required improved safety measures on board and even set conditions for the meals served. The act, which came in the wake of a Senate investigation into the sinking of the *Titanic,* also reduced some of the total rule of the captain and made clear what sailors' legal rights were while at sea.

With the onset of war in Europe, La Follette emerged as a strong opponent against America's entry into the conflict that became known as World War I (1914–18; a war in which Great Britain, France, the United States and their allies defeated Germany, Austria-Hungary, and their allies). In April 1917, when Wilson asked Congress to pass his Armed Neutrality Bill, which allowed for the arming of American merchant ships, La Follette was one of just six senators who opposed the bill. He was even responsible for launching a Senate filibuster, or lengthy debate session, in order to delay voting on it.

La Follette warned that some American companies would profit richly from the war and called attention to the fact that these businesses seemed to be trying to influence politics and even foreign policy. He objected to Wilson's bill that authorized a military draft, asserting that it was the poor who were killed in warfare, not the rich, who were generally able to avoid conscription. That remark was considered almost an act of treason (an attempt to overthrow the government) and there was an unsuccessful attempt to expel him from the Senate.

The press was critical of La Follette for these views, but his popular support remained strong and he was easily reelected to the Senate in 1922. He was a key figure in the buildup to the Teapot Dome scandal that nearly brought down the administration of Warren G. Harding (1865–1923; served 1921–23). La Follette authored the Senate resolution that called for an investigation into charges of political dishonesty in Harding's administration. The inquiry that followed found that Harding's secretary of the interior, Albert B. Fall (1861–1944), had granted access to Navy-owned oil reserves—two in California and one in Teapot Dome, Wyoming—to oil companies owned by his political supporters. In return Fall received generous personal loans. Fall would become the first U.S. cabinet member to be sentenced to prison for misconduct committed in office.

Candidate for president

La Follette was a strong supporter for the elevation of the Bureau of Labor into a new, cabinet-level Department of Labor in 1913. He supported the regulation of telephone rates and was an early champion of women's rights and civil rights. In 1924 he made his final bid for office, this one for the U.S. presidency. La Follette ran as an independent candidate, on the Progressive Party ticket, with Burton K. Wheeler (1882–1975) as his vice-presidential running mate. Wheeler was a progressive-minded Democrat and also a senator. Their campaign pitted them against Republican Calvin Coolidge (1872–1933; served 1923–29) and the Democratic candidate, John W. Davis (1873–1955).

La Follette's 1924 campaign was viewed by many historians as the most radical presidential race in American electoral politics. La Follette's Progressive Party platform proposed several daring ideas, including the government takeover of

La Follette speaks to a group of women during his presidential campaign in 1924. *(© Corbis.)*

the railroads, the elimination of private utility companies, and the passing of laws that protected workers' rights to organize a union. It also called for an end to U.S. involvement in Latin America, where U.S. troops were stationed and some local elections were being illegally influenced in favor of pro-American candidates. Finally, La Follette argued that in the event of another armed conflict, a national plebiscite, or popular vote, had to be held before a declaration of war was announced.

The response from La Follette's opponents, and from media and corporate interests, was swift and extreme: newspapers warned that America would descend into chaos if La Follette was elected. Some of his enemies even claimed he was linked to agents of Soviet Russia, the world's first communist nation (a nation adhering to socialism, an economic system in which the means of production and distribution is owned collectively by all the workers and there is no private property or social classes). However, he won endorsements from the American Federation of Labor, railroad workers' unions, farmers, and many African-American organizations. In the voting La Follette carried his home state of Wisconsin and came in second place in eleven other states. He won five million votes, or about one-sixth of the total. But his health was already suffering, and he died in June 1925. Forever remembered in Wisconsin as "Fighting Bob" La Follette, his sons carried on his political legacy. Bob Jr. (1895–1953) followed him into the U.S. Senate, while Phillip (1897–1965) served as Wisconsin's only Progressive Party governor.

La Follette's political movement spurred the formation of liberal parties in other Midwestern states. More importantly, however, it helped shift the Democratic Party to the left, making it more progressive and an advocate of change. Party leaders recognized that La Follette's ideas had great popular support among the working classes and minorities, and they adjusted their ideals accordingly. When Franklin D. Roosevelt (1882–1945; served 1933–45) was elected president in 1932 in the midst of the Great Depression (1929–41; a time of great economic hardship world-wide), Democrats in Congress enacted many sweeping reforms that protected workers' rights and regulated big business and the financial markets.

For More Information

Books

Thelen, David P. *Robert M. La Follette and the Insurgent Spirit*. Madison: University of Wisconsin Press, 1985.

Periodicals

McCann, Dennis. "Belle Case La Follette Was Her Husband's Key Political Adviser." *Milwaukee Journal Sentinel* (October 15, 1998).

Nichols, John. "Portrait of the Founder, Fighting Bob La Follette." *Progressive* (January 1999): p. 10.

Web Sites

La Follette and His Legacy. http://www.lafollette.wisc.edu/publications/otherpublications/LaFollette/LaFLegacy.html (accessed on July 7, 2005).

Julia C. Lathrop

Born June 29, 1858 (Rockford, Illinois)
Died April 15, 1932 (Rockford, Illinois)

Social worker

"The charities of Cook County will never properly perform their duties until politics are divorced from them."

Julia Clifford Lathrop was an active member of Hull House, the settlement house founded in Chicago, Illinois, by **Jane Addams** (1860–1935; see entry) in 1889. Located in one of the city's poorest neighborhoods, Hull House was established to provide much-needed social services to Chicago's newly arrived immigrants. Lathrop was a key figure in its first forty years of existence, and her pioneering social work eventually took her to Washington, D.C. There she served as the first director of the newly created U.S. Children's Bureau from 1912 to 1921.

Vassar graduate

Lathrop was born in June 1858, in Rockford, Illinois. Her maternal grandparents had been one of the first families to settle in the town. Her ancestry on her father's side stretched back to the establishment of the Massachusetts Bay Colony in the early 1600s. Her father, William, was a successful lawyer and one of the founders of the Republican Party in Illinois. He was already serving in the Illinois state legislature by the time Lathrop was born, and he authored a bill that permitted women lawyers to become members of the Illinois bar.

Julia C. Lathrop. *(© Corbis.)*

Lathrop was the first of five children in her family. Her mother, Adeline, had been a member of the first class of Rockford Seminary, later known as Rockford College, and Lathrop spent a year there herself in 1876, the same year her father won election to the U.S. House of Representatives. At school she met **Ellen Gates Starr** (1859–1940; see entry), who later established Hull House with Addams. Addams also attended Rockford Seminary, but she entered the same year that Lathrop transferred to Vassar College in Poughkeepsie, New York. Vassar was one of the new women's colleges in the eastern United States, which offered its students a challenging academic program.

Lathrop earned her Vassar degree in 1880 and went to work in her father's office back in Illinois. She studied law in her spare time but became increasingly unsure about the direction of her life. There were few professions open to women in her day, and even those who had earned college degrees were expected to devote their energies to a home, husband, and children. After a decade of drifting with no goal in mind, Lathrop found her purpose when she learned about Addams's plans for Hull House. Like Lathrop, Addams spent much of her twenties searching for a worthwhile career but had been discouraged by her family from pursuing her studies. Addams borrowed the idea for a settlement house from one she had visited in London. They were called settlement houses because of their mission to work with the poor, which was based on the idea that only by living alongside those in the neediest of circumstances could the aid workers discover the best methods to help them.

Hull House, which opened its doors in September 1889, was a shabby mansion located in one of Chicago's worst areas. The second-largest city in the nation at the time, Chicago had suddenly emerged as a center of manufacturing and industry, and sons and daughters from America's farms traveled there looking for jobs. Even more immigrants came from overseas, hoping to find work as well, causing the city's population to double between 1880 and 1890, and then again between 1890 and 1900. The jobs were plentiful, but the city could not keep up with the demand for housing, and in the neighborhood surrounding Hull House a single tiny dwelling would usually be shared by three or four families. These homes did not have indoor plumbing and often had only a few windows to provide access to fresh air. Garbage collection in the area was unreliable, and in such conditions the young, the old, and the weak were at risk from outbreaks of disease, which regularly swept through the city's poorest areas.

Public service

Lathrop joined Addams and Starr at Hull House in 1890. One of her first efforts was the formation of a club for the older men of the neighborhood to discuss the works of the ancient Greek philosopher Plato (427 BCE–347 BCE). In 1893 newly elected Illinois governor John P. Altgeld (1847–1902) appointed Lathrop as the first woman on the Illinois Board of

Public Charities. Altgeld had won office on campaign pledges to improve working and living conditions in the city, and he recognized that the Hull House women were a committed and ready task force who could help him achieve his mission. He appointed several other settlement workers to public service jobs or commissions, but Lathrop's duty to help those in Cook County institutions was among the toughest. The city had an official poorhouse, as well as orphanages and homes for the elderly who had no family to care for them. There were also homes for the blind and deaf, and a place where the developmentally disabled and the criminally insane were taken.

Lathrop saw that the county-run system was dishonest and inefficient. The staff members of the institutions had usually received their jobs through political favors given out by local elected officials, and as a result they were not necessarily committed to helping the residents. Reforming the system became one of Lathrop's most

Illinois governor John P. Atgeld appointed Lathrop the first woman on the Illinois Board of Public Charities.
(Courtesy of The Library of Congress.)

important missions. She recorded her visits in "The Cook County Charities," which was included in a book written by another Hull House activist, **Florence Kelley** (1859–1932; see entry). *Hull-House Maps and Papers: A Presentation of Nationalities and Wages in a Congested District of Chicago, Together with Comments and Essays on Problems Growing Out of the Social Conditions* was published in 1895, and Lathrop's chapter described in shocking detail the conditions inside what was commonly referred to at the time as the insane asylum. "Here are gathered usually about eight hundred men and women, paupers, incurably insane," she wrote. "Can words express more pitiable condition? Certainly there are no creatures in a state of more painful helplessness." Lathrop went on to note that the wards, or the long corridors that housed the residents' beds, were clean, but sunless. Meals consisted of "mush for breakfast; for dinner, beef and potato and another vegetable ... often cabbage; for supper, stewed apples or rice; with coffee or tea for breakfast and dinner, and tea for supper, and bread and butter for all meals," she wrote. "Unfortunately, this sounds better than it is in fact. Few persons could see the food as prepared and served (excepting the bread) without a sense of physical revolt."

Lathrop dedicated several years to improving the conditions of such institutions from her seat on the Illinois Board of Public Charities. She argued in favor of a civil service examination for administrators and a hiring process that favored those who had some professional training in their field. She knew that European nations were finding new and more humane ways to help the mentally ill, and so she traveled to England, France, Belgium, and Germany in 1898 and again in 1900 to see what they had accomplished. By 1901, however, when jobs in state homes were still being handed out as political favors, she resigned from the board in protest. Another governor reappointed her in 1905, and she served for six more years.

Work with juvenile offenders

As the dawn of the new century neared, Lathrop had already moved on to her next major project: the creation of the first court of law for juvenile offenders. The Cook County Juvenile Court began hearing cases in July 1899, and she and the other Hull House women played an active role in its establishment and early administration. The court operated under a relatively new concept at the time, one that argued that underage (those under the age of 16) criminals should be treated differently than adults, and at the very least not housed alongside far more seasoned criminals while awaiting trial. Cook County became the model for the juvenile court system in other states, and even those in many European countries.

At the start, however, there were several problems that prevented the Cook County Juvenile Court idea from running smoothly. For example, no funds had been set aside to pay the salaries of probation officers, who were charged with monitoring underage criminals. There was also no site to house the young offenders before trial. Lathrop and other Hull House workers raised money for both efforts and even established a transportation service to the courthouse from the detention center. Another Hull House resident, Alzina Stevens (1849–1900), became the first probation officer for the juvenile court. For many years Lathrop served as head of the juvenile court committee, which functioned as an advocacy group to oversee the new system.

Lathrop's commitment to helping others was an inspiration to the founders of the Chicago Institute of Social Science, which was only the second American school created specifically for social work. She consulted with them to create a course of studies, as well as lecturing at the school and serving as director of its research department along with Sophonisba Breckinridge (1866–1948), another Hull House worker. The school became part of the University of Chicago in 1920. Because she was independently wealthy, Lathrop donated her time and services and did not take a salary from the institute.

A historic first

Lathrop's efforts on behalf of juveniles brought her national fame. In 1912 she was appointed by President William H. Taft (1857–1930; served 1909–13) to serve as the first director of the newly created U.S. Children's Bureau. Kelley, her Hull House colleague, had been one of the most committed campaigners for the establishment of the bureau, whose mission was to protect the health and welfare of America's children. Lathrop's appointment was a historic one, for she became the first woman in the United States to head a federal bureau after a presidential nomination and confirmation by the Senate.

In Washington Lathrop oversaw her bureau's first major mission: to reduce infant mortality (death) rates. Because of her years of work with Chicago's poor, she knew that some children did not survive their first year because of the effects of poverty, such as unsanitary living conditions and poor medical care. Under her guidance the bureau launched a public awareness campaign, and it was Lathrop's idea to make sure that the free educational pamphlets it began to publish for mothers were written for the average reader and not in the language of a doctor or nurse. The Sheppard-Towner Act was another one of her achievements during this part of her career. It was passed by Congress just after she resigned as head of the Children's

Bureau in 1921 and authorized the establishment of partnership programs between the federal government and states' public health departments to reduce maternal and infant mortality rates. Lathrop was also instrumental in the federal government's decision to enact a uniform birth registration law. The newly collected statistics showed that by 1930 a dramatic decrease in infant mortality had occurred, due in part to the Bureau's efforts.

Under Lathrop's leadership the U.S. Children's Bureau also worked to end child labor. Many years later child labor would come to be considered a human rights violation, but in this era it was entirely legal and commonplace. Thousands of children in every industry received low wages and worked under dangerous conditions in order to help feed their families. Some never learned to read and write, and others were permanently injured or even killed on the job because of dangerous machinery. A new federal law banning the use of children in the workforce was passed in 1916 and went into effect the following January. It was challenged in the courts by an association of business interests and declared unconstitutional. Not until 1938, with the passage of the Fair Labor Standards Act, would child labor be permanently outlawed.

Lathrop celebrated her sixty-third birthday the year she retired from the Children's Bureau, but she remained active. In 1922 the U.S. secretary of labor named her to a committee charged with investigating conditions on Ellis Island, where new immigrants were processed when they arrived in America. She also supported women's suffrage (right to vote) in the years before Congress approved the Nineteenth Amendment to the Constitution, which gave women the right to vote in the 1920 national elections for the first time. She went on to serve as president of the Illinois League of Women Voters. Her experiences with the establishment of the Cook County Juvenile Court were the basis for a chapter she wrote for a 1925 book, *The Child, the Clinic and the Court.* From 1925 to 1931 she also worked for the League of Nations—an international organization that was the forerunner to the United Nations—as an evaluator for its Child Welfare Committee.

Aside from her time in Washington, Lathrop lived most of her years at Hull House. She was known for her habit of going to bed immediately after dinner and then waking up in the middle of the night in order to read and write. In her final years she lived with her sister in Rockford. She died there on April 15, 1932. She was the subject of Addams's book, *My Friend, Julia Lathrop,* published in 1935.

For More Information

Books

Diliberto, Gioia. *A Useful Woman: The Early Life of Jane Addams.* New York: Scribner/A Lisa Drew Book, 1999.

Linn, James Weber. *Jane Addams: A Biography.* Chicago: University of Illinois Press, 2000.

Periodicals

Alexander, Amy Reynolds. "Reformer Julia Lathrop Attention to Detail Got Her Results." *Investor's Business Daily* (January 5, 2001): p. A3.

Web Sites

Urban Experience in Chicago: Hull-House and Its Neighborhoods, 1889–1963. http://tigger.uic.edu/htbin/cgiwrap/bin/urbanexp/main.cgi?file=new/show_doc.ptt&doc=351&chap=132 (accessed on July 7, 2005).

Lewis H. Latimer

Born September 4, 1848 (Chelsea, Massachusetts)
Died December 11, 1928 (Flushing, New York)

Inventor

Lewis H. Latimer had an honored career as an inventor, skilled mechanical draftsperson, and patent expert. Patents are legal documents giving an inventor the exclusive right to make, use, or sell an invention for a certain term of years. Latimer worked with **Alexander Graham Bell** (1847–1922; see entry) in preparing the drawings that were important to Bell's patent application for the telephone and spent much of his later career with the firm founded by **Thomas Edison** (1847–1931; see entry). Latimer's achievements were even more remarkable because he was an African American executive and technical expert in the United States before the civil rights movement, when minorities who attained such prominence were rare.

Son of escaped slaves

Latimer was born on September 4, 1848, in Chelsea, Massachusetts, just outside of Boston, Massachusetts. His parents, George and Rebecca, had settled there after fleeing a Virginia plantation in the Norfolk area six years earlier. They had stowed away on a Boston-bound ship, and when they

Lewis H. Latimer. *(Queens Library, Long Island Division. Reproduced by permission.)*

emerged on board, Latimer's light-skinned father posed as a slave owner and the master of Rebecca Latimer for the rest of the journey. The Virginia plantation owner, however, learned of their whereabouts and came to Boston to bring them back. Abolitionists (antislavery activists) took up their cause and hid Rebecca, but George was jailed and a Massachusetts court ruled that the owner had the right to take him back. A standoff outside the jail that lasted nearly a month ended when abolitionists raised the money to buy George's freedom from the master. The Latimers' situation attracted widespread attention and helped spur the passage of a state law that prohibited

Massachusetts authorities from aiding in the capture of fugitive slaves from the Southern states.

Latimer did well at Phillips Grammar School in Boston and even skipped a grade, but his formal education ended at the age of ten. He went to work to support the family, helping his father, who worked as a barber, and selling copies of the *Liberator,* the newspaper published by William Lloyd Garrison (1805–1879), a noted abolitionist. He also assisted his father in a second line of work, paperhanging (the application of wallpaper), which was a trade that would later prove useful. The family's financial situation worsened when George abandoned the household, and Rebecca went to work on an ocean liner. She sent her youngest son to live with a farm family, but Latimer hated the endless, dirty chores that farm life required. He and another boy managed to escape and make their way back to Boston. Latimer found a job waiting tables and then ran errands for a law firm.

In 1864, in the final year of the American Civil War (1861–65; a war between the Union [the North], who were opposed to slavery, and the Confederacy [the South], who were in favor of slavery), the sixteen-year-old Latimer enlisted in the Union Navy. He served aboard the U.S.S. *Massasoit* on the James River in Virginia, and when the war ended he returned to Boston once again. In 1871 he was hired as an assistant in the office of two patent lawyers, Crosby and Gould. The firm also employed a staff of draftsmen, who created the detailed drawings necessary for patent applications. Latimer bought a secondhand book on mechanical drafting and taught himself the subject in his spare time. He convinced one of the draftsmen at the office to let him try to do a drawing one day, and his work was so good that he was soon being given regular assignments. Crosby and Gould eventually made him the firm's head draftsman.

Worked with Alexander Graham Bell

Latimer's drawings for the ideas of others gave him his own ideas for inventions. With a friend, W. C. Brown, he devised a "Water Closet for Railway Cars," which was an improved version of the toilet then in use aboard trains, and it was patented in February 1874. In early 1876 Latimer was enlisted to work with Alexander Graham Bell, a Scottish immigrant who ran a Boston school for the deaf. Bell had hired Crosby and Gould to handle the paperwork for a new device that had come out of his efforts to teach the hearing-impaired to speak. Bell's primary job and commitment to his students meant that he could only sit down with Latimer later in the evening to describe the details of his invention. "I was obliged to stay at the office until after 9 p.m. when he was free from his night classes, to get my instructions from him, as to how I was to make the drawings for the application for a patent upon the telephone," Latimer recalled years later, according to Nathan Aaseng in *Black Inventors*. Latimer's dedication to his work helped Bell's patent for the telephone beat the submission of another inventor, Elisha Gray (1835–1901), by just four hours. Both were filed at the U.S. Patent Office on the same day, and if Latimer had made any mistake in his drawings, this would have allowed Gray to win the telephone patent.

Latimer took a job at another law firm. Unfortunately, the firm's financial situation worsened, and he found himself out of work. By then he had married, and he and his wife, Mary, moved to Bridgeport, Connecticut, where he worked as a paperhanger for a time. Finally he found a part-time job as a draftsman in a machine shop and through that met Hiram S. Maxim (1840–1916) in 1880. An inventor himself, Maxim was the founder of a Bridgeport company, U.S. Electric Lighting, and would later be known for creating the first fully automatic machine gun. Maxim was impressed by Latimer's drawing skills, and by the fact he had been with Crosby and Gould, where Maxim had also once worked. He immediately hired Latimer as a draftsman, and shortly after that the company moved its operations from Bridgeport to the New York City area.

U.S. Electric was a rival of Thomas Edison's New Jersey firm. Edison held the patent for his 1879 invention, a light bulb with a carbon fiber inside an airless vacuum tube. The carbon fiber, when charged, made the bulb give off a steady glow, and it was a vast step forward for the possibility of easy, cheap, and safe lighting. An improved filament (a thin conductor made to glow by the passage of an electrical current) was necessary to help the light bulb become a mass-produced item, however, and U.S. Electric was one of the companies working to come up with a solution to that.

A better way to make a bulb

Latimer was fascinated by the idea of electrical lighting and went to work on finding a better filament. He began studying the subjects of chemistry and electrical engineering in his spare time and tried out various manufacturing processes during his workdays at U.S. Electric. The process for making the filament involved wood, cotton, and carbon, and he undertook numerous trial-and-error experiments to come up with a better combination. He finally devised a method that involved cellulose (a chemical combination found in the cell walls of plants) and carbon, and the result was a much longer-lasting filament. He filed the necessary patent application paperwork for "Process of Manufacturing Carbons" in February 1881, and it was granted in January 1882. His filament became significant in the evolution of electric lighting from something that only the rich could afford to something cheap to produce and affordable for almost anyone.

Latimer and a colleague, Joseph V. Nichols, also devised a new way to connect the carbon filament to the wiring in a lamp, and they received a patent for that as well. Since both projects had been done at Maxim's company, however, the two men did not own the exclusive rights or make any money from their ideas. But Latimer did become the company's chief engineer and traveled to its newly established factories to supervise the setup of the filament manufacturing process. He also devised a circuitry for street lamp lighting that allowed the whole system to stay lit even when one of the bulbs burned out. The innovation became standard in streetlight installations in New York City, Philadelphia, Pennsylvania, and even London, England, and Maxim sent Latimer to ensure the processes went smoothly. "Electrical measurements had not then been invented and all our work was by guess," Latimer wrote in his logbooks, according to the Web site *Blueprint for Change: The Life and Times of Lewis H. Latimer.* "Office bell wire was the only kind on the market, and our method of figureing [sic] was that it was a good guess that that size wire would carry a certain number of lamps without dangerous heating. A number of mysterious [sic] fires about this time were probably the fruit of our ignorance."

Latimer even learned French so that he could work more effectively with municipal engineers in Montreal, Canada, on their system. In London, however, he encountered prejudice because of his skin color. He wrote about this in the same logbooks. "The prevailing motif [theme] seemed to be humility of the workman and the attitude that nothing that I can do can repay you for permitting me to earn an honest living," he remarked about his London assignment. "My assistant and myself were in hot water from the first moment to the end of my engagement, and as we were incapable of assuming a humility we could not feel, there was a continual effort to discount us."

Later career achievements

It was Latimer's understanding of the patent application process that brought him to the attention of Thomas Edison, who hired him in 1884 as a draftsman for the Edison General Electric Light Company in New York City. At the time Edison's firm was engaged in numerous patent-infringement (violation) lawsuits, and Latimer became a key player in those battles. Once he was promoted to the position of associate in the company's legal department, Latimer investigated the work of other electrical firms that were asking the courts to overturn Edison's patent rights. He prepared drawings for the teams of lawyers, served as an expert witness in court testimony, and proved particularly useful in contradicting the claims of his former boss, Maxim. Meanwhile, he continued to work on his own inventions. Among these was the Latimer Lamp, an improvement on Edison's lamp that came into wide use for a few years, as well as an instrument for cooling and disinfecting rooms that was an early version of the air conditioner.

After most of the Edison patent issues had been settled, Latimer authored a classic early textbook, *Incandescent Electric Lighting,* which was published in 1890. It was one of the first books to describe the subject in detail in the decade since so many improvements had been made, and it helped train a generation of new electrical engineers. Latimer's text provided information based solely on the Edison lighting system, which guaranteed the company's dominance in the industry for many years to come. Two years later the firm united all its properties and became General Electric.

In 1896 Latimer was named to the Board of Patent Control, which had been created by General Electric and the Westinghouse Company, a leading competitor. The board's task was to pool the patents of both companies in electrical systems. Latimer would serve on the board for the next fifteen years, until it was dissolved. He also taught mechanical drafting at the Henry Street Settlement, a well-respected community help center for the poor and immigrants in the Manhattan area of New York City. After retiring from General Electric in 1911, Latimer worked as a consultant for a New York law firm, Hammer & Schwarz, on patent law. But his eyesight began to fail, and he was forced to give up work on his own inventions. In 1918 he became a founding member of the Edison Pioneers, an elite group of twenty-eight Edison employees who had been instrumental in making the company an impressively innovative one. He was the sole minority member.

Latimer spent his retirement years in Flushing, a section of Queens, New York. A founder of the Flushing Unitarian Church, he was also an accomplished painter and poet and played the flute and violin. He corresponded with several notable African Americans of his era, among them abolitionist Frederick Douglass (c. 1818–1895), educator **Booker T. Washington** (1856–1915; see entry), and Richard Greener (1844–1922), the first black graduate of Harvard University. In 1902 Latimer launched a petition drive to bring more minority representation to the New York City school board.

Latimer and his wife had two daughters, Emma Jeannette and Louise. He suffered a stroke in 1924, the same year his wife died, but many of the love poems he wrote to Mary were published in booklet form by his friends the following year as a gift for him on his seventy-fifth birthday. He died on December 11, 1928. In 1968 a public school in Brooklyn, New York, was named in his honor.

For More Information

Books

Aaseng, Nathan. *Black Inventors*. New York: Facts on File, Inc., 1997.

Turner, Glennette Tilley. *Lewis Howard Latimer*. Englewood Cliffs, NJ: Silver Burdett Press, 1991.

Periodicals

Fouche, Rayvon. "Lighting Made Easy." *Footsteps* (January-February 2005): p. 8.

Web Sites

"Edison's Miracle of Light." *PBS.* http://www.pbs.org/wgbh/amex/edison/filmmore/index.html (accessed on July 7, 2005).

Singer, Bayla. *Inventing a Better Life: Latimer's Technical Career, 1880–1928.* http://edison.rutgers.edu/latimer/invtlife.htm (accessed on July 7, 2005).

Blueprint for Change: The Life and Times of Lewis H. Latimer. http://www.queenslibrary.org/gallery/latimer/ (accessed on July 7, 2005).

Mary Elizabeth Lease

Born September 11, 1853 (Ridgway, Pennsylvania)
Died October 29, 1933 (Callicoon, New York)

Activist
Public speaker

"The great common people of this country are slaves, and monopoly is the master."

Mary Elizabeth Lease was a tough, outspoken woman in an era when women were expected to be subordinate and avoid conflict with men. Lease, however, was angry at the wrongs she saw in the world and refused to keep silent no matter how society perceived her. She gained national recognition during the crusade for reform in the 1890s due mainly to her powerful oratorical (speech-making) skills. With a quick mind, a powerful voice, a way with words, and a strong dislike for rich American industrialists, she stirred both anger and hope in farmers who were struggling to pay bills and feed their families. In hundreds of speeches made in just a few years she rallied crowds to fight for reform against the wealthy financial backers and industrialists.

Difficult beginnings

Lease was born in Ridgway, Pennsylvania, in 1853. Her parents were immigrants from Ireland, forced to flee their native land because her father faced a possible death sentence for rebelling against the ruling English. Lease's young life was overwhelmed by poverty and loss. Two of her brothers and her

Mary Lease. *(© Corbis.)*

father died in battle against the Confederacy during the American Civil War (1861–65; a war between the Union [the North], who were opposed to slavery, and the Confederacy [the South], who were in favor of slavery). Lease developed a bitter hatred for the Confederacy—and consequently the Democratic Party to which many Southerners later belonged—that lasted for the rest of her life.

After the war Lease completed her schooling at a Catholic girls' school in Allegany, New York, with the aid of neighbors. She initially taught in New York but moved to Kansas to teach around 1870. There she met and married a druggist's clerk, Charles L. Lease, in 1873. They established a small farm and lived contentedly on it for a couple of years, but, because of an economic downturn that had begun in 1873, prices for crops fell sharply and their farm eventually failed. The young couple lost everything. They moved to Texas, where two of their children died in infancy. The economic situation had not improved and they eventually failed at farming once again. Like many at that time, Lease blamed her losses on the railroad companies, which charged farmers higher rates than they charged Eastern businessmen. Also to blame, according to Lease, were the lenders who charged high interest rates (a percentage of the sum borrowed) for loans to farmers. When lack of profits made it impossible for farmers to pay back their loans, it often led to the banks taking their land as repayment. In 1883 the Leases moved to Wichita, Kansas, and settled there with their four surviving children.

Lease's first speeches

In Kansas Lease began studying law while also becoming active in several causes: labor issues, prohibition, women's suffrage (right to vote), and eventually the situation of the farmers. On St. Patrick's Day, 1885, she delivered her first public speech, "Ireland and Irishmen," in defense of the Irish struggle for independence from England. Lease's speech impressed all who attended, enabling her to find work as a paid lecturer, which helped to pay her family's bills. In the same year Lease was admitted as a lawyer to the Wichita bar. She opened a law office but, for reasons that are not clear to historians, she never actively practiced law. In 1886 she founded and became president of the Hypatia Club, an organization of women who aimed to improve themselves intellectually. The club was still in existence in the early twenty-first century.

In 1887 Lease became a lecturer for the Farmers' Alliance, a branch of loosely organized societies that sought to bring farmers together to promote their interests, such as calling for government regulation or ownership of the railroads, monetary reform that would help farmers, and the elimination of the national banks. Lease also briefly worked as an associate editor for a reform newspaper, the Wichita *Journal*. In 1888 farmers and laborers tried to form a union, the Union Labor Party, to represent both interest groups. This was a cause that Lease took up with great enthusiasm. She gave a stirring speech at the state convention of the new party in Wichita. Shortly after, she became a candidate for a county office. Although she narrowly lost her campaign, her candidacy in itself was impressive in a time when women were not even eligible to vote.

A speaker for the Populists

The Union Labor Party soon failed due to lack of interest, and the members of the Farmers Alliance and labor groups went on to form a new third political party, the People's Party of America, also known as the Populists. The Farmers' Alliance had always aimed to influence Democrats and Republicans to promote legislation beneficial to farm interests, but by 1890 many of its members felt this was useless. They believed the two major parties were ignoring their interests because they were strongly attached to the wealthy and powerful northeastern industries. Kansans were at the forefront of the efforts to create the third political party, and thus the Populist Party was founded in Topeka, Kansas, in 1890. Lease eagerly went to work as a stump speaker (someone who traveled to other towns and regions to make public addresses for a political candidate) for the party. She was tireless in her work, making hundreds of speeches in Kansas and across the nation.

In 1889 Lease took an active role in the successful campaign to unseat U.S. senator John J. Ingalls (1873–1891), a Kansas Republican. She reportedly made over 160 speeches during the 1890 election. She was often mistakenly called Mary Ellen, and because her speeches were so full of anger and contempt for the Republican candidate, her enemies dubbed her "Mary Yellin'." Her speeches also fiercely attacked the nation's powerful industrialists, the federal government, and the upper classes. "Wall Street owns the country," she proclaimed in an 1890 speech, as quoted in William E. Connelly's *A Standard History of Kansas and Kansans*. "It is no longer a government of the people, by the people and for the people, but a government of Wall Street, by Wall Street and for Wall Street. The great common people of this country are slaves, and monopoly [the exclusive right to produce or sell a product] is the master." She went on to call Ingalls "the errand boy of Wall Street, the silver-tongued

William Jennings Bryan and the Election of 1896

William Jennings Bryan (1860–1925) was known as the "Great Commoner" for his representation of the poor, the working class, and the farmers in his impassioned speeches and political campaigns. Bryan was born and raised in Illinois, where he practiced law for a few years. In 1887 he moved to Lincoln, Nebraska, where he ran for Congress in 1890. Bryan won his Congressional seat as a Democrat in a strongly Republican district, which was probably an early indication of his oratorical (speech-making) skills.

One of the issues that Bryan championed was free silver. In 1893 the United States experienced a depression, or a period of drastic decline in the economy. Farm failures were common. Many farmers became advocates of free silver, demanding that the government issue new dollars backed by silver as opposed to paper money being backed only by gold. Since gold was used as the standard value for the dollar, the dollar could be redeemed for a certain amount of gold and the nation had to have gold reserves that could cover the supply of money. Those who advocated free silver believed using silver as well as gold to back the currency would increase the money supply and lead to inflation (a rise in the amount of money in circulation in relation to a smaller amount of available goods and products, leading to a rise in prices). Higher prices for their crops due to inflation would benefit the farmers, particularly in the effect it would have on loans they had borrowed when money was worth less. Inflation would hurt the banks and insurance companies that had loaned them money because the money they collected on the debts was not worth as much as it was when it was borrowed. During his first term in the House of Representatives, Bryan gave a masterful three-hour speech in defense of the free silver cause. He claimed lawmakers had to decide between wealthy industrialists and the downtrodden masses. Bryan earned national fame for his speech-making, but in 1894, after two terms in office, he failed in a bid to become a U.S. senator. Nevertheless, he continued to make speeches in favor of the free silver cause.

At the age of thirty-six, Bryan impressed the audience at the 1896 Democratic presidential convention in Chicago with

champion of special privilege, [and] a dishonest, soulless, shameless charlatan [fraud]." Many believed Ingalls' loss was due to Lease's campaign against him.

Approval and criticism

Lease quickly became one of the most famous figures of the Populist movement. Her speeches were so rousing she was said to have enlisted hundreds of new Populist Party members

William Jennings Bryan. *(© Corbis.)*

a famous address that came to be known as the "Cross of Gold" speech. Delivering a carefully planned and rehearsed text as if it were a spontaneous outpouring, he declared that farms could survive without the cities, but cities could not survive without farms. He called on his supporters to defy big business with its gold standard, or the backing of currency with gold. "Having behind us the producing masses of this nation and the world, supported by the laboring interests and the toilers everywhere, we will answer their demand for a gold standard by saying to them: You shall not press down upon the brow of labor this crown of thorns; you shall not crucify mankind on a cross of gold."

The next day Bryan was nominated as the presidential candidate of both the Democratic Party and the Populist Party, and he ran under both parties. He campaigned against Republican candidate William McKinley (1843–1901; served 1897–1901). Bryan came very close to winning the election. He captured the vote of many rural Americans with his wonderful voice and exciting delivery, despite what many historians termed an overly dramatic and simplistic platform. Ultimately the Democrats failed to persuade eastern workers to support the free silver cause. Industrialists convinced their employees that Bryan was a radical, even a revolutionary, and McKinley narrowly won the election. McKinley took the presidency, and the Populist movement and Bryan's influence in the nation were largely over.

with each one she gave. She was an imposing figure at six feet tall, and observers noted that her voice had an unusually powerful and appealing quality. Lease had great natural charm and was able to translate the frustrations and emotions of her audiences into words. The farmers and labor unions loved her, but the press and the major party politicians criticized her mercilessly. Most went far beyond disagreeing with what she was saying, attacking her looks, her self-confidence, and her "unwomanly" argumentative behavior.

Lease did not respond well to the personal attacks. She once claimed that the major party politicians were out to get her and had tried to poison her lemonade three times.

The Populists gained strength, and in 1892 they nominated General James B. Weaver (1833–1912) of Iowa as the party's presidential candidate. Lease campaigned heavily in the South and West for Weaver. Though he did not win the election, Weaver won more than one million popular votes and claimed the majority vote in four states, a major accomplishment for a third-party candidate. In 1893 the Populists gained control of the Kansas state government when Populist governor Lorenzo Lewelling (1846–1900) was elected. Lease had become very well connected with those in power in the state, and many urged her to run for senator. She declined, instead accepting the governor's appointment as president of the State Board of Charities, the highest office held by a woman in Kansas at that time.

By 1893 some members of the Populist Party were looking into a possible merger of their party with the Democrats, whom Lease still hated as it was the party to which most of the former Confederates belonged. When it became clear that Governor Lewelling was in favor of the merger, Lease began criticizing him in public. Lewelling had her removed from the board just months after her appointment, and she reacted by launching an attack on him in the newspapers. She took her case all the way to the Kansas Supreme Court, which ruled in her favor, saying that Lewelling had not had the authority to dismiss her from the board.

The end of a movement and a career

The Populist Party merged with the Democrats for the 1896 presidential elections, with young orator William Jennings Bryan (1860–1925) as the candidate for both parties running against Republican candidate William McKinley (1843–1901; served 1897–1901). The Populists supported Bryan by calling for struggling working-class Americans to vote for him in order to overthrow the party serving the interests of the powerful and wealthy industrialists. Despite her objections to the merger, Lease joined in the Bryan campaign. Although it was a very close race, Bryan lost, signaling the end of the Populist movement.

Lease left her husband in Kansas and moved with her children to New York City in 1897. There she filed for a divorce, which was complete in 1902. In her new home she earned her living as a political writer for the *New York World*. Though she continued to serve as a public lecturer for several causes, particularly women's suffrage, Prohibition (the forbidding of alcoholic beverages), and birth control, she was no longer the celebrity she was during the Populist campaigns. She acknowledged in her old age that her anger was gone, though not her desire to reform the wrongs done to the country's women, workers, and farmers. In 1931 Lease bought a farm in New York State, running it with hired labor. She died there on October 29, 1933.

Lease published one book in her lifetime, *The Problem of Civilization Solved* (1895). Most academics agreed that it was a mixture of poorly conceived ideas, promoting racism and the separation of cultures. The publication caused historians to regard Lease with less respect, but she was still remembered for her courage in daring to stand up to the strongest forces of a male-dominated society and provide a loud and clear voice for the interests of the farmers and the working poor.

For More Information

Books

Clanton, Gene. *Populism: The Humane Preference in America, 1890–1900.* Boston, MA: Twayne, 1991.

Stiller, Richard. *Queen of Populists: The Story of Mary Elizabeth Lease.* New York: Thomas Y. Crowell, 1970.

Women Public Speakers in the United States, 1800–1925. Edited by Karlyn Kohrs Campbell. Westport, CT: Greenwood Press, 1993.

Periodicals

"Cheered Mary E. Lease." *New York World* (August 11, 1896). This article can also be found online at http://projects.vassar.edu/1896/leasespeech.html (accessed on July 7, 2005).

Web Sites

Connelly, William E. *A Standard History of Kansas and Kansans,* 2000. http://skyways.lib.ks.us/genweb/archives/1918ks/v2/1142.html (accessed on July 7, 2005).

Francis Cabot Lowell

Born April 7, 1775 (Newburyport, Massachusetts)
Died August 10, 1817 (Boston, Massachusetts)

Industrialist

Francis Cabot Lowell played a key role in bringing the Industrial Revolution to the United States in the early nineteenth century. He introduced highly advanced technology to New England's growing textile industry and devised new methods of managing workers and the production process. Lowell's textile factories produced on a much larger scale than anything the United States had seen prior to that period. Lowell also established one of the earliest forms of the modern-day corporation, which prospered long after his death and was a model for all American business.

Early work in the shipping industry

Lowell was a member of a large aristocratic New England family. He grew up in Newburyport, Massachusetts, and was the son of prominent judge John Lowell (1743–1802) and Susanna Cabot (1754–1777), the daughter of an immensely wealthy shipping family. Francis enrolled at Harvard University in 1789, where he excelled in mathematics. When he graduated in 1793, he began working in a Cabot family

144

Francis Cabot Lowell. *(Courtesy of The Library of Congress.)*

trading firm as a partner. He was a successful businessman well on his way to becoming wealthy when he married Hannah Jackson in 1798. His wife's family provided Lowell with more connections to the shipping business. By 1810 he was a major merchant in his own right, and he traded with companies in Europe, Canada, India, and China.

Lowell got into the shipping business at a very dangerous, though profitable, time, when major conflicts were occurring in Europe, mainly between England and France. The English were trying to stop foreign trade with France, while the French were denying the English access to other European ports. As the tensions grew worse, England announced its intention to seize goods carried in neutral ships that were intended for French ports—a not-very-subtle threat to American merchants. In 1807 an English warship seized an American ship and removed four sailors from it who they claimed had deserted from the English navy. Americans were outraged. That same year Congress passed an embargo, an act forbidding almost all foreign trade. The embargo was so damaging to the U.S. economy it was lifted in 1809, but trade with England and France was still forbidden. For New England traders like Lowell there were great profits to be made since the price of English textiles rose as the supply steadily decreased. On the other hand, the risks of the business were extreme, and many ships and their cargos were lost in the conflict. Lowell's business thrived, but the stress damaged his health. When his doctor recommended he take a trip overseas to regain his strength in 1810, he and his wife set out for England.

Studying textile technology in England

Lowell had thought of building a textile mill before making the trip to England, believing that New England could prosper if it replaced part of its cloth trade with its own manufacturing facilities. While visiting the industrial city of Manchester, England, Lowell used his position as a prominent Boston import-export merchant to gain access to the world's largest textile mills, which were normally closed to Americans out of a well-founded fear of industrial espionage (spying). Lowell was impressed by the technology he saw, particularly by an automated weaving machine called a power loom (a frame or machine used to weave thread or yarns into cloth). American technology could not even begin to compete with what he was seeing in the Manchester mills. However, it was illegal to bring the English looms, or even the plans for them, to the United States, as the English wanted no competition in their production of the finished cloth.

Lowell was determined to bring the power loom to the United States. While he was in Manchester he studied the looms in the mills, making sketches and drawings when he could and memorizing mechanical details. He returned to New England in 1812 with his sketches and a mission. He hired Paul

Moody (1779–1831), a mechanic considered to be a genius by many of his peers. Lowell described what he had seen to Moody, giving him the sketches and explaining the mechanics he had observed. Under Lowell's direction Moody proceeded to build a power loom that was not only equal, but in many ways superior, to the English power loom. Using this machine it would be possible for the first time in the United States to carry out the full cotton manufacturing process in one building. Factory workers, called operators, could run machines to clean the raw cotton fibers, spin the fibers into threads, and then weave the threads into cloth. Other U.S. mills were already producing cotton textiles, but with his new technology Lowell expected to reduce costs enough to compete with English imports. To set up the factory he envisioned, though, would require a great deal of money, and even though he was wealthy, Lowell did not have the funds to accomplish such a large project.

An early corporation

Most English and American companies in the beginning of the nineteenth century were sole proprietorships or partnerships. A sole proprietorship was a company owned by an individual who had the authority to manage the company and was directly responsible for its debts and entitled to its profits. A partnership was a business created by a contract between two or more persons who managed the company jointly and shared its debts and profits. Although Lowell did not have the money to create his textile mill venture as a sole proprietorship, there were several problems with the idea of forming a partnership as well. To raise capital (accumulated wealth or goods devoted to the production of other goods) beyond the initial investment, all the participants had to agree to contribute or else new partners would have to be found, which could cause major holdups in the company's expansion. Another possible difficulty was that one partner could suddenly find himself responsible for the full debts of the company, rather than just his own share. Also, partnerships were not usually able to stay in business after the death of one of the partners. Lowell realized he needed a better plan and decided to organize his business as a joint-stock company. A joint-stock company is a group of people that organize a business and then sell shares of it as stock to

Moses Brown

Francis Cabot Lowell was not alone in his attempt to create humane working conditions in the new U.S. textile factories. Moses Brown (1738–1838), often considered the first textile manufacturer in the country, was equally concerned with the conditions of life the new industry would provide for its workers. Brown was an unusual mix of industrialist and reformer with sharp insight into the problems facing industrial America.

Brown was born into a family of merchants in Providence, Rhode Island. His father died while he was very young, and he was raised and trained in business by his uncle, Obadiah Brown. The elder Brown's interests included not only the West Indies trade but also insurance, moneylending, and candle manufacturing. When Obadiah died in 1762, Moses and his three older brothers took over and greatly expanded their uncle's business. By the 1770s the Browns were one of the great mercantile families of New England.

In 1773 Moses Brown's first wife died. In his grief Brown withdrew from business for several years. He became a Quaker (a member of the Religious Society of Friends, a Christian group noted for its opposition to war, oath taking, and rituals) and began to take an active part in the antislavery movement in Rhode Island. He freed his own slaves, helped others to escape, and gave aid to freedmen of African descent. Brown's brothers were pro-slavery and they did not understand his new religion. It caused conflict in his family, but Brown was an independent thinker and stuck with his beliefs.

After the American Revolution (1775–83; the American colonists' fight for independence from England), Brown was convinced that the United States should become more economically independent from England. The early signs of American industry drew Brown back to the commercial world. He was particularly interested in the prospect of textile manufacturing in the United States. In 1789 he formed a company with his son-in-law, William Almy, to spin and weave cloth in Providence. After two years in business, they

investors. Those who purchase stock shares are entitled to part of the profits as well as part of the losses.

Lowell needed about $400,000 to build his mill and set it in operation. He organized a business, the Boston Manufacturing Company (also called the Boston Associates), and began to sell shares of it. He sold one hundred shares of the company stock at $1,000 per share, raising enough money to build the first textile factory. Then, with the power loom ready and the business company established, Lowell applied for a patent (a legal document issued by a government granting exclusive had been unable to obtain effective machinery. Brown investigated methods to spin thread and noted that English inventor Richard Arkwright (1732–1792) had developed a method using water power to run spinning frames and carding machines (machines that cleaned, untangled, and collected fibers). Around that time Samuel Slater (1768–1835), a mill overseer at the famed Arkwright Mills in England, arrived in the United States. Brown immediately invited him to his mill and asked him to re-create the Arkwright machinery. From memory, Slater built copies of the machinery he had known and used in England, producing the first water-powered cotton mill in the United States. Slater joined the company and soon Brown withdrew from the business world again. Although Slater is often credited with creating the first water-powered textile mills in the country, Brown's lesser-known part in the process was significant.

Brown's withdrawals from business were attempts to apply himself more fully to his religion. Eventually he seemed to successfully combine his instinct for business with his religious impulses. In 1770 he helped move Rhode Island College from Warren to Providence. It became Brown University, named to honor the great contributions of his family. Although to some degree he shared the Quaker suspicion that higher education weakened devotion to religion, he worked for decades to found a Friends' school. In 1819 the New England Yearly Meeting Boarding School became a reality, and in 1904 it was renamed the Moses Brown School.

Brown never lost interest in the Industrial Revolution, which was in its early stages in New England. He was highly curious about technology and often wondered how industry would treat its workers in the years to come. He knew that workers in England's textile industry suffered under miserable conditions, and he hoped that the U.S. textile industry might handle its workforce differently. In an impassioned report to Secretary of the Treasury Alexander Hamilton (1757–1804), he urged strong measures to protect the incomes and safety of laborers and to monitor child labor. He was, in a sense, asking for reforms to some conditions that had not yet occurred in the United States.

authority to an inventor to make, use, or sell an invention for a certain number of years) for his power loom. He purchased land along the Charles River in Waltham, Massachusetts. In 1814 the company erected buildings in Waltham and fitted them with looms and machines based on Lowell's model, all powered by water. By the end of 1814 the mills were operating.

One of the main elements in the successful operation of such a large business was keeping it well funded for expansion, and Lowell's joint-stock company did just that. He raised $300,000 for additional factories by selling more shares of company stock. According to economic education specialist Albert Barnor in his online article "Francis Cabot Lowell," this attracted investors: "If the company did well, they would receive dividends [a share of the profits] on the amount they had invested. If they liked how the company was performing, they could invest additional money. If they wanted to end their investment, they could sell their shares to others. They could also bequeath their shares in their wills." This type of corporation would be the business organization of the future, and Lowell was one of the first Americans to develop it.

The Lowell girls

Lowell was interested in all aspects of his new business. He had devoted a considerable amount of attention to the labor and management of his mills before they went into operation. He came up with an innovative labor program that he hoped would provide a humane alternative to the system of child labor that had long been in use in England. Lowell believed he had found an ideal workforce for his mills—the unmarried daughters of New England farm families. The "Lowell girls," as they were called, usually ranged in age from about sixteen to thirty. Most worked two or three years at the mill before returning home to marry and start a family. They were cheap labor, as they were willing to accept significantly lower wages than male workers, and they were quick, intelligent, and dedicated. New Englanders were not used to the idea of women living independently and working for wages. In order to convince farmers to allow their daughters to come to the mills, Lowell knew he would have to provide safety in the workplace and a socially acceptable living environment for the young women, with curfews, required church attendance, and chaperones (adult supervisors). He envisioned establishing the country's first planned industrial communities, and he set up rows of boardinghouses near the factories for the workers. Called the Lowell System, or the Waltham System, farm girls and young women who came to work at the textile factory were housed in the supervised dormitories or boardinghouses and were provided with educational and cultural opportunities.

Although Lowell would not live to see it, by 1831 women made up almost forty thousand of the fifty-eight thousand factory workers in the textile industry. His early death also prevented him from seeing the conflicts that arose between the workers and management in the Lowell mills. Though there was some resentment about the mills' paternalistic, or fatherly, treatment of its workers, initially many young women found working at the Lowell mills for a few years before marrying a great adventure. They worked very hard but found time to take advantage of educational opportunities in the growing city. By the 1840s, though, competition in the textile industry put pressure on the management to obtain more work from employees at less pay. The frustrated Lowell girls protested against long workdays and low wages, staging two major strikes. By 1848 mill managers had stopped following Lowell's ideal of creating a humane workplace. By then, most of the farmers' daughters had left the textile industry in disgust. They were replaced by recent immigrants who were in desperate need of work.

Despite Lowell's death, the company expands

The United States had finally gone to war with England over trade and territorial disputes in the War of 1812 (1812–15). This had made trade with England nearly impossible and created a huge demand for American-made cloth, but the war ended around the time the mill in Waltham finally opened. Suddenly inexpensive English textiles were available in the United States again, which posed a serious threat to Lowell's new business. Lowell went to Washington, D.C., where he helped to convince Congress to impose a tariff (a fee on imported goods) on imported cotton cloth to aid American manufacturers. His influence had beneficial results for his new and prospering business, but Lowell would not live to see the outcome. His health, which had been poor for some time, declined further. He died at the age of forty-two in 1817.

The Boston Manufacturing Company went on to build a complete factory town along the powerful Merrimack River in Massachusetts, naming it Lowell in his honor. The company built more mills along the Merrimack at Lawrence, Massachusetts, and Manchester, New Hampshire. Soon the largest waterwheel in the nation was built on the river and supplied power to a dozen large factories. A waterwheel was a wheel that rotated due to the force of moving water, and the rotation of the wheel was then used to power a factory or machine. By 1836 the Boston Manufacturing Company

Lowell, Massachusetts, became a bustling town due to the success of the Lowell mill. *(© Bettmann/Corbis.)*

employed six thousand workers at the Lowell mills. By 1845 just one of Lowell's mills could produce in a week more cotton cloth than was produced in the entire country in the year of 1810. While numerous competitors followed Lowell's example in building factories along New England's rivers, the Lowell mills were for several decades the largest industrial enterprise in America in terms of profit, value of production, and number of employees. The city of Lowell had a population of about twenty thousand by 1848, and its mills produced fifty thousand miles of cotton cloth each year.

For More Information

Books

Brogan, Hugh. *The Penguin History of the USA.* 2nd ed. London and New York: Penguin Books, 2001.

Hindle, Brooke, and Steven Lubar. *Engines of Change: The American Industrial Revolution, 1790–1860.* Washington DC and London: Smithsonian Institution Press, 1986.

Rivard, Paul E. *A New Order of Things: How the Textile Industry Transformed New England.* Hanover, NH: University Press of New England, 2002.

Web Sites

Barnor, Albert, with Lynn Elaine Browne. "Francis Cabot Lowell." *Economic Adventure.org.* http://www.economicadventure.org/decision/index.cfm (accessed on June 7, 2005).

"Francis Cabot Lowell: Consolidated Manufacturing." *Who Made America? They Made America: PBS.* http://www.pbs.org/wgbh/theymadeamerica/whomade/lowell_hi.html (accessed on July 7, 2005).

Elijah McCoy

Born May 2, 1844 (Colchester, Ontario, Canada)
Died October 10, 1929 (Eloise, Michigan)

Inventor
Engineer

American inventor Elijah McCoy patented a lubricating (reducing friction between two solid objects) device for locomotive engines that was widely used in the railroad industry for more than forty years. McCoy's oil cup, which dripped a steady flow of oil into an engine while it was running, was a major time-saver for the train engineers of the era. Previously, they had to halt the train and manually oil the engine and its parts to keep it running smoothly. McCoy had once done that very job himself, and his idea came from that experience. He never earned much money from this or from any of his other inventions, however, and died penniless.

Educated in Scotland

McCoy was born in 1844, in Colchester, Ontario, in Canada. His parents were escaped slaves from a Kentucky plantation. They had made it to Canada, where slavery was illegal, by using the Underground Railroad, a secret network of safe houses that helped fugitive slaves reach freedom in the free states and Canada. He was one of twelve children in his family, and they

Elijah McCoy. *(Fisk University Library. Reproduced by permission.)*

lived on a farm. His father had received the land from the government as thanks for his part in stopping an 1837 rebellion against English colonial rule. Eventually the McCoys crossed the U.S.-Canadian border to Michigan. They settled in Ypsilanti, and McCoy's father found a job in the logging industry.

As a youngster McCoy liked to take things apart to see how they worked, and he usually managed to reassemble whatever it was and put it back in working order. He earned good grades and was employed in a machine shop after school to help support the large household. In 1860, the year he turned sixteen, he completed grammar school. His parents were eager to send him to college, but there was little opportunity at the time for blacks to do so in the United States. The country was on the verge of the American Civil War (1861–65; a war between the Union [the North], who were opposed to slavery, and the Confederacy [the South], who were in favor of slavery).

Though it was a great financial sacrifice for them, McCoy's parents sent him to Edinburgh, Scotland, where he studied mechanical engineering. He then worked as an apprentice, or someone who is bound to work for someone else for a specific term in order to learn a trade, to complete his education, and returned home certified as a master mechanic and engineer. By then the Civil War had ended, but discrimination against African Americans had not, and McCoy had a difficult time finding a job as an engineer. Despite his credentials, few firms would hire a black man in a job that required him to give orders to white employees.

Instead McCoy took a job as a fireman on the Michigan Central Railroad, which ran between the cities of southeastern Michigan, Indiana, and Illinois. In the steam locomotive world, a fireman was the worker who kept the fire going in the engine compartment. Also called a boilerman or coal-stoker, the fireman had to shovel coal into the burner of the furnace. That generated the heat that created the steam, which powered the engine. It was difficult work, and McCoy sometimes had to shovel as much as two tons of coal each hour. Though the job was one of the few open to African Americans, it was also considered a step in the process of becoming a locomotive engineer.

Developed automatic engine lubricator

Another one of McCoy's duties on the train was to oil the engine. This occurred frequently. The train would be halted, and he would dash out to the running board of the engine compartment and pour oil onto the parts. It was a terribly inefficient method to keep the engine running smoothly, and McCoy dreamed of a device that would keep an engine lubricated on its own, even while the train was running. Other inventors had come up with various types of automatic lubricating devices, but they did not work consistently and never caught on in the locomotive industry.

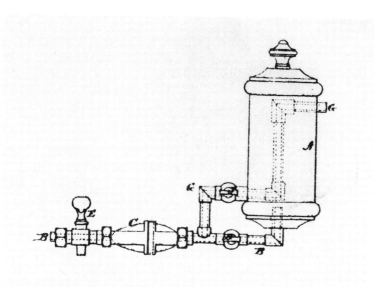

A drawing from Elijah McCoy's patent application for his automatic engine lubricator. *(Schromberg Center for Reseach in Black Culture.)*

In his workshop in Ypsilanti, McCoy began working on a way to solve this problem. First he built an engine that had channels running through it that were connected to one another. These channels would let oil flow through the engine. The hardest part of the challenge was to get the oil to drip steadily. If it came out too quickly, the oil would flood the engine and damage it. McCoy's idea was a drip cup made from either metal or glass, that held the oil in a reservoir (a place where something is stored). The cup was activated by steam pressure from the engine itself. The steam rose and when it reached the cup, the heat activated a piston. A piston is a solid cylinder (tube-shaped part) that moves back and forth. The piston was connected to the reservoir, and its movement tapped the opening of the reservoir in which the oil was stored. Thus the oil flowed out at a steady rate.

McCoy's invention represented a major advance for steam engines of the day. The constant stops to oil the engine were thought to be costing the railroads about 25 percent of their profits at the time. With McCoy's drip cup the necessary lubrication of the parts came regularly and there was less friction inside the engine, which meant that its parts did not wear out

The Real McCoy

Elijah McCoy's automatic engine lubricator became standard on train equipment in the last decades of the nineteenth century, but the inventor had assigned his patent rights to investors, which meant that other companies could buy the design and produce their own lubricators. According to traditional belief, train engineers of the era would ask if an automatic lubricator was "the real McCoy" or a cheaper imitation. This tale is widely repeated in literature about McCoy and his invention.

Language historians have tried to discover the real story behind the phrase "the real McCoy." Over the years, it became a colloquialism (a word or phrase used in casual conversation) that meant "genuine." The term may actually have been linked to a popular brand of whiskey made by an Edinburgh distillery, G. Mackay and Company. "The real McKay" was a slogan the company used in its advertising around 1870, but was thought to have been a colloquialism for authentic Scotch whiskey since at least the mid-1850s. Two other theories relate the term to either an American cattle baron of the era or to U.S. boxing champion Norman Selby (1872–1940), who called himself "Kid McCoy."

as quickly. The device also reduced the risk of potentially deadly engine fires, which happened when the parts were not properly lubricated, and even made engines quieter. McCoy applied for and received a patent (a legal document giving an inventor the exclusive right to make, use, or sell an invention for a certain term of years) from the U.S. Patent Office. Patent No. 129,843 for "Improvement in Lubricators for Steam Engines" was granted in July 1872. The product quickly became popular, and McCoy's employer, the Michigan Central Railroad, was the first to use it on their trains. Soon it was being manufactured and attached to steam engines on other railroads. He patented three more improvements for it over the next two years.

The "real McCoy"?

McCoy still encountered prejudice because of his skin color. Sometimes when a company found out that he was black, they would cancel their order for his lubricating device. He failed to earn much money from it, either, since he agreed to assign the rights to his patents to others. McCoy probably did this in order to obtain the necessary funds to start his own company and work on other inventions. This meant that his design could be sold to other companies, and imitations of poor quality soon came onto the market. Because of this, his self-lubricating device had many imitators, and this may have given rise to the phrase "the real McCoy." Supposedly engineers would ask if their train was equipped with the McCoy lubricator or one of the many, sometimes inferior, imitations. Nevertheless, it was used on many trains until about 1915, and also made countless steam engines that powered ocean liners, steamships, and factory machinery run more smoothly.

McCoy was able to quit his Michigan Central job in 1882. He moved to Detroit, Michigan, where he worked on other inventions and earned some income from consulting work. Occasionally he would appear to deliver a scheduled lecture, but when the event's organizers saw that he was black, he would be sent away. He continued with his inventions and in his spare time he volunteered with youth clubs in the city. He encouraged Detroit teenagers to pursue any educational opportunity available to them.

Other patents that McCoy received were for steam and air brakes on trains, but he also invented a new type of automobile tire, a folding ironing board, and even a lawn sprinkler. **Booker T. Washington** (1856–1915; see entry) mentioned McCoy in his 1909 book, *Story of the Negro.* Washington pointed out that McCoy had more patents to his name than any other African American inventor.

In 1920, when he was well into his seventies, McCoy founded the Elijah McCoy Manufacturing Company in Detroit to produce an air-brake lubricator that he had recently patented. Two years later McCoy and his wife were involved in an automobile accident. Mary Delaney McCoy was also active in community service in the city and cofounded the Phillis Wheatley Home for Aged Colored Ladies in 1898. She died in 1923 from injuries suffered in the accident, and McCoy's health declined as well. He spent the final years of his life at the Eloise Infirmary, which was a state home for the poor outside of Detroit. He died there on October 10, 1929. A state historical marker was placed at his longtime Detroit home, at 5730 Lincoln Street, and a nearby street was named in his honor.

Mary McCoy

Elijah McCoy's second wife, Mary Eleanora McCoy, was a noted Detroit, Michigan, philanthropist (person who made an active effort to promote human welfare) and clubwoman, as African American women involved in community service were known in her day. She was born Mary Eleanora Delaney on January 7, 1846, in Lawrenceburg, Indiana. Her parents, Jacob Delaney and Eliza Montgomery Delaney, were staying there on their way north to Canada. Lawrenceburg was a stop on the Underground Railroad.

McCoy attended a home-based mission school where the children of slaves were taught to read and write. Around 1869 she also studied at the Freedman's School of St. Louis, Missouri. That same year she married Henry Brownlow, a St. Louis man. Historians do not know if he died, or if the couple divorced. On February 25, 1873, she married Elijah McCoy, whose first wife had died, and they settled in Detroit. They had one child together.

McCoy, along with other middle-class women of color, was active in the movement to establish clubs in the city. These were organized to provide much-needed social services and aid to the poorer members of the community. In 1895 she became one of the founders of In As Much Circle of King's Daughters and Sons Club, one of the first such groups in Detroit organized by black women to help the underprivileged. That same year she teamed with other African American women in the area and established the Michigan State Association of Colored Women. She also served as vice president of the Federated Colored Women's Clubs of Michigan. That group later merged into the National Association of Colored Women (NACW). At the NACW's 1914 gathering McCoy presented to the national president, Margaret Murray Washington, a gavel carved out of cherrywood taken from a tree that once sat on the property of John Brown (1800–1859), the noted antislavery activist.

The list of McCoy's efforts to help Detroit's black citizens was an impressive one. She was a founder of the Phillis Wheatley Home for Aged Colored Women, along with Fannie Richards (1840–1922), a notable local educator and activist. Some years earlier Richards had become the first black teacher when the Detroit public school system was ordered by a court to desegregate (stop having separate facilities for whites and blacks). McCoy also held a leadership post with the Lydian Association of Detroit and was active in the women's suffrage (right to vote) movement, as well as the National Association for the Advancement of Colored People (NAACP). At the parade before the inauguration of President Woodrow Wilson (1856–1924; served 1913–21) in 1913, she was chosen to carry the flag at the head of the Michigan delegation of Democratic Party supporters.

That same year, McCoy was appointed by Michigan's governor to serve on the state commission that participated in the Half-Century Exposition of Freedmen's Progress. This Chicago event honored black achievement in America in the fifty years since slavery had been abolished.

For More Information

Books

Aaseng, Nathan. *Black Inventors.* New York: Facts on File, Inc., 1997.

Web Sites

Elijah McCoy. http://www.africawithin.com/bios/elijah_mccoy.htm (accessed on July 7, 2005).

J. P. Morgan

Born April 17, 1837 (Hartford, Connecticut)
Died March 31, 1913 (Rome, Italy)

Financier

"Morgan had some grounds for thinking that the country ought to leave its financial affairs to him. Over the past half century, his bank had helped transform the United States ... into the strongest industrial power in the modern world."

Jean Strouse.

By 1900 John Pierpont (J. P.) Morgan had amassed one of the largest fortunes in the United States, and over the next decade his financial empire grew to rival the economies of large nations. His finance company was so well funded it was able to back new industries, buy railroads, and arrange mergers between giant corporations. The majority of the American public believed that Morgan's money and skill were advancing the rapid growth of American industry, but many nonetheless viewed the powerful Wall Street banker as a robber baron, a term sometimes used to refer to the ruthless and greedy industrialists of the latter half of the nineteenth century. In several ways Morgan had more influence over the American economy than the federal government, and some Americans were alarmed that one private citizen had obtained such power in a democratic nation. Morgan, however, believed he was working for the advancement of the United States. Throughout his career he organized industries in an attempt to eliminate competition among them and to stabilize the nation's economy. Morgan also directly helped the government avoid financial crises on three occasions. At a time when the nation's banking system was barely

J. P. Morgan. *(AP/Wide World Photos. Reproduced by permission.)*

functioning, Morgan's company served as the chief financial institution of the country, playing a huge, if somewhat secretive, role in the shaping of the industrialized United States.

The education of a future banker

Morgan was born on April 17, 1837, in Hartford, Connecticut, to a wealthy family whose roots in the United States dated back to 1636. J. P. was the oldest of five children and the only son of Junius Spenser Morgan and Juliet Pierpont

Morgan. Junius ran a successful dry goods wholesale business that had been purchased for him by his own wealthy father. He taught J. P. about business and sent him to expensive schools in the United States and Europe. While always a good student, Morgan was particularly gifted in math. When he was fourteen his family moved to Boston, Massachusetts, and Morgan graduated from the city's well-respected English High School three years later. Even as a child Morgan traveled extensively. By the age of fifteen he had visited most of the famous cities of Europe. During his travels he developed a lifelong passion for fine art, beginning a collection while still in his teens.

After Morgan's high school graduation, his father became a partner in a thriving London, England, firm, George Peabody & Company, which handled financial transactions for trade between Europe and the United States. J. P. spent several years traveling, first to fight a lingering illness, and later to study in Europe. He graduated from the University of Göttingen in Germany at the age of twenty, and then went to work at his father's London office. He returned to New York City in 1857.

In early 1860 Morgan married Amelia Sturges. Sturges was suffering from tuberculosis, a disease that affected the lungs, so for their honeymoon the pair sailed to North Africa in the hopes the climate there would improve her health. It did not, and she died within a couple of months. Morgan fell into a deep depression and turned to work to escape from his sorrow. In 1865 he wed Frances Tracy. Together they had four children: one son, J. P. Morgan Jr., and daughters Louisa, Juliet, and Anne. The couple separated around 1875.

Entering the world of finance

In New York Morgan was hired at the banking firm Duncan, Sherman & Company. He spent much of his first months as a copyist. The company had no typewriters and every business document had to be written in longhand and then copied in the same manner. Soon Morgan advanced to more interesting work, researching possible investments around the country. On his own time he began to do what seemed to come naturally to him: engineering money deals. One of his early ventures was to purchase a shipload of coffee in New Orleans and then sell it to merchants in New York at a profit.

In 1861 the twenty-four-year-old Morgan founded his own firm to act as the American agent for his father's London firm. That same year the American Civil War (1861–65; a war between the Union [the North], who were opposed to slavery, and the Confederacy [the South], who were in favor of slavery) began, and Morgan, like thousands of other men who could afford to do so, hired someone to take his place in the Union Army. During the war he drew criticism for his role in financing what came to be known as the Hall Carbine Affair, in which Morgan loaned money to a person who used it to buy obsolete (no longer useful) firearms from the U.S. government and then sold them back to the government at a profit. At the same time Morgan was taking part in gold speculation (engagement in a risky business transaction with the hope of making quick or large profits), purchasing gold in the United States and then selling half of it overseas. The overseas sales drove up the price of gold in the United States, and he could then sell the other half at a profit. When his father heard about these dealings, he convinced J. P. to bring an older and wiser partner into his firm in 1864. In 1871 Junius Morgan arranged a merger of his son's company with the New York branch of a Philadelphia bank, and the firm became Drexel, Morgan and Company.

Entering the railroad business

After the war the U.S. government was deeply in debt, and Morgan's company became one of its major refinancing agents, an institution that loaned money so that the borrower could merge several loans into one that could be paid off at a more reasonable pace and rate of interest. Morgan had already built up a large supply of capital (accumulated wealth or goods devoted to the production of other goods), and he could also get funding from his father's London connections. He began to purchase companies that had fallen into financial trouble during the war. He would buy out several businesses within one area and reorganize them so they had no competition and could operate profitably.

One of the businesses Morgan began financing was the railroad industry. Competition among railroad builders had resulted in unstable rates and wasted profits in the industry. From the 1860s through the 1880s, new railroad construction had occurred at an extremely rapid pace. Many powerful businessmen were only concerned with personal gain and did not care how long or well their companies operated. A result of this competition was that the railroad network became over-built. Competing companies were racing to put down track in order to lay claim to the best sites, regardless of whether those areas even needed rail service. Often two lines operated by competing companies would run side by side. In order to keep their customers, each railroad line would be forced to continually lower its rates, which often led them to operate without profit or even at a loss. Hundreds of railroads collapsed in the last three decades of the nineteenth century. Morgan quickly saw that the future of American railroads lay in building large systems in which a single corporation controlled all lines and operated without competition in its area. He resolved to correct the mistakes that had been made by the greedy railroad businessmen and stabilize the industry—at great profit to himself.

Morganization

Morgan began buying up shares in the New York railroads. In 1869 he gained control of the Albany and Susquehanna Railroad from financial backers Jay Gould (1836–1892) and James Fisk (1834–1872). Then in 1879 the state began looking into charges that William Vanderbilt (1821–1885), the owner of the New York Central Railroad, was controlling his railroad rates in a discriminatory fashion, in a way that may have conflicted with New York state law. Rather than face investigation, he turned over 250,000 shares of the railroad to Morgan to quietly sell in Europe. The $25 million deal Morgan arranged greatly enriched his company and made him famous for the excellent monetary return he obtained for Vanderbilt. Morgan was even granted a seat on New York Central's board of directors. He went on to finance many failing railroads, successfully reorganizing them to eliminate the disorderly conditions caused by competition between them.

By 1885 Morgan had become a driving force behind America's railroads. He held private meetings at his home with other railroad leaders, a group that called itself the Interstate Commerce Railway Association, to discuss how to eliminate potential competition on profitable routes. He initially tried to create railroad pools, or agreements among rival companies to share their profits or divide up territories to avoid destructive competition and maintain higher prices, but many of them failed so he went on to forge mergers, in which one of the stronger railroad companies in an area bought up its competitors. His strategy became known as Morganization. He acquired bankrupted lines (those that could not pay their debts), gave them enough new capital to survive, made strict cost cuts, and oversaw agreements with rival lines to reduce unnecessary competition. He placed many of the largest systems under the control of boards of directors, or of voting trusts, that he and his associates closely controlled. Voting trusts are agreements in which people with voting powers who owned stock transferred their voting rights to directors while still retaining ownership. By 1900 he had gained financial control over the largest railroad empire in the country. He had made a great fortune, but he had also stabilized the troubled industry, bringing the rocky era of warring railroad companies to a close.

A financial statesman?

In 1893 the United States experienced a major financial panic due to a shortage of gold in the country. Bank failures (the collapse of banks that were unable to meet their credit obligations) began in April and spread rapidly. Some six hundred occurred in the first months of the panic, especially in the South and West, and four thousand banks had failed by the end of the year. An estimated fourteen thousand businesses collapsed during the same period, and the economy suffered a severe four-year depression. The United States had no central banking system at the time, and Morgan and the other bankers knew the nation's monetary system was in danger of failing. Morgan created a business group to provide the government with $65 million in gold, half of it borrowed from other nations. This action likely saved the American commercial banking system from collapse, averting years of painful financial decline, but the nation as a whole was not grateful. Morgan had profited enormously from the deal and the press was critical of his actions. Congress launched an inquiry, but Morgan refused to reveal how much profit he had actually made in the transaction.

J. P. Morgan & Company building in New York City. *(© Bettmann/Corbis.)*

The supreme capitalist

Junius Morgan died in 1890, leaving his son J. P. a great deal of money. By then the younger Morgan was head of his own firm, J. P. Morgan & Company. He was such a powerful force on Wall Street that businesses from all around the country moved to New York to be near his company's financial services. The city had become the hub of business activity for the nation and was home to its wealthiest people. Morgan was at the center of it all, a position in which he was quite comfortable due to his privileged upbringing.

After his success with the railroads, Morgan expanded the range of his financial activities. During the 1870s he had become interested in the work of inventor **Thomas Edison** (1847–1931; see entry), finding merit in Edison's experiments with electricity when no other businessmen did. Morgan and a couple of associates supported Edison's work for nearly two decades, which eventually led to the foundation of the Edison General Electric Company. In 1892 Morgan acquired the lighting company Thomson-Houston Electrical and merged it with the Edison Company to form General Electric (GE), which quickly became the country's main electrical equipment manufacturing company.

In the 1890s Morgan began to buy small steel-producing companies. Soon he owned a major share of the steel industry, which brought him into competition with **Andrew Carnegie** (1835–1919; see entry) and his huge and successful Carnegie Steel Company. In 1901 Morgan bought Carnegie Steel for $480 million. He then merged it with his ten other steel companies, creating U.S. Steel. U.S. Steel became the first billion-dollar company in the world and produced 67 percent of the country's steel. Within months Morgan began purchasing businesses that provided products or services his company used to manufacture and transport the steel, such as the Shelby Steel Tube Company and the Bessemer Steamship Company. U.S. Steel controlled massive iron deposits and coal reserves. The company also owned the largest shipping line on the Great Lakes, eighty blast furnaces (furnaces in which blasts of air were pumped into the fire to speed up the process of removing the iron from the iron ore), and 149 steel plants and mills. U.S. Steel continued to expand, acquiring seven more companies between 1902 and 1908 and constructing the world's largest steel mill at Gary, Indiana.

By the turn of the century U.S. Steel operated with expenses and revenues greater than all but a few of the world's governments. It had eliminated most of its competition and controlled every step in the steelmaking process from mining coal and ore to the making of nails and steel beams, so it did not have to pay high prices to other companies for their products or services. It was one of the world's biggest monopolies, companies that had the exclusive right to produce or sell a product. Morgan had succeeded in making a fortune for his company while at the same time making the steel industry more efficient so it could thrive in the following decades.

Trust-busting begins

By the time Morgan formed U.S. Steel, the American public had become distrustful of monopolies and trusts. Trusts were formed when companies within an industry combined in order to eliminate competition. Complaints had pressured Congress into passing the Sherman Antitrust Act in 1890, which barred any "contract, combination in the form of trust or otherwise, or conspiracy, in restraint of trade" and made it a federal crime "to monopolize or attempt to monopolize, or combine or conspire ... to monopolize any part of the trade or commerce among the several states." The 1890 act was rarely enforced in its early years, however. Morgan did not think it applied to him, since he felt his work as the nation's banker and financial backer was too beneficial to the country to be challenged. He was proved wrong in 1901.

That year James J. Hill (1838–1916), the head of the Great Northern Railroad and a friend of Morgan, and Edward H. Harriman (1848–1909), the head of the Union Pacific Railroad, engaged in a competition with each other to purchase controlling stock in the Northern Pacific Railroad, which did not have the power and money to stop these powerful and wealthy men from buying up controlling amounts of its stock. Hill sought Morgan's help, so Morgan sent word to his staff to purchase all the Northern Pacific stock they could. Such vast amounts of money and stock changed hands that the business dealings of these financial giants affected the nation's economy. Stock prices soared and fears about railroad failures caused a financial panic that ruined many businesses. Realizing that neither side could win, Morgan, Hill, and Harriman decided to form a $400 million holding company (a company formed to own stocks and bonds in other companies, usually for the purpose of controlling them) called the Northern Securities Trust Company. They hoped to bring order and efficiency to the northwestern railroad market by bringing their combined interests—the Great Northern Railroad, the Northern Pacific Railroad (over which Hill had finally gained control), and the Chicago, Burlington & Quincy Railroad—under the control of one board of directors. The merger resulted in one of the largest holding companies formed up to that point.

In March 1902 President Theodore Roosevelt (1858–1919; served 1901–9) instructed the U.S. attorney general (the chief lawyer of the federal government) to file a lawsuit against the Northern Securities Trust Company. By order of the federal court in a ruling upheld by the U.S. Supreme Court, in 1904 the company was dissolved, or broken down into its separate companies, to conform to the regulations in the Sherman Antitrust Act. Roosevelt stunned the business world when he finally applied the eleven-year-old act, and he soon became known as the "trust-buster." No one was more surprised by the government's actions than Morgan.

The friend and enemy of the government

On October 23, 1907, a major financial panic began with a few business failures that frightened the public. This caused a ripple effect through the nation's economy, starting with the New York banks, when hordes of panicky customers suddenly began to withdraw their money at the same time, causing the banks to run out of cash. The bank failures led to more business failures and a general downturn in the economy. As they had in the past, antigovernment officials and leading business executives looked to Morgan to make things better, and he went right to work. Morgan set up a syndicate (group) of the most powerful banks in New York. For three weeks this syndicate acted like the nation's central banking system, providing ready cash to financial institutions in need. Morgan obtained pledges to provide financial assistance from the Bank of England, oil industrialist **John D. Rockefeller** (1839–1937; see entry), and several other major financial backers. He recruited the best analysts available to investigate the resources of the various New York banks and trust companies to determine which were capable of being saved and then acted to do so. He even resorted to locking leading New York trust company presidents in his library overnight in his efforts to negotiate deals that would support the country's financial institutions. When the crisis calmed down in mid-November, the financial community credited Morgan with saving the nation. However, the incident had revealed to the public the immense power wielded by Morgan, a private citizen. More and more Americans began to demand reforms of the financial system.

The Federal Reserve Act of 1913

During the eighteenth and nineteenth centuries, the United States had a banking system that was significantly inferior to those of other industrial nations. Americans had opposed any type of central bank since the founding of the country, when the largely agrarian (farming) population favored local and state government control over any form of federal government activity, which they distrusted. Even when two national banks were founded, one in 1791 and the other in 1816, both were soon eliminated due to fears that the federal government was taking over powers that belonged to the states. As the nation expanded, hundreds of state banks were established under a wide assortment of state laws. Each state bank operated using its own methods; they issued their own paper money in amounts that suited their needs or tightened up their money supplies without any central coordination. The policies often conflicted with one another from state to state, and bank failures were widespread.

To correct some of these problems, Congress passed the National Bank Acts of 1863 and 1864, which combined to create a national bank system. National banks could issue banknotes—a fairly stable paper currency—and by 1865 state banks stopped issuing paper money. The nation's banking system, now made up of both state and national banks, continued to be inefficient, however. All banks faced the problem that the country's supply of currency was rigidly fixed to the nation's gold reserves. Additionally, no one had the authority to raise or lower the existing money supply to meet the changing needs of the nation.

By the turn of the twentieth century, the United States had become a rich and powerful industrial nation, but its economy was still hindered by the disorganization of its banking system. Major financial panics (periods

The Pujo Money Trust investigation

By 1912 the reform movement led to an important government investigation into the state of the nation's money. The Pujo Money Trust Investigation Committee was formed to explore whether money trusts or large combinations of financial institutions existed and were creating a concentration of the nation's wealth in the hands of a few powerful bankers and industrialists. Representatives from the largest U.S. financial institutions were called to testify, including key executives from J. P. Morgan & Company. The Pujo committee hearings uncovered astonishing facts about American financial institutions. Most impressive was the discovery that 341 directors of corporations with a net worth of more than $25 billion were controlled by Morgan and a few others. A United Press article on December 12, 1912, reported the details:

when people feared that the economy was shaky and many withdrew their money from the banks, leading to bank failures, the closing of companies, and widespread unemployment) hit the United States in 1873, 1893, and 1907, with smaller panics occurring in the years between. After the panic of 1907, Congress began to look into the possibility of forming a central bank that could stabilize the economy.

In December 1913 the Federal Reserve Act was passed. The act is generally regarded as the most far-reaching piece of legislation covering banking and currency in the nation's history. It established a Federal Reserve system to set the nation's monetary policies, regulate banks, stabilize the economy, and provide banking services for the federal government and other public and financial institutions. It was the only institution authorized to issue the nation's currency. Unlike any previous American banking systems, Federal Reserve banks had the power to increase or decrease the amount of currency in circulation according to the needs of the economy. Generally, if the prices of goods fell too low, the Federal Reserve could increase the currency supply. When people had more money, they were willing to spend more on products, and businesses could raise their prices. If, however, there was a larger amount of ready money than goods and services on the market, which was called inflation, prices would rise, and a decrease in the money supply could help lower prices.

The Federal Reserve Act provided for the establishment of no more than twelve Federal Reserve Banks. These twelve so-called "bankers' banks" were not available to individuals and provided services only to member banks. The twelve banks were controlled by a seven-member Board of Governors appointed by the president and overseen by the secretary of the treasury. All national banks were required to belong to the Federal Reserve.

Domination of $25,325,000,000 of the nation's wealth by 18 leading financial firms was the stupendous evidence, purporting [intending] to show actual existence of a money trust, presented to the Pujo investigating committee today. Five firms, the J. P. Morgan, the Guaranty and the Bankers trusts companies, the First National and the National City bank, are said to have 341 directors in 112 corporations, with aggregate [total] resources of $22,245,000,000. The firm of J. P. Morgan & Co. was held up as the "heart" of the alleged combination.

Seventy-five-year-old Morgan was called to testify before the committee and complained about the government's desire to look into his financial affairs. He refused to discuss his business and his worth during the questioning, holding to his belief that business could not be carried out in "glass pockets"—in other words, that a businessman must be able to make his deals in private. He declared that in all of his dealings he had acted in the interest of the nation, a claim most historians agreed with. The public, however, believed that no one individual should ever again be allowed to have such tremendous power over the economy with no regulation. Within a year Congress passed the Federal Reserve Act, creating a central banking system that would greatly improve the government's ability to handle financial crises and provide funds for major national enterprises.

The Pujo investigation badly affected Morgan's health. In March 1913, a few months after he testified, he died at the Grand Hotel in Rome, leaving behind a fortune estimated at $68 million. Prior to his death, the state of New Jersey had begun an antitrust suit against U.S. Steel. Two years after his death, in 1915, the case was dismissed, with the court ruling that there was no acceptable evidence of unfair pricing or monopolization by U.S. Steel in the steel market. The U.S. Supreme Court upheld the ruling in 1920, finding U.S. Steel to be an acceptable form of combining business for efficient production. The Court explained that U.S. Steel had not been formed with the intent to monopolize or restrain trade or to restrict competition, and that despite its gigantic size, the corporation did not abuse its market powers to fix prices or to increase profits by reducing the wages of its employees or lowering product quality or output. Rather, according to the Court, the formation of the steel trust was a natural result of the existing industrial technology, which made mass production efficient. Morgan had spent most of his life working by this principle.

Morgan had been generous with his fortune throughout his life, donating large amounts to social and cultural institutions such as churches, hospitals, schools, and above all, the arts. He owned an extensive collection of fine art, most of which he bequeathed to New York's Metropolitan Museum of Art, of which he had served as president. He was also the owner of a superb rare book and manuscript collection that included several historically significant pieces, such as the first Bible ever printed in North America. His rare books and manuscripts, at first housed at his mansion at Madison Avenue and 36th Street in New York, were moved to the Pierpont Morgan Library.

Morgan played a significant role in the history of U.S. industrialization. He served as an important link between those who had funds and those who needed them. As a result of having so much money and power, he was frequently seen as either a force of good or the source of evil in the business world. In either case, he paved the way for large, efficient, and powerful corporations in industrial America.

For More Information

Books

Brands, H. W. *Masters of Enterprise: Giants of American Business from John Jacob Astor and J. P. Morgan to Bill Gates and Oprah Winfrey.* New York: Free Press, 1999.

Chernow, Ron. *The House of Morgan: An American Banking Dynasty and the Rise of Modern Finance.* New York: Atlantic Monthly Press, 1990.

Strouse, Jean. *Morgan: American Financier.* New York: Random House, 1999.

Periodicals

"Investigation Shows Morgan, 17 Firms Control $25.3 Billion." *UPI's 20th Century Top Stories* (December 18, 1912).

Web Sites

"John Pierpont Morgan, 1837–1913." *Obits.com.* http://www.obituary.com/morganjp.html (accessed on July 7, 2005).

"John Pierpont (J. P.) Morgan." *People of Connecticut.* http://www.netstate.com/states/peop/people/ct_jpm.htm (accessed on July 7, 2005).

George Washington Murray

Born September 24, 1853 (Sumpter County, South Carolina)
Died April 21, 1926 (Chicago, Illinois)

Inventor
Legislator
Farmer

G eorge Washington Murray was an inventor, educator, and politician in late nineteenth-century America. Born into slavery, he rose to prominence as one of the first African Americans to serve in Congress. He farmed for several years in South Carolina and invented a number of farm tools in the 1890s.

Patents and politics

Murray was born in September 1853, in Sumpter County, South Carolina. He spent his early years in slavery on a plantation in Rembert and was nine years old when the historic Emancipation Proclamation freed all slaves in the Southern states during the American Civil War (1861–65; a war between the Union [the North], who were opposed to slavery, and the Confederacy [the South], who were in favor of slavery). By then his parents had either been sold off to other owners or died, and he was an orphan. He had no formal schooling but entered South Carolina University in 1874. He studied there for two years until a new rule segregated the school and its black students were forced to leave.

Murray earned his undergraduate degree from the State Normal Institute in Columbia, South Carolina. For a time he taught school while also supporting himself as a farmer. He was active as a lecturer for the Colored Farmers Alliance, a separate chapter of the nationwide Farmers' Alliance. The Alliance was a political organization formed in 1876 that worked to improve the often difficult economic situation of farmers in the United States. Though the black farmers' chapter to which Murray belonged met separately, the Farmers' Alliance was, for a time, the only biracial group in the American South.

Murray's first three patents (legal documents that gave an inventor the exclusive right to produce his invention for a certain number of years) for farm tools were all granted on the same day in April 1894. His inventions were a direct result of his own experience as a farmer, and efforts to lessen some of the hard labor involved. They were for a furrow opener, a stalk-knocker-cultivator, and a marker, each of which was designed to speed the planting and harvesting process. The U.S. Patent Office approved his applications for four more devices in June of that year. These included a fertilizer distributor and a cotton chopper.

Murray's career as an inventor was secondary to his political achievements. He was active in the Republican Party, which had been formed several decades earlier in opposition to slavery, and in 1888 he was named chair of the party in Sumpter County. He ran for a seat in the U.S. House of Representatives in 1890 but lost. His efforts brought him to the attention of the White House, however, and U.S. president Benjamin Harrison (1833–1901; served 1889–93) appointed him customs inspector for the Port of Charleston, South Carolina.

In 1892 Murray won the South Carolina congressional race and went to Washington to take his seat in the U.S. House. He had won the election due to his successful challenge of a local law designed to discourage blacks from voting. He was reelected for a second term and was the sole African American representative in the Fifty-third Congress between 1893 and 1895. He spent much of his Washington career fighting to preserve the few rights that African Americans had managed to keep since the end of the Reconstruction era in the South. The Reconstruction Act of 1867 and a series of laws the following year had been passed by Congress to provide the Southern states, which had seceded from the

African American Inventors before the Civil War

When George Washington Murray patented several of his farm tool inventions in the 1890s, he joined an impressive list of other African American innovators. The first of these was a New York City tailor by the name of Thomas L. Jennings (1791–1859). Jennings was the first black to earn a patent from the U.S. Patent Office after it was established in 1790. Jennings developed a method of dry-scouring clothes in 1821 that was an early form of dry cleaning. His business thrived, and he used some of his personal wealth to fund the abolitionist (antislavery) cause.

Benjamin Banneker (1731–1806) was one of the more well-known black inventors in early American history. As a young man the Maryland native borrowed a pocket watch and took it apart to see how it worked. He made detailed drawings of its parts and built from those a clock that chimed on the hours—

the first of its kind. It worked steadily for the next forty years. He achieved some fame from it and in 1791 joined a team of surveyors working to measure the land that became the District of Columbia. That job is thought to have made him the first African American federal appointee. Later in life Banneker became an astronomer and published an annual almanac (a publication containing astronomical and meteorological data).

Norbert Rillieux (1806–1894) was born in New Orleans and was the son of a successful French planter and a woman who was a slave. Thanks to the support of his rich father, Rillieux received some schooling. He worked as a blacksmith and then as a machinist before going to France to teach. There he became fascinated with the newly developed steam engine, and back in Louisiana he used what he had learned to create an effective new method for turning the juice of the sugar cane plant into very small particles of sugar. He received a patent for what was called the multiple effect evaporator, and it

Union during the Civil War, with a plan for reentry into the Union and the return of full political status. The act included several laws that granted blacks political rights in their home states, and when they went to the polls they often chose African American candidates. This caused terrible tensions in the South, and Reconstruction became an explosive issue in the 1876 presidential election. The brief period of black political power ended the following year with the election of President Rutherford B. Hayes (1822–1893; served 1877–81), who withdrew federal troops from the Southern states. This returned much of the political power to white Southerners, many of whom were determined to bar African Americans from the political process at all levels, including voting in local elections.

began to be widely used in the sugar industry. Rillieux's device helped make sugar cheap to produce and contributed greatly to the rise of the sugar-producing industry and world trade.

Some sources referred to a Maryland man, Henry T. Blair, as the first African American to receive a patent, but that was before Jennings's patent was discovered. Blair was born around 1807 and in his twenties applied for and received two patents. One was for a corn seed planter in 1834 and the other was granted in 1836 for a cotton planter. His patent applications are marked with an "X" instead of a signature, a common practice for documents when the signee could not read or write. He died in 1860.

Lewis Temple, born a slave in Virginia in 1800, eventually escaped or bought his freedom. He settled in Massachusetts and became a blacksmith. His New Bedford shop sold supplies to the whaling industry, and his customers sometimes told him stories about whales that escaped. The mighty creatures sometimes managed to wriggle free of the barbed-head harpoon that whalers used to capture them, and so Temple created a new kind of toggle harpoon in 1848. His had a movable head and was known by the names Temple's Toggle or Temple's Iron. Though he did not patent it, it came into widespread use on New England whaleboats. He died in 1854.

James Forten was a successful Philadelphia sailmaker who had learned the skill from his father. Born into a free black family in 1766, he was educated at a progressive Quaker school in the city and joined his father in the sail-making firm where he worked. Forten devised an improved sail support that was said to have made it possible for ships to sail from America's Pacific Coast all the way to China for the first time. Later Forten's employer loaned him the money to buy the business, and it continued to thrive. He was active in the abolitionist movement and founded the American Anti Slavery Society in Philadelphia in 1833. He died nine years later.

A historic list

The Reconstruction period had given many former slaves their first experience with politics, and the few like Murray who managed to win or hold onto office had to fight against tremendous odds. White Southerners still tried to restrict black political power at the local level, creating, for example, a law that forced voters to pass a reading test. As most of the freedmen had not had the benefit of an education during their years as slaves, few could pass the test. Such tactics were finally outlawed decades later by the Voting Rights Act of 1965. Murray also worked to win increased federal funding for African American schools, and he made one notable public speech during a debate on a planned Cotton States Exhibition that would show-case the achievements of the South in the post–Civil War period. He hoped to convince his colleagues to approve a special section at the exhibition that would focus on the achievements of black inventors, and he read aloud a list of more than ninety inventions patented by African Americans, eight of which were his.

Murray's words that day and the historic list of African American inventors were recorded in the official daily proceedings of Congress, the *Congressional Record*. Addressing the speaker of the house, Murray declared:

> *The colored people of this country want an opportunity to show that the progress, that the civilization which is now admired the world over, that the civilization which is now leading the world, that the civilization which all nations of the world look up to and imitate—the colored people, I say, want an opportunity to show that they, too, are part and parcel of that great civilization.*

Murray's political career was over by 1898. There was a battle within the South Carolina Republican Party over the status of blacks within it, and an 1898 U.S. Supreme Court decision upheld a poll tax that forced certain voters to pay to vote. Some Southern states had enacted the new poll tax law to prevent blacks from voting. The law exempted an adult male voter from the tax if his grandfather had voted, which meant few whites had to pay. Since blacks had only won the right to vote with the Fifteenth Amendment of 1870, and many in the South were poor sharecroppers who could not afford to pay the poll tax, the Supreme Court decision made it extremely difficult for black politicians like Murray to count on African American voters to elect them to office.

Murray returned to farming in Sumpter County. He became involved in a real estate deal that attracted the attention of local authorities, and he was convicted of fraud in 1904. Forced to flee the state, he moved to Chicago, Illinois, where he was a writer and lecturer during the last twenty years of his life. He authored *Race Ideals* in 1914 and *Light in Dark Places* in 1925; both were privately published. He died in April 1926. There would not be another African American to serve in the House from South Carolina until 1992 and the election of James Clyburn (1940–).

For More Information

Books

"George Washington Murray." In *Black Americans in Congress, 1870-1989.* Prepared under the direction of the Commission on the Bicentenary by the Office of the Historian, U.S. House of Representatives. Washington, DC: Government Printing Office, 1991.

Periodicals

Gaboury, Willaim J. "George Washington Murray and the Fight for Political Democracy in South Carolina." *Journal of Negro History* 62 (July 1977): 258-69.

Web Sites

"Congressman George Washington Murray Urged Black Voting." *The African American Registry.* http://www.aaregistry.com/african_american_history/366/Congressman_George_Murray_urged_Black_voting (accessed on July 7, 2005).

Patent Points to Ponder: Colors of Innovation. http://inventors.about.com/library/inventors/blkidprimer6_12aa.htm (accessed on July 7, 2005).

A. Philip Randolph

Born April 15, 1889 (Crescent City, Florida)
Died May 16, 1979 (New York, New York)

Labor activist
Civil rights activist

"A community is democratic only when the humblest and weakest person can enjoy the highest civil, economic, and social rights that the biggest and most powerful possess."

American labor leader and civil rights crusader A. Philip Randolph was instrumental in shaping some of the first federal laws designed to give African Americans equal rights in the workplace. For several decades Randolph served as president of the Brotherhood of Sleeping Car Porters, a union of black employees in the passenger rail service industry. He rose to national prominence as its leader and then turned his attention to the manufacturing industry when the factories were preparing for wartime production in the early 1940s. By warning U.S. president Franklin D. Roosevelt (1882–1945; served 1933–45) that he planned to lead black workers in a civil rights march on Washington, Randolph convinced Roosevelt to sign an executive order that forced factories with government contracts to stop discriminating against African American workers. Many years later Randolph did lead a march on Washington when he was the behind-the-scenes organizer of the August 1963 March on Washington for Jobs and Freedom, at which Dr. Martin Luther King Jr. (1929–1968) delivered his famous speech, "I Have a Dream."

A. Philip Randolph. *(Fisk University Library. Reproduced by permission.)*

Early ambitions

Born Asa Philip Randolph in April 1889, Randolph was a Florida native and the son of a minister in the African Methodist Episcopal (AME) church. The family lived in Jacksonville's thriving African American community. The city had a number of black-owned businesses, some black police officers on its public safety patrol, and even a black judge. Such achievements were rare in a Southern city at the time, and for Jacksonville they ended with the 1896 U.S. Supreme Court decision *Plessy v. Ferguson.* That case granted states and municipalities the right to segregate (separate) blacks and whites in public facilities. Like many African Americans, Randolph's father was deeply upset with the ruling. He refused to let either Asa or his older brother, James, take the streetcar to school after seating was segregated on the line, nor were they allowed to use the public library's blacks-only reading room.

In 1907 Randolph graduated from the Cookman Institute, Florida's first high school for black students, as valedictorian of his class. His parents could not afford to send either of their sons to college, and so Randolph worked in a series of low-paying jobs over the next four years. In 1911 he and a friend boarded a passenger steamboat headed for New York City. They worked in the galley, or ship's kitchen, in order to pay their way, and Randolph later recalled it as one of the hardest jobs he had ever had. He arrived in New York City with high ambitions: he planned to become a classical stage actor and was particularly devoted to the works of English dramatist William Shakespeare (1564–1616). Tall and with a deep baritone voice, Randolph was a commanding figure, and he would later put those qualities to use persuading audiences and even heads of state to see his point of view.

Randolph settled in Harlem, the area of Manhattan where many African Americans lived and where the Harlem Renaissance (the flourishing of African American art, music, literature, and culture) emerged a decade later. He took acting classes and auditioned for roles but failed to win any theater parts. To make ends meet, he took a number of low-wage jobs, including washing dishes and operating an elevator. When he learned that the City College of New York offered free tuition to city residents he began taking classes there. Some were in political theory, and he became especially interested in socialism, an economic system in which the means of production and distribution is owned collectively by all the workers and there is no private property or social classes. Like other politically minded young blacks in Harlem, Randolph imagined that a more equal economic system in America, as opposed to the current capitalist one, would help bring an end to discrimination against blacks and other minorities. (Capitalism is an economic system in which the means of production and distribution are privately owned by individuals or groups and competition for business establishes the price of goods and services.)

In 1914 Randolph married Lucille Green, a hair salon owner in Harlem who shared many of his political ideals. Both joined the Socialist Party in New York City, and Green also introduced him to Chandler Owen (1889–1967), an energetic Columbia University student. Randolph and Owen became soapbox orators (people who gave speeches from improvised platforms) in Harlem, urging passersby to become more politically active. In 1917 they were hired by the union of black hotel waiters in the city and given the task of starting a new magazine, the *Hotel Messenger*. One article that criticized a few union members cost them their jobs, but they decided to launch their own publication. Lucille Green provided the original funding for *The Messenger*, and its first issue appeared in November 1917.

Confrontation and opportunity

The Messenger was radical in its tone. It urged African Americans to fight prejudice and discrimination by joining the Socialist Party, and its articles and editorials were critical of American capitalism. When America entered World War I (1914–18; a war in which Great Britain, France, the United States and their allies defeated Germany, Austria-Hungary, and their allies), *The Messenger* took an antiwar stance. Randolph's articles pointed out that in America racism was permitted by law, and blacks should question fighting and dying for a country that treated many of its citizens so unjustly.

Randolph's writings and public speaking engagements attracted government attention. He was arrested during a 1918 speech in Cleveland, Ohio, and the U.S. attorney general even tried to prevent the U.S. postal service from delivering *The Messenger* to subscribers. After the war, tensions lessened, although not in Harlem. There a new African American activist named Marcus Garvey (1887–1940) was attracting large crowds with his speeches. The Jamaican immigrant headed the Universal Negro Improvement Association, a black nationalist group that urged African Americans to return to Africa. Garvey even owned a steamship line that provided transportation to Africa. Randolph and Garvey disagreed sharply, with Randolph asserting that America belonged partly to the descendants of slaves who helped build the economy of the nineteenth century. He also considered Garvey's steamship venture a scam in which Garvey and his associates profited from the goodwill donations of middle-class blacks. The battle between the two sides escalated, and in September 1922 Randolph opened a package that contained a severed human hand. He suspected Garvey's group, but he certainly had other enemies by then. The attorney general had once called him the most dangerous black man in America.

The turning point in Randolph's career came in 1925, when Pullman Company porters in the New York area asked him to organize the Brotherhood of Sleeping Car Porters (BSCP). Pullman was an important brand name in American transportation at the time and had been for decades. Founded by George Pullman (1831–1897) in Chicago, Illinois, nearly sixty years earlier, the Pullman Company built luxury sleeping cars, known as Pullmans, for passenger rail service. In the period just after the end of slavery in the United States, George Pullman recruited former slaves to serve as porters inside the sleeping cars, which his company leased to the railroads. By the 1920s the term Pullman porter stood for excellent customer service. They prepared the sleeping berths, handled baggage, and even shined shoes. For decades it was one of the most respected jobs a black man could hold in America.

The Pullman porters were an underpaid and overworked lot, however. They earned an average of $67 a month and had to buy their uniforms with that money, along with the shoe polish they used on the job. They worked four hundred hours a month, or eleven thousand miles—whichever came first—and were expected to be at their departure train station a few hours before the train was scheduled to leave so that they could load baggage. They were not paid for those hours, however, because the four-hundred-hour count did not begin until the train pulled out. Some federal protections had been won for other railroad workers, but the porters were not included in that legislation. There had been attempts to organize a porters' union since 1909, but the Pullman Company had a long history of opposing labor groups. Some of the porters who had tried to form a union lost their jobs.

Battle for recognition

The Pullman porters needed a leader who was not a porter, and Randolph agreed to take the job. The BSCP was formally founded in August 1925 with the motto "Stands for Service

Not Servitude." Over the next twelve years, Randolph worked tirelessly to organize BSCP chapters in the major American cities that were home to large numbers of Pullman porters. Membership in the brotherhood rose quickly, with 4,600 members out of a total Pullman porter workforce of 10,000 by 1928. They failed to make any progress in gaining formal recognition as a union, however, as the company chose to ignore it entirely. Randolph sent numerous letters to the Pullman headquarters, none of which received any reply, but behind the scenes the Pullman executives worked quietly to damage his reputation, with little success.

Randolph launched a campaign to help boost public awareness of, and support for, the BSCP. He argued that a Pullman union would help the company become more efficient and therefore more profitable. His goal was to force the company to reduce working hours to 240 per month, which was the federal guideline for other railroad employees, and increase the porters' wages to $150 a month. With the onset of the Great Depression (1929–41; a time of great economic hardship worldwide), Randolph's job became much more difficult. Jobs were scarce in every industry, and the Pullman Company harassed BSCP members. By 1933 membership had dropped to just 658 porters, and the union was evicted from its Harlem office. Randolph was broke as well but refused to abandon his cause. New York City mayor Fiorello LaGuardia (1882–1947) saw that his shoes had holes in them and offered him a government job, but Randolph declined it.

The issue was resolved in 1934, when Franklin D. Roosevelt, a union-friendly Democrat in his first term in the White House, signed into law a bill that gave the porters the same protections as other groups of railroad industry employees. Pullman still refused to negotiate a contract with the BSCP, but Randolph called on some politicians in Washington who knew and respected him for help. The contract between the BSCP and the Pullman Company was finally signed in August 1937, and it reduced working hours for the porters to 240 a month. Wages were set at a minimum of $89.50 per month, much lower than the $150 that Randolph had wanted, but the contract was significant nonetheless as the first economic agreement between a white-owned institution and a group of African Americans.

Battles abroad and at home

Although Randolph had quit the Socialist Party many years before, he remained committed to the needs of the black working class and an end to discrimination. A new war loomed on the horizon when Germany, controlled by the fascist Nazi Party, invaded Poland in 1939. (Fascism is a system of government characterized by dictatorship, government control of the economy, nationalism, and the suppression of all opposition.) Germany and its allies began invading other European countries, and though the United States did not enter what became known as World War II (1939–45; a war in which Great Britain, France, the United States, and their allies defeated Germany, Italy, and Japan) until late 1941, it was providing military aid to England. The U.S. economy began to rebound from the Great Depression as factories were converted over to wartime production and began adding shifts and the workers to staff them.

In January 1941 Randolph launched his mission to force the federal government to ban racial discrimination in employment and hiring practices in these plants, as well as in the military. U.S. troops were segregated into black and white units at the time, and American military officials feared that if soldiers were on equal footing, racial tensions would prevent them from working together as an effective group responsible for one another's lives. Randolph was determined to change both of these practices. He announced his intention to lead a march of black workers on the nation's capital on July 1. This was known as the March on Washington Movement (MOWM), and the nation's black newspapers, which had tremendous influence in the African American community at the time, picked up the cause. One of them even created the Double V campaign, which called for victory against fascism, but also victory at home over racism. It was an important symbolic effort, for the United States entered the war against a Germany that had, in the past decade, stripped its Jewish citizens of their jobs and then their civil rights.

Randolph believed that fifty thousand blacks would march on Washington, a number he later doubled. He asked to meet with President Roosevelt, but Eleanor Roosevelt (1884–1962), the First Lady and a longtime civil rights supporter, was sent instead. She urged him to call off the march and asked how 100,000 travelers would be fed and sheltered if they arrived as

Blacks and the Labor Movement

African American workers often found it very difficult to gain steady employment before the Civil Rights Act of 1964 outlawed discrimination in all forms, including in hiring practices. The organized labor movement in America that emerged in the late nineteenth century did not offer much help to minority workers. The unions served to protect the job security and safety of their mostly white members. Many of the unions had charters that prohibited black workers from joining and similar rules that discriminated against persons who had been born in foreign countries.

Early in the nineteenth century, African American tradesmen worked as caulkers at the Washington Navy Yard. They sealed the seams of warships to make them seaworthy, and there is evidence that they went on strike in 1835. Later, the Association of Black Caulkers was formed in 1858 in Baltimore, Maryland, when the workers were harassed by immigrants who wanted their jobs. There were a few other organizations for black workers in the years before the late 1860s. In 1850 free blacks in New York City established the American League of Colored Laborers. There was also a Waiter Protective Association of New York formed in that decade. In 1869 the Colored National Labor Union held its first convention in Washington, D.C.

By 1886 the newly formed American Federation of Labor (AFL) served as an umbrella organization (an association of related institutions, who work together to coordinate activities or pool resources) for twenty-five skilled-trade unions. There were not very many African Americans in such professions, but the AFL did have a rule against accepting a union that barred blacks. That changed after 1895 when the International Association of Machinists joined the AFL. It had been created from the merger of two other unions, one of which did not allow African American members. After this the AFL negotiated a deal in which it allowed the establishment of segregated locals, or union chapters.

In 1902 there were more than one million union members in the United States, but only forty-one thousand of those were African American. That changed with the migration of blacks from the South to the industrial cities of the North from 1914 to 1918. In the 1930s there was a split inside the AFL, and the unions that broke away organized themselves into the Congress of Industrial Organizations (CIO). The CIO actively recruited black workers into its unions. An executive order signed by President Franklin D. Roosevelt in 1941, thanks to the work of A. Philip Randolph, brought thousands of new workers into both AFL and CIO ranks. When the ALF and CIO merged in 1955, Randolph was elected vice president of the newly formed union. Over the next decade the AFL-CIO emerged as an active participant in the civil rights movement.

planned. Randolph coolly told the First Lady that he expected them to use District of Columbia hotels and restaurants, although the city was deeply segregated at the time, and the police force was almost entirely white. Both Roosevelts realized, therefore, that the potential for violence was enormous. On June 25 the president signed Executive Order 8802, also known as the Fair Employment Act. It ended discrimination in hiring practices at any company that had contracts with the federal government. It also included a rule that prevented labor organizations at such factories or workplaces from barring black members.

Executive Order 8802 was a massive victory for Randolph and a significant one for black workers. He called off the march and then went to work on his other mission to desegregate the U.S. armed forces. Again his powers of persuasion and his commanding words helped drive change. The war had ended, and a new peacetime military conscription bill was being debated in Congress. (Conscription, also known as the draft, is a process in which persons were compelled, or forced, to enlist in the military.) President Harry S. Truman (1884–1972; served 1945–53) invited Randolph and other black leaders to the White House in early 1948. While there, Randolph warned Truman that unless discrimination ended in America, blacks might not fight for their country again if another war occurred. Several days later Randolph testified before the Senate Armed Services Committee, and again stated that black men might resist a military draft if the armed forces continued to be divided into separate units by race, and that he would publicly support them if they did. In 1948 Truman signed Executive Order 9981, which ended segregation in the U.S. armed forces.

The 1963 march

Randolph was still the president of what had become the International Brotherhood of Sleeping Car Porters, and he spent the remainder of his career fighting discrimination inside organized labor. He held a seat on the executive council of the American Federation of Labor-Congress of Industrial Organizations (AFL-CIO) and founded the Negro American Labor Council (NALC) in 1959. Four years later he organized another march on Washington, this one known as the March on Washington for Jobs and Freedom. A record 200,000 protesters turned out for the August 1963 event, and it became a pivotal moment in the civil rights struggle in twentieth-century America. The last speech of the day was scheduled to

A. Philip Randolph organized the 1963 March on Washington. *(© Bettmann/ Corbis.)*

be given by Dr. Martin Luther King Jr., who headed the Southern Christian Leadership Conference (SCLC). After Randolph introduced the minister, King delivered his stirring "I Have a Dream" speech, in which he envisioned an America free of racism and poverty, one in which "all men are created equal," as the Declaration of Independence stated.

King's speech is linked so dramatically to the 1963 March that he is sometimes mistakenly credited with being its organizer. In fact Randolph and his longtime associate Bayard Rustin (1910–1987) were the driving forces behind the event. The march helped sway public opinion and succeeded in convincing lawmakers to reconsider the status of blacks in America. A year later Congress passed the Civil Rights Act of 1964, followed by the Voting Rights Act of 1965. Both were historic pieces of legislation that sought to forever end discrimination against blacks and other minorities in the United States.

In 1968 Randolph retired as president of the International Brotherhood of Sleeping Car Porters, which later became part of the Brotherhood of Railway and Airline Clerks. He died in New York City in May 1979. Though his name is sometimes forgotten in the history of the civil rights movement in America, he was a well-known figure in his day and a hero to African Americans. Randolph spent his long career fighting on behalf of the black worker at a time when a man or woman could be fired simply on the basis of skin color alone and few would dare to challenge an employer. His role in securing equal treatment and legal protection for African Americans, from both the federal government and from organized labor, helped lift thousands of black families out of poverty.

For More Information

Books

Miller, Calvin Craig. *A. Philip Randolph and the African-American Labor Movement.* Greensboro, NC: Morgan Reynolds, 2005.

Reef, Catherine. *A. Philip Randolph: Union Leader and Civil Rights Crusader.* Berkeley Heights, NJ: Enslow Publishers, 2001.

Periodicals

Chenoweth, Karin. "Taking Jim Crow out of Uniform: A. Philip Randolph and the Desegregation of the U.S. Military." *Black Issues in Higher Education* (August 21, 1997): p. 30.

Hill, Norman. "A. Philip Randolph. (Labor)." *Social Policy* (summer 2002): p. 9.

Web Sites

A. Philip Randolph Pullman Porter Museum. http://aphiliprandolphmuseum. org/ (accessed on July 7, 2005).

John D. Rockefeller

Born July 8, 1839 (Richford, New York)
Died May 23, 1937 (Ormond, Florida)

Industrialist
Philanthropist

J ohn D. Rockefeller was one of the most successful industrialists in the history of the United States. His creation of the powerful Standard Oil Trust in the late nineteenth century permanently changed the course of business in the country. Rockefeller was a disciplined, serious, and ambitious man, driven by a desire for order and efficiency. When the oil industry was new, he quickly saw that competition among small companies would lower profits for everyone, and he attempted to take over the entire business to keep this from occurring. To gain the monopoly, or the exclusive possession or right to produce a particular good or service, he evaded and broke laws and destroyed the careers of many rivals. In contrast to his less desirable actions, however, Rockefeller was also a great philanthropist who gave substantial amounts of money to help institutions and organizations. The American public was split in its opinion of the man. Some thought him an evil genius seeking to gain too much control over the economy, but he was viewed by others as a kind man who tried to help his fellow man. Regardless of how America saw him, Rockefeller always seemed sure of the rightness of his own path.

"It has seemed as if I was favored and got increase because the Lord knew that I was going to turn around and give it back."

John D. Rockefeller (© Bettmann/Corbis.)

A troubled childhood

Rockefeller was born in 1839, in Richford, New York, and was the second of six children. Rockefeller's parents were very unlike each other. His father, William Avery Rockefeller, was a lively and charming man. He had a good sense of business and taught John about money. Unfortunately he was also a very dishonest man who could not settle down to family life. Rockefeller's mother, Eliza Davison Rockefeller, was a devout Baptist and a highly disciplined and reserved woman. She was extremely strict with her children. Eliza served as the sole caregiver of her family most of the time because William worked as a peddler and traveled from town to town to sell his goods. In 1849 William was arrested and charged with rape, but for some unknown reason the case never went to court. Sometime in the 1850s he assumed the false identity of Dr. William Levingston, a traveling doctor who claimed to be able to cure cancer. In 1855, using his fake name, William Rockefeller married a woman in New York and from then on lived as a bigamist (someone with two spouses). Several times a year William returned to stay with his first family, always bringing them money and taking an active interest in John's future. As a boy Rockefeller probably did not know much about the secret life of his father, whom he adored.

Rockefeller was much more like his mother. Both were serious to the point of being grim, moral, quiet, and hardworking, and both were committed to their church and religion. The family lived modestly, often finding it difficult to pay their bills, especially when William was away for long periods. Rockefeller learned to be enterprising as a child. If he saved enough money to buy a bag of candy, he would divide the candy up and sell it in individual pieces at a profit. When he was just twelve years old, he saved up $50 and loaned it to a farmer at a 7 percent interest rate (a percentage of the sum borrowed).

The Rockefeller family relocated several times, and in 1853, when John was fifteen, they moved to Cleveland, Ohio. Rockefeller had picked up some schooling before the move, but it was not until the family settled in Cleveland that he was able to attend two years of high school without interruption. He worked very hard at his studies and was good in math. His father urged him to pursue business, so he attended a three-month commercial education program that taught him bookkeeping and banking practices. At that time Rockefeller also joined the Erie Street Baptist Church and rapidly became an important member of the struggling congregation. He swept floors and washed windows, served as a clerk, raised money for a Sunday school library, and became one of the church's trustees (someone who was given responsibility for a property or organization). Out of his first meager earnings he contributed almost 10 percent of what he received to charities.

Becoming a businessman

After finishing his business course, Rockefeller applied for work at every large commercial establishment in Cleveland. At the age of sixteen he found a job as a clerk in a commission house, a firm that bought and sold futures contracts (binding agreements to buy or sell goods at a later date) in groceries and grains. After working at the company for three and a half years, during which he gained the confidence of many Cleveland businessmen and bankers, the nineteen-year-old Rockefeller quit his job and joined with a partner to form a business handling grain, hay, meats, and miscellaneous goods. Both partners invested $2,000 in the business. Due largely to Rockefeller's hard work and wise decision-making, the company made a modest profit in its first year, despite heavy competition in the field. The second year of business, 1861, marked the beginning of the American Civil War (1861–65; a war between the Union [the North], who were opposed to slavery, and the Confederacy [the South], who were in favor of slavery). Orders from the Union army, a rapid growth of agricultural shipments to industrial centers, and a heavy European demand for foodstuffs brought large profits to the partnership, and Rockefeller made his first small fortune. He soon began to foresee, however, that the trade in farm products would soon bypass Cleveland due to the spread of railways through the West. Rockefeller was ready for change when the oil industry began to attract widespread attention in the mid-1860s.

Before the 1850s fuels made from oil were not practical because oil could only be obtained through a difficult process that involved skimming it from the tops of ponds and other nonmoving bodies of water. When the first modern oil well was drilled in Pennsylvania in 1859, crude oil suddenly became available in large quantities, and in 1861 the first oil refinery (a building in which a raw material was processed to free it from impurities) opened in the United States. Because there were railroad lines that directly connected Cleveland to the oil fields of Pennsylvania, Rockefeller thought he could compete in the refining business. In 1865 he invested in an oil refinery, although few businessmen at the time thought there was much of a future in the industry. He bought out his partner's share in the refinery and began to focus on it full-time, borrowing large amounts of money to expand the refinery and taking in new partners to help him build up the business. By the end of the year, his refinery was producing at least twice as much oil as any other in Cleveland, and by 1868 it was the largest refinery in the world.

A family and church man

In 1864 Rockefeller married Laura Celestia Spelman (1839–1915), the daughter of a wealthy merchant. Their marriage, unlike that of Rockefeller's parents, was a union of shared values and beliefs. Both preferred a quiet, family-centered life to socializing, and they did not like showy displays of wealth. The Rockefellers had four children that reached adulthood: Bessie, Alta, Edith, and John Davidson Jr. Another child, Alice, died in infancy. Despite the long hours he worked, Rockefeller was a concerned and loving father to his children. He tried to pass on his moral and religious beliefs to his children, and he made them work for the things they wanted, but he was not strict like his own mother had been. His son, John Jr., as quoted by Ron Chernow in *Titan: The Life of John D. Rockefeller, Sr.,* called his father "a beloved companion." He went on to explain: "He had a genius with children. He never told us what to do or not to do. He was one with us."

Rockefeller's primary passions were work, family, and church. Even after he became extremely wealthy, he continued to attend a modest Baptist church with a congregation made up mainly of working-class people. Helping others was always part of his belief system. He was known to quietly press envelopes filled with money into the hands of needy members of his congregation as they left the church, and both Rockefeller and his wife taught Sunday school classes for decades. Rockefeller had no problem separating the ruthless activities he used to create his oil monopoly with his charitable and religious actions. He believed that human beings had a religious obligation to do their work as well as they were able and, consequently, to make as much money as possible. He was not concerned about the wide and growing gap between the rich and the poor since it was, in his opinion, all part of God's plan. Rockefeller never doubted that he had been chosen by God to create his corporation, make a huge fortune, and then give his money to worthy causes. In an interview with the *New York Times* (quoted by Chernow), Rockefeller explained that these views had long guided him: "I remember clearly when the financial plan, if I might call it so, of my life was formed. It was out in Ohio under the ministration of a dear old minister who preached, 'get money, get it honestly, and then give it wisely.' I wrote that down in a little book."

The Standard Oil monopoly

In its early years the oil industry was subject to destructive cycles of success and failure, with oil prices soaring to high levels and then dropping steeply. It was relatively cheap to build a small refinery, so when oil prices were high, newcomers seeking quick profits rushed to get into the business. Their production, added to that of the older refineries, flooded the market with oil, causing prices to fall. Low prices led to lack of profit and soon the small companies began to collapse. Only the large companies like Rockefeller's had enough money to hold out until prices rose again. In this climate Rockefeller and his new partner, Henry Flagler (1830–1913), knew that they had to run their refinery as efficiently as possible. They invested heavily in the most advanced equipment and machinery, putting most of the money they made back into the company and borrowing large sums to constantly expand. They paid particular attention to keeping their business expenses as low as possible by avoiding waste, producing in large quantities, and obtaining reasonable rates from companies that provided them services.

Low shipping rates were essential to maintaining a profit in the oil industry. Railroads commonly gave favored shippers rebates, or partial refunds, of their publicly stated rates. The larger the shipper was, the higher the rebate he received. Rockefeller made deals with the railroads to get the biggest rebates and the lowest rates possible, offering large-scale and consistent business in return. This allowed him to sell his refined oil for a lower price than his competitors. He cut other costs by investing in businesses that provided supplies to his refinery. Since oil was initially shipped in barrels, Rockefeller bought a plant to make the company's barrels. The company needed wood for the barrels, so Rockefeller bought his own timber tracts, or wooded areas for logging. He owned his own warehouses, bought his own tank cars, and owned or produced much of the raw materials and transportation he needed to operate. Later, when oil began to be transported in underground pipeline systems, Rockefeller and his associates invested in the pipeline industry and engaged in an industrial war with competitors in the field until his company had a monopoly. Rockefeller aimed to control every aspect of oil production and sales, from the drilling process to the delivery of the oil to the customer's door.

In 1870 the Standard Oil Company was incorporated, which meant all its separate businesses were united into one large company. At the time it controlled about 10 percent of the country's oil industry. Rockefeller was unhappy with the disorder in the industry, and he had a solution—the Standard Oil Company would buy out its competition, eliminating the inefficient newer companies and placing the more successful rivals under his able management. He began to build his empire in 1871, when he purchased twenty-one of Cleveland's twenty-six refineries. He offered the owners a good price for their businesses, giving them the option of taking payment in Standard Oil stock or in cash. Many felt they had to sell because Rockefeller's connections to the railroads meant that Standard Oil would always receive better shipping rates and would therefore be able to drive them out of business. Some others claimed they had been threatened with financial ruin if they did not sell, and this led some historians to call Rockefeller's purchasing plan the Cleveland Massacre.

By the end of 1872, Rockefeller and his associates controlled all the major refineries in Cleveland, New York, Pittsburgh, Pennsylvania, and Philadelphia, Pennsylvania. Over the next decade, the Standard Oil Company continued to expand, and in 1879 its thirty-seven stockholders controlled between 90 and 95 percent of the country's refining capacity. Because most of Rockefeller's transactions had been done in secret, many Americans were surprised to suddenly find that Standard Oil had become an industrial giant.

Standard Oil continued to grow during the 1880s. Under the direction of Rockefeller's brother, William, the firm expanded into the international market. Standard Oil products became well known in Asia, Africa, South America, and Central Europe. By the 1890s Standard Oil had pioneered a nationwide system to deliver oil directly to homes and businesses in almost every American town. Although consumers benefited greatly

John D. Rockefeller Jr.

John D. Rockefeller Sr.'s reputation for ruthless business methods was lessened somewhat in the next generation by his son and heir, John D. Rockefeller Jr. (1874–1960). John Jr. was brought up in a loving but solitary family atmosphere. The social life of the family centered on the Baptist Church, and young Rockefeller and his four sisters were taught to live morally upright, religious lives. Rockefeller was a shy, sensitive child who adored his father. At an early age he had to deal with stories in the press that claimed his father was a corporate criminal, and at the age of thirteen he experienced a nervous collapse.

After graduating from Brown University in 1897, young Rockefeller—largely to please his father—entered the offices of the family's Standard Oil Company in New York City to prepare himself to supervise his father's vast business interests. Rockefeller disliked the business world, so he occupied himself increasingly with managing his father's estates and philanthropic (related to the giving of money or gifts to promote human welfare) enterprises. The Rockefeller Institute for Medical Research, the General Education Board, and the Rockefeller Foundation were financed by the elder Rockefeller, but his son participated actively in their management.

From 1900 to 1908 Rockefeller became more closely involved with Standard Oil.

When the company was accused of unfair competitive practices, he separated himself from active policy making. He could not escape from hostilities toward his family name, however. In 1913 there was trouble at the Colorado Fuel and Iron Company, in which his family held large amounts of stock. The workers there went on strike, demanding improved conditions, better wages, and union recognition. The strike was violently suppressed by management, and Rockefeller was connected to management by his family's control of the company. Hurt by accusations from labor leaders that he had sided with the owners, Rockefeller drafted a plan for worker representation in company affairs that became a model for industrial relations during the 1920s. He explained his plan in speeches and articles and came to be considered a leader in labor reform.

Among the best-known philanthropies in which Rockefeller played a major part were conservation and national park projects in the West; the purchase of the Barnard Cloisters, a medieval museum in upper Manhattan, for the Metropolitan Museum of Art; the creation of the Rockefeller Center in New York City; and a donation of the land for the United Nations building. Modest and unaffected by his wealth, Rockefeller helped remove the bad associations from the family name and awakened other businessmen to their social responsibilities. He died on May 11, 1960, in Tucson, Arizona.

from this practice, criticism of Standard Oil's business tactics increased. One major complaint was that the company required the stores that sold its products to agree to sell only Standard products.

The Standard Oil Trust

In 1882 the Standard Oil Company owned controlling or substantial amounts of stock in forty associated companies around the nation. The company needed the legal power that would allow it to operate all these companies. The Standard Oil Trust was formed by an agreement that placed all properties owned or controlled by the Standard Oil Company in the hands of nine trustees (directors), including Rockefeller, Flagler, and Rockefeller's brother, William. The trustees exercised general supervision over all Standard Oil companies and over the other companies in which Standard held stock. Standard Oil Company (Ohio) stock was exchanged for trust certificates. The trust certificates provided shares of ownership of the whole trust, which included the assets of all regional Standard Oil companies, one of which was Standard Oil of New Jersey, the third largest U.S. refinery at the time. The trust also permitted Standard Oil to work around state laws that might restrict its operations, because, in name, the ownership had been delegated to the trustees, rather than a company. But in effect the trust created a giant new centralized company.

Standard under attack

Standard Oil had developed a bad reputation not long after its creation. Rockefeller destroyed many careers in his attempts to eliminate his rivals in the industry, and he often used dishonest methods to make business owners sell to him or stop competing with Standard Oil. Some of his company's executives and managers resorted to illegal means, including violence and intimidation, when dealing with competitors. Though Rockefeller was not personally associated with these illegal ventures, he was nonetheless openly ruthless when making business decisions. The press frequently printed stories about Standard Oil's underhanded tactics and its complete domination of the industry. Political cartoons about Rockefeller appeared in newspapers and magazines. Journalist Henry Demarest Lloyd (1847–1903) began a campaign against Standard Oil in 1881 with his *Atlantic Monthly* article "Story of a Great Monopoly." Lloyd was considered to be one of the first muckrakers, a group of journalists who searched for and exposed corruption in public affairs. His most important book, *Wealth Against Commonwealth* (1894), strongly criticized the Standard Oil monopoly.

By the 1880s, after hundreds of mergers and consolidations, the railroad, steel, and other monopolies like Standard Oil were so powerful that no government commission could regulate them, and public resentment grew. In 1889 Kansas enacted the first state antitrust legislation, and the effort soon spread across the South and the West. By 1900 twenty-seven states had created laws prohibiting or regulating trusts. Many trusts were simply too big to be controlled by the laws of any one state, however, and public pressure mounted for the federal government to take action. But the federal government was in no hurry to respond. The business trusts, including Standard Oil, donated heavily to political campaigns and frequently bribed legislators.

In 1890, finally responding to the public outcry against big business and monopolies, Congress passed the Sherman Antitrust Act, which made unfair restraint of trade, or unreasonably limiting one's competition, illegal and outlawed monopolies. On March 2, 1892, the Ohio Supreme Court convicted Standard Oil of violating the Sherman Act. The court decision led to the breaking up of the Standard Oil Trust back into its independent companies. Standard responded by taking advantage of favorable state laws in New Jersey, and the New Jersey refinery became the trust's parent holding company, a company whose primary function was to own the stocks of other corporations. Rockefeller remained president, and the management of the trust was still supervised by the directors who sat on the boards of the companies controlled by the parent company. The supposedly separate companies were therefore able to continue acting as a single unit.

The end of the oil career

In 1894 journalist **Ida M. Tarbell** (1857–1944; see entry) began writing a nineteen-article investigative series on Standard Oil that ran from 1902 to 1904 in *McClure's* magazine. Tarbell exposed many of the dishonest business practices Rockefeller used to get rid of his competitors in the oil industry. Tarbell also criticized Rockefeller's personal life, even publishing information about his bigamist father that had, until then, been kept secret. The reporting in the series was judged by historians to be fair and accurate despite the fact that Tarbell had a personal grudge against Rockefeller, as one of the rivals he had put out of business was her father. The series was extremely popular and was published in book form in 1904 as *The History of the Standard Oil Company.* Tarbell's writings focused public resentment on the Standard Oil Trust at a time when the corporation could not afford the attention, since the public was hostile to its monopolizing and the federal government was just beginning to investigate it for violations of the Sherman Antitrust Act. Rockefeller, always private and withdrawn, never publicly responded to Tarbell's articles, which hurt his company's reputation deeply. Within one year of the book's release, the federal courts brought charges against Standard Oil for being a monopoly and restraining trade. Many believed that Tarbell's book, and the public's reaction to it, played a part in the government's decision to break up the powerful trust.

In 1891 Rockefeller suffered from a mysterious illness that caused him to, among other things, lose his eyebrows and all his hair. His poor health was often attributed to the negative press that surrounded the retired industrialist. Despite the press, Rockefeller was always proud of all he had accomplished. He continued to believe that monopolies were the most efficient form of business and that their existence was necessary to raise the American standard of living.

Rockefeller stepped down as the president of Standard Oil in 1896 and retired from the business entirely a year later. Because his name was so closely associated with the company's power and success, the executives of Standard asked that he keep the title of president even though he would no longer play an active role in the company. The public was unaware of his retirement and continued to hold him accountable for the company's questionable business methods for many more years.

In 1911 the Supreme Court ruled that the Standard Oil Trust was in violation of the Sherman Antitrust Act. The Court ordered the trust to be dissolved, separating the parent holding company, Jersey Standard, from its thirty-three major subsidiaries. Many of the individual companies continued to operate under the name Standard Oil. These included the Standard Oil Company of Indiana (later American), the Standard Oil Company (Ohio), Standard Oil Company of California (later Chevron), Standard Oil of New Jersey (later Exxon), and Standard Oil of New York (later Mobil).

John D. Rockefeller at his desk. *(© Hulton Archive/Getty Images.)*

Rockefeller, the philanthropist

Rockefeller had always donated his money to those in need and causes that helped American society. His generosity was so well-known that he was chased daily by people who wanted help for themselves or for a charitable organization. Rockefeller spent hours of his spare time listening to people's requests for donations. In one case in 1882, two women from New England asked his church's congregation to help them fund improvements on a school they operated for freed female slaves. Rockefeller was eager to help, for he gladly supported institutions that gave people a chance to improve themselves. Though he only gave the women $250 that day, in the end he donated most of the money that created the campus for Spelman College, a historically African American liberal arts college for women located in Atlanta, Georgia. The school was given his wife's maiden name.

In his early philanthropic endeavors, Rockefeller depended on the Baptist Church to provide guidance for his gift-giving. The church wanted its own university, and in 1892, backed by Rockefeller's donation of $600,000, the University of Chicago opened. The university would eventually receive a total of about $80 million from Rockefeller and his son. While investigating the prospects of the university before making his donation, Rockefeller met Frederick T. Gates (1853–1929), a talented young Baptist leader and businessman. In 1891 Rockefeller, overburdened by philanthropic demands, asked Gates to open an office in New York to assist him in planning his donations. Rockefeller did not want to give his money away impulsively; he wanted a rational plan like the one he had followed in building Standard Oil. For most of the rest of his life, with substantial help from Gates, Rockefeller applied his business talents to organized giving.

While Standard Oil faced the federal courts and received steady criticism from the press, Rockefeller focused his attention almost entirely on his philanthropy. Sometime in the 1890s he decided to create an institution to carry out medical research and find cures for disease. What made his idea so radical was that he wanted his institution to pay its scientists and doctors to work full-time to conduct their research, a concept never before tried. Gates put together the plans for the Rockefeller Institute for Medical Research (later known as Rockefeller University), which opened its doors in 1901 and quickly became a world-famous center for research and graduate education in the bio-medical sciences. In 1902 he established the General Education Board, an institution funded with $129 million to promote U.S. education that did not discriminate on account of sex, race, or religious beliefs. The board helped to establish high schools in the South in a cooperative effort with local communities. In 1909 he established the Rockefeller Sanitary Commission for Eradication of Hookworm Disease to cure and prevent the disease in which parasites infest the body.

The Rockefeller Foundation was formed in 1913 in New York "to promote the wellbeing of mankind throughout the world," according to the foundation's Web site. In its first year Rockefeller contributed $35 million, and the next year $65 million. Its professional staff was charged with the duty of spending the foundation's money on projects that, according to an early memorandum to the trustees (quoted on the Rockefeller Foundation Web site), went "to the root of individual or social ill-being and misery." The foundation's first act was to grant $100,000 to the American Red Cross to build its headquarters in Washington, D.C., and to create a memorial to medical personnel during the Civil War. By the early twenty-first century, the foundation had given more than $2 billion to institutions and causes all over the world. As writers for *American Experience, PBS* noted on the organization's Web site, the Rockefeller Foundation represented "permanent corporate philanthropy on a scale never before seen—a charitable trust to parallel the oil trust that had made it possible."

Rockefeller's donations went far beyond these most famous examples of his philanthropic works. He was never personally involved in the organizations he created, leaving their operations and policies up to the experts appointed to run them. He was quite modest about his generosity and often told interviewers that he believed he had contributed more to the American people by building an efficient oil industry than by his philanthropy. Historians estimated that the total of Rockefeller's lifetime donations was somewhere more than $500 million, and many of his institutions were still in existence in the early twenty-first century.

Rockefeller lived to be ninety-eight years old. He died on May 23, 1937, in Ormond, Florida.

For More Information

Books

Chernow, Ron. *Titan: The Life of John D. Rockefeller, Sr.* New York: Vintage Books, 1998.

Coffey, Ellen Greenman. *John D. Rockefeller: Richest Man Ever.* San Diego, CA: Blackbirch Press, 2001.

Nevins, Allan. *John D. Rockefeller: The Heroic Age of American Enterprise.* New York: Charles Scribner's Sons, 1940.

Rockefeller, John D. *Random Reminiscences of Men and Events.* New York: Doubleday, Page & Company, 1909.

Web Sites

Chernow, Ron. "The Philanthropist as Quarry: John D. Rockefeller's Acts of 'Retail' Generosity." *The Philanthropy Round Table.* http://www.philanthropyroundtable.org/magazines/1998/november/chernow.html (accessed on July 7, 2005).

Rockefeller Foundation. http://www.rockfound.org/Documents/180/intro.html (accessed on July 7, 2005).

"The Rockefellers." *American Experience, PBS.* http://www.pbs.org/wgbh/amex/rockefellers/peopleevents/index.html (accessed on July 7, 2005).

Samuel Slater

Born June 9, 1768 (Derbyshire, England)
Died April 21, 1835 (Webster, Rhode Island)

Industrialist

S amuel Slater was often called the founder of the American Industrial Revolution. In 1789 he arrived in the United States from his native England with the construction details of the power looms committed to memory. It was a time when the new American nation was eager to learn the secrets of England's thriving textile industry, but the sale of such information to the former colonies was prohibited by English law. Slater settled in Rhode Island, where he built machines that made cotton yarn and were the first such looms in the country. He went on to launch his own immensely successful textile company, and it made him one of the first industrial leaders in the United States. The Slater mills built along New England riverbanks helped bring an end to England's dominance in the textile industry, but they also forever changed the American economy. During Slater's lifetime America would emerge as a manufacturing powerhouse, and its textile mills were the first large-scale factories to fuel the new economy.

"I understand you have taught us how to spin."

U.S. president Andrew Jackson.

The new textile industry

Born in June 1768, Slater was the son of William Slater, an educated, moderately prosperous farmer in Belper, Derbyshire,

Samuel Slater. *(Courtesy of The Library of Congress.)*

England. As a youngster Samuel attended a local school, where he did well in math. William died when Samuel was fourteen, but he had already arranged with a neighbor the contract for his son's apprenticeship. Working as an apprentice (someone who is bound to work for someone else for a specific term in order to learn a trade) was the traditional first step in the path to a career in one of the skilled trades in the eighteenth century. Jedediah Strutt (1729–1797) was a successful hosiery manufacturer who had been the co-inventor of a special attachment to the hand-operated machinery that made stockings. Strutt's device gave the stockings a ribbed pattern that became quite popular in England, and the location of his Derbyshire factory made this kind of hosiery known as "Derby rib" for many years.

In the 1780s, when Slater began his apprenticeship, England had become the leader in international textile manufacturing. The country had numerous distant colonies that provided a source of raw materials and a vast shipping industry to provide the transportation necessary for busy trade. It was a series of mechanical innovations that had made textiles much easier and cheaper to produce, however, and all were the product of English inventors earlier in the eighteenth century. Before then cloth manufacturing had been done by hand, at home or in home-based workshops, and the process was long and required large amounts of labor in return for small profits. The source of fiber was sheep's wool, or plants like flax or cotton. The fibers had to be gathered from the sheep or from the cotton fields and then washed and picked clean of debris. Carding was the next step, which involved the separation of the fibers, and those were then combed, or flattened with a special toothed device. From there the fibers went onto a spinning wheel and were spun into yarn with the help of a hand crank or foot pedal. There were different thicknesses of yarn, with thread as the thinnest type. The yarn then went onto a loom and was woven by hand into cloth. The process took so long that only the rich could afford finely woven cloth; everyone else wore what was called "homespun," which had a rough texture similar to that of burlap.

The dawn of the English textile industry began with John Kay (1704–1780), who created a flying shuttle in 1733 that speeded up the process of loom-weaving. A shuttle is a device that carries threads across the loom, a frame or machine used for weaving thread or yarns into cloth. The flying shuttle allowed a weaver to simply pull a cord and the shuttle shot across the loom by itself. In 1770 James Hargreaves (1720–78) invented a spinning jenny (named after his daughter), which was a spinning wheel with multiple spools. The jenny meant that a worker could produce several skeins of yarn (lengths of yarn wound around a reel) much more quickly. A year earlier an ambitious barber named Richard Arkwright (1732–1792) devised a spinning frame that drew, twisted, and wound the yarn at an astonishing speed. After trying to make an early mechanical version

Slater based his water-powered mill on the designs of Richard Arkwright (above).

that was powered by a team of horses, Arkwright improved on his own design by creating what was known as the Water Frame, which used a waterwheel to control the movement of the frame. Awkwright used the Water Frame at his mill in Cromford, in Derbyshire, England, which was one of the first factories in the world. Although there had been other enterprises where workers arrived daily for a shift, Arkwright's enterprise was the first to be built specifically to house machinery.

When Slater began his apprenticeship in 1783, Strutt had gone into business with Arkwright to build cotton manufacturing machinery to meet the growing demand across England for yarn. Slater trained there for six years, becoming supervisor of machinery construction as well as a staff manager and skilled repairperson. He was eager to start his own company, but by that time entering the business required a great deal of money to buy the machines and raw materials. However, Slater knew that state legislatures in the newly independent American states were quietly advertising in England for skilled textile machinery operators, and the machines, too, if they could be had. American consumers paid very high prices for English-made cloth after the conclusion of the American Revolution (1775–83), when the American colonists fought England to win their independence.

Unfortunately for Slater, England had laws preventing the export of textile manufacturing machinery, and the wealthy and influential textile mill owners had also persuaded the English government to ban the immigration of skilled textile workers to America. Even sketches for the machinery could not be taken across the ocean. In an effort to reduce their dependence on English cloth, state legislatures in the United States were offering cash bonuses to skilled workers, and Slater decided to try his luck.

He began memorizing the layout of the machines, and when he sailed for Philadelphia, Pennsylvania, in September 1789, he told English officials at the dock that he was a farm laborer. He did not even tell his family of his plans, instead writing them afterward of his whereabouts. He needed his apprenticeship certificate to get the bonus, and he hid it from authorities in his simple outfit that a humble farmhand might wear.

Moses Brown

When he arrived in America, Slater went to New York City and took a job with a textile manufacturing firm there. He was dismayed by the outdated equipment and knew that a textile company would need to have access to a livelier water source to power the Arkwright-style frame he hoped to build. He moved on to Providence, Rhode Island, which had a vast harbor connecting it to the Atlantic Ocean, and a river, the Seekonk. There he met a prominent local businessman, Moses Brown (1738–1836), whose family established Brown University. Brown hoped to enter the textile business with his new firm Almy & Brown. In nearby Pawtucket, Rhode Island, on the Blackstone River, Brown had rented an old fulling mill, where wool was washed before it was spun into yarn. Brown installed as many of the old wooden spinning frames as he could fit inside, but they were inefficient. Slater was disappointed when he saw the old hand-cranked equipment and told Brown that he could build a version of Arkwright's water-powered machinery instead. Brown agreed, and a deal was struck in which Slater would get to keep the mill's profits once it went into operation.

It took Slater nearly a year to build the Arkwright-style frame and connect it to the water source. He lured skilled mechanics away from the nearby shipbuilding yards to help him, and finally in December 1790 his first machine—the first of its kind in the United States—went into operation. Impressed, Brown and William Almy, his son-in-law, took Slater into partnership with them, and they decided to build an entirely new mill from the ground up. This was also in Pawtucket, and became known as Slater Mill. The mill has often been called the birthplace of the American Industrial Revolution.

In 1791 Slater married Hannah Wilkinson, the daughter of a successful Rhode Island nail manufacturer. Hannah had an idea for making sewing thread out of fine cotton yarn and sketched out the process. At the time linen, which was expensive, was the standard for sewing thread. She applied for a patent (a legal document granting an inventor the exclusive right to produce or sell an invention for a certain number of years) from the newly created U.S. Patent Office, established in 1790, and was the first American woman ever to receive one. Hannah's new husband, her father, and her brothers were interested in setting up a business venture with the idea, and they went into partnership together in 1798.

The new firm was called Samuel Slater & Company. Its first mill was near Pawtucket, but the company soon found it needed more workers than were available in the town in order to expand. There was a ready source of labor on New England's farms, where sons and daughters were eager to escape the difficult work, and so Slater sent his brother, John, who had joined him in America, to find a new mill location. John found one in Smithfield, Rhode Island, again on the Blackstone River. There was already a saw and grist mill there used by nearby loggers and farmers. The saw mill cut timber for the building industry, and the grist mill ground corn and other agricultural products prior to sale. The geography of New England was particularly favorable to the establishment of the textile industry, with its many rivers flowing through hilly lands and waterfalls. This meant that most of the rivers flowed downward from their source and offered a ready supply of power for the mills' heavy waterwheels.

Birth of New England's first industry

The site that Slater's brother found was ideal for the new mill, and when it began operations in 1803, it was the largest and most technologically advanced industrial facility in its time. Other company mills would be established in East Webster, Massachusetts, Jewett City, Connecticut, and Amoskeag Falls, New Hampshire. The Amoskeag Falls facility was built on the banks of the Merrimac River, and out of it grew the manufacturing center of the city of Manchester.

Slater's company was a great success, with its mills producing cotton and yarn that were cheaper but just as strong as the English imports. This reduced the demand for English-made textiles and launched the manufacturing era

The Slater Mill. *(© Bettmann/Corbis.)*

in the northeastern United States. Slater products dominated the cotton yarn market in Rhode Island, Massachusetts, and New Hampshire. His main competitor was **Francis Cabot Lowell** (1775–1817; see entry), a Massachusetts businessman from a prominent old Boston family. Lowell toured England's textile mills in 1811 and, like Slater, memorized what he saw and reconstructed the machinery back home. Lowell set up his first textile mills in the Boston area in the early 1820s and founded the mill town of Lowell, Massachusetts.

Slater met the heavy demand for labor by hiring child workers. This was a standard practice in many U.S. businesses in those years, and families were eager to have the extra income at a time when there were either no laws requiring children to attend school or ones that were rarely enforced. Children were considered especially well-suited for textile mill work because they had smaller hands and could move about the loom more quickly. The machinery was dangerous, however. Gears and other parts were exposed without any safety devices, and fingers, hands, and even lives were lost to them. Slater tried to treat his young employees better than most New England factory owners, and at his mills they worked shorter hours than was standard in the industry and were provided with decent meals. To lure entire families as a source of labor, Slater provided a ready-made community. He built apartment blocks, schools, churches, and even a company store. Farms in outlying areas, also owned by the company, provided the food. Wages were often paid in the form of credit slips that could be redeemed at the company store, which helped keep Slater's company operating at a profit. His strategy was widely copied in other industries during the Industrial Revolution.

During his lifetime Slater became quite famous in New England and throughout the rest of the nation. In 1833 U.S. president Andrew Jackson (1767–1845; served 1829–37) visited Slater's impressive home in Pawtucket and called him the "Father of American Manufactures." Slater's wife died in 1812, and five years later he married Esther Parkinson, a Philadelphia widow. He had nine children by his first marriage, and several of his sons entered the family business. The Old Slater Mill in Pawtucket, his first project, became a national historic site. When he died in April 1835, Slater owned thirteen New England mills and was reportedly worth one million dollars.

For More Information

Books

Tucker, Barbara M. *Samuel Slater and the Origins of the American Textile Industry, 1790–1860*. Ithaca, NY: Cornell University Press, 1984.

Periodicals

Fisk, Karen. "Arkwright: Cotton King or Spin Doctor?" *History Today* (March 1998): p. 25.

Web Sites

Samuel Slater: Father of the American Industrial Revolution. http://www.woonsocket.org/slater.htm (accessed on July 7, 2005).

Slater Mill: A Living History Museum. http://www.slatermill.org/ (accessed on July 7, 2005).

Ellen Gates Starr

Born March 19, 1859 (Laona, Illinois)
Died February 10, 1940 (Suffern, New York)

Labor activist
Teacher

Ellen Gates Starr did not achieve the same kind of fame enjoyed by her close colleague, **Jane Addams** (1860–1935; see entry), but Starr did play an important role in the founding of Hull House in Chicago, Illinois, in 1889. Starr and Addams established the pioneering settlement house in one of the city's poorest neighborhoods, where thousands lived in unhealthy, overcrowded conditions. Hull House was founded on the principle that to help the poor one must live among them, and the two single, well-educated women from wealthy families astonished many in the city by doing just that. Starr stayed with Hull House for much of her life and took an active role in Chicago's early labor union movement.

> "After we have been there long enough and people see that we don't catch diseases . . . there are at least a half dozen girls in the city who will be glad to come and stay a while."

Family influence

Starr was born in March 1859, in Laona, Illinois. She came from an old New England family, and legend held that her great-grandfather, who fought in the American Revolutionary War (1775–83; the American colonists' fight for independence from England), walked home barefoot from the battle site at

Valley Forge, Pennsylvania, to his hometown of Ipswich, Massachusetts. Starr's father, Caleb, was a former sea captain, a politically involved farmer, and an occasional writer and book lover who read to his three children nightly. He settled in Illinois when he married Starr's mother, Susan Gates Childs, in 1848.

Caleb Starr was active in the Grange movement, a nationwide organization of farmers formed to protest the high rates railroads charged to ship produce and grain. He was also a supporter of women's rights and the suffrage movement to win a constitutional amendment that would allow women to vote in national elections. He was committed to working for social justice and taking an active role in helping those less fortunate, and these beliefs had a strong influence on his daughter.

Caleb's sister, Eliza Allen Starr, would also serve as an important role model for the young Ellen. Eliza was an art historian and writer and was active in Roman Catholic circles, although the family was Presbyterian. From her Starr inherited a passion for the arts, particularly European painting and sculpture, and she would later convert to Roman Catholicism also. She began to study Renaissance Italian art in 1877 after she entered the Rockford Female Seminary, an Illinois school that served as a kind of junior college for women from well-to-do families. It was there that she first met Jane Addams, who was from another Illinois town, Cedarville.

Starr and Addams

While at Rockford Starr wrote articles for the school magazine on poetry and the art treasures of Florence, Italy. Caleb had struggled financially over the years, however, and could only afford to send her to Rockford for one year. After that he was forced to sell his farm and move the family to Durand, a town near the Wisconsin border. There he opened a pharmacy, but it failed.

After leaving Rockford Starr went to work as a teacher. Her first job was at a school in Mount Morris, Illinois. She and Addams wrote each other regularly, and she would occasionally visit Addams at her family's Cedarville home. In 1879, when Starr was twenty years old, she moved to Chicago to take a teaching job there. The Kirkland School for Girls was a private school on Chicago's North Side that served the wealthy families of the neighborhood. Starr taught English and art appreciation, and the contacts she made there would play an important role in the fundraising efforts for Hull House some years later.

Starr took some time off from teaching to tour Europe with Addams in 1887. They went with a third friend, Sarah Anderson, and occasionally split off while each pursued her own interests. During the winter they spent in Rome, Starr studied the Renaissance art she loved, and in the spring the three went on to Spain. She then went on to Paris to take a job as chaperone for two American girls while Addams and Anderson went to London to visit Toynbee Hall. This was the first so-called settlement house, located in the city's poverty-stricken East End. Founded by a minister and staffed by Oxford University students, Toynbee Hall offered a variety of social services designed to help the poor. Addams wanted to establish a settlement house like this in Chicago, and when she and Starr returned to the United States, they began eagerly making plans. In January 1889 they moved into a boardinghouse for women on Washington Place in downtown Chicago. They spent their days calling on civic leaders, ministers, and wealthy citizens who were known to support charities, telling them about their plans for what would become Hull House.

A rough neighborhood

The American economy had undergone rapid changes in the years since Starr and Addams were born. Vast amounts of people had moved from rural areas to urban ones as new manufacturing and commercial enterprises sprang up and farming became increasingly unprofitable. The new factories required a large labor force, and young men and women from rural villages flocked to Chicago, which had become the second-largest U.S. city and a major railway transportation hub. Still others came by ship from various European lands to escape religious persecution or political unrest. The factory jobs offered steady wages, but the newcomers quickly discovered that housing and food costs in the city were very high.

Housing was a particular problem during this era. Chicago had rebuilt quickly since a massive fire in 1871 had destroyed large sections of the city, but the available shelter could not keep up with the growing population. Cheap housing was built in the areas surrounding the factories, manufacturing enterprises, and even the meatpacking houses where cattle and pigs were slaughtered. The smell from the nearby stockyards was said to be unbearable.

Addams found a shabby mansion on Halsted and Polk streets, in the center of one of Chicago's worst slums, or severely overcrowded urban areas characterized by the most extreme conditions of poverty, run-down housing, and crime. She spent nearly $5,000 of her own money on repairs, and she and Starr moved into Hull House in September 1889. They were alone there except for a housekeeper they had hired. At first their neighbors considered the two women to be somewhat odd; few could understand why anyone would choose to live in that neighborhood if they had better options.

Starr and Addams spent their first months visiting their neighbors, and for this the custom of the day required them to take one of the young men or ministers who worked with Hull House along as a chaperone. They introduced themselves and invited the neighbors and their children to visit Hull House. The mansion was soon hosting a number of clubs and classes. Starr gave lectures in literature, art, history, and English as a second language. Women she had taught at the Kirkland School came to help, and their husbands or parents donated funds to the struggling enterprise.

A shift in priorities

Art remained Starr's passion during her Hull House years. She convinced Edward Butler, a wealthy Chicago patron of the arts, to give them $5,000 to establish an art gallery in 1891. This became the first building associated with Hull House that was not on the immediate property. Starr knew from her travels in Europe and her interest in art that many of the European immigrants who came to Chicago and other American cities quickly forgot the handicrafts that had been passed down to them from generation to generation in their native countries. Woodworking, decorative embroidery, and other artisan traditions were often dismissed by art historians, but Starr knew that the skill needed for such tasks, and the appreciation for color and form they taught, gave even the poorest people a sense of satisfaction and a way to beautify their humble homes.

At Hull House Starr was determined to help keep such traditions alive. She wrote about the subject in a chapter titled "Art and Labor," which appeared in her 1895 book *Hull-House Maps and Papers: A Presentation of Nationalities and Wages in a Congested District of Chicago, Together with Comments and Essays on Problems Growing Out of the Social Conditions*. She discussed what she called "the fatal mistake of our modern civilization," asserting that "we have believed that we could force men to live without beauty in their own lives, and still compel them to make for us the beautiful things in which we have denied them any part."

Over time Starr's interests shifted from art to the labor movement, and this helped change the direction of Hull House, too, as its women associates became more active in the organized labor movement along with her. In the early twentieth century there were almost no laws protecting workers, and child labor was commonplace. Injuries and even deaths from poorly maintained equipment or unsafe working conditions occurred frequently. The neighborhood surrounding Hull House was home to a number of sweatshops, or factories in which workers work long hours in poor conditions for very low wages. The women of Hull House called attention to such conditions, and public awareness eventually forced state lawmakers to enact laws that regulated working conditions for women and children in the state.

The labor movement

As the labor movement became stronger in Chicago, Starr raised money to help striking workers and their families and even joined the picket lines herself. (A strike is a work stoppage by employees to protest conditions or make demands of their employer.) Most low-wage workers suffered various abuses on the job, but women workers were particularly vulnerable to harassment by male supervisors in the garment factories. Organizing them into labor unions, or organizations of workers formed to protect and further their mutual interests by bargaining as a group with their employers over wages, working conditions, and benefits, and urging them to stand up for their rights was especially difficult, because many lived on their own in boardinghouses and faced immediate homelessness if they could not pay their rent. They could also be easily replaced by other workers, or even by children, who were willing enough to accept a wage of seven or eight cents an hour.

Starr did not just speak in support of the unions, she joined them. She was a founding member of the Chicago chapter of the Women's Trade Union League, a labor group organized in 1903 that played a significant role in the formation of both the International Ladies' Garment Workers' Union and the Amalgamated Clothing Workers of America, two early and important unions in American labor history. When the Chicago local chapter of the Amalgamated Clothing Workers went on strike in late 1915, Starr wrote about it in an article that appeared in the *New Review* the following year.

In Chicago and elsewhere, picket lines often erupted into violent clashes between strikers and the police, and Starr was even arrested once during a 1914 restaurant workers' strike. She faced charges of disorderly conduct, and her defense attorney was a young labor lawyer named Harold Ickes (1874–1952), who would go on to serve in the cabinet of U.S. president Franklin D. Roosevelt (1882–1945; served 1933–45). The courtroom was filled with laughter when the arresting officer testified that the tiny, almost frail Starr attacked him. She was released, but her increasing labor activism made some of the more conservative donors to Hull House uneasy.

Over time Starr and the women of Hull House—Addams, **Florence Kelley** (1859–1932; see entry), and the others who came there to live, teach, and work to improve conditions for Chicago's poor—grew apart. The friendship between her and Addams, in particular, cooled as Starr grew increasingly religious in her later years. She had converted to the Episcopalian faith in 1883, but around 1910 she became dismayed at the wealth of the congregations in Chicago's churches of that denomination. She started to attend services at the Roman Catholic parishes near the Hull House neighborhood, which served a largely working-class and immigrant population, and eventually converted to the faith herself.

Beloved Mr. Dodge

Starr was also a bit eccentric and had a temper that flared occasionally. For a time she wore only purple, and for many years she wore a raincoat she had named Mr. Dodge. It had been left to her by an elderly man, a retired machinist, who came to Hull House to find chess partners. Starr found him a few worthy opponents, and when he died he willed his estate, worth some $3,000, to her. After 1916 she was less active at Hull House but remained committed to other causes. She was a member of the Socialist Party of Chicago. (Socialism is an economic system in which the means of production and distribution is owned collectively by all the workers and there is no private property or social classes.) She also gave lectures in which she urged others to work at solving the social problems caused by rapid industrialization.

In 1929 Starr underwent surgery for a spinal abscess (a collection of pus surrounded by hot, painful tissue) and was left partially paralyzed from it. She spent her last years at the Convent of the Holy Child in Suffern, New York, cared for by Benedictine nuns. She herself was an oblate, or person who entered Roman Catholic monastic life without taking full religious vows. She died there in 1940. In her early years at Hull House, she had founded a program with the local elementary school to expose schoolchildren to the art she loved so much. Her idea was for a lending library of prints and sculpture that rotated through the Chicago schools, and it eventually became the Public School Art Society. It was still in operation in Chicago more than a century later as Art Resources in Teaching (ART).

For More Information

Books

Diliberto, Gioia. *A Useful Woman: The Early Life of Jane Addams.* New York: Scribner/A Lisa Drew Book, 1999.

Linn, James Weber. *Jane Addams: A Biography.* Chicago: University of Illinois Press, 2000.

Starr, Ellen Gates. "Art and Labor." In *Hull-House Maps and Papers: A Presentation of Nationalities and Wages in a Congested District of Chicago, Together with Comments and Essays on Problems Growing Out of the Social Conditions.* New York: Thomas Y. Crowell, 1895.

Periodicals

Starr, Ellen Gates. "The Chicago Clothing Strike." *New Review* (March 1916): pp. 62–64.

Web Sites

"Urban Experience in Chicago: Hull-House and Its Neighborhoods, 1889–1963." *University of Illinois at Chicago.* http://www.uic.edu/jaddams/hull/urbanexp/contents.htm (accessed on July 7, 2005).

Ida M. Tarbell

Born November 5, 1857 (Hatch Hollow, Pennsylvania)
Died January 6, 1944 (Bridgeport, Connecticut)

Journalist

As a child Ida M. Tarbell watched her father, an independent oilman, struggle unsuccessfully to compete in a field dominated by **John D. Rockefeller** (1839–1937; see entry) and his massive Standard Oil Company. Rockefeller's attempts to gain complete control over the oil industry led to the destruction of many small oil refineries, such as the one owned by Tarbell's father, and she grew to despise the wealthy industrialist. Decades later Tarbell became a successful investigative journalist whose publications helped bring about the fall of the powerful oil company, forever linking her name with that of the man she held responsible for much of her family's early troubles.

"I've tried to lean neither to one side nor the other in my Standard Oil articles, but merely to tell the truth, corroborated by court documents and pamphlets issued at various times. . . ."

An early introduction to the oil business

Tarbell was born on November 5, 1857, in a log cabin in the tiny village of Hatch Hollow in Erie County, Pennsylvania. Her parents, Franklin Sumner Tarbell and Elizabeth McCullough Tarbell, had both been trained as teachers, but around the year of her birth Franklin bought a farm in Iowa. Tarbell and her

Ida Tarbell. *(UPI/Corbis-Bettmann. Reproduced by permission.)*

mother were about to follow him to Iowa when a financial panic (a time when people feared the economy was shaky and withdrew their money from banks, leading to bank failures, the closing of companies, and widespread unemployment) shut down their local bank, depriving them of the money they needed to travel. The farm in Iowa failed and Franklin came back home to Pennsylvania in 1859.

Franklin returned to Pennsylvania the same year that the nation's first oil well—the Drake well—was drilled in Titusville, Pennsylvania, only thirty miles from Hatch Hollow. During the first half of the nineteenth century, crude oil (liquid petroleum in its natural state), which could be used to make a flammable oil called kerosene for lighting lamps, was considered an impractical fuel source. The oil could only be obtained by a difficult process of skimming it off the tops of ponds or other bodies of still water. As more wells were drilled in 1859, crude oil suddenly became available in large quantities. Adventurous and enterprising young men from all over the country rushed to Pennsylvania when it became clear there was money to be made in the oil business. Tarbell's father was one of these men. He moved the family into a rough shack near the new wells in Rouseville, Pennsylvania, and went into business building wooden oil storage tanks. Later, as these early wells began to dry up, the Tarbells moved to Titusville, building a house there in 1870. Tarbell remembered her childhood as a happy one. The Tarbells lived modestly and were very religious people, regularly attending Sunday school and prayer meetings. Both parents were educated and their large collection of books and magazines kept the young Tarbell busy when she was not out playing among the oil rigs.

Franklin's wood tank business prospered for several years, but by 1871 wooden tanks were being replaced by iron ones for oil storage, and the business failed. Franklin then decided to become an independent oil producer and refiner (someone who runs a factory in which oil in its natural state is broken down into commercial products such as oil lamp fuel). In 1872 news reached Titusville that the Standard Oil Company and several other large oil refineries had entered into a secret pact with the railroads that served the oil fields. The pact was known as the South Improvement Company, and its purpose was to keep shipping rates low for its members and high for nonmembers like Franklin. The higher shipping rates would effectively close down many of the smaller independent producers since they would not be able to compete with the South Improvement members.

Soon after the citizens of Titusville heard about the secret agreement, the railroads posted their new rates, which were double what they had been the week before. Tarbell, who was fifteen at the time, witnessed the reactions of the angry independent oilmen when they learned about the rates. Some advocated the hanging of South Improvement Company members and the burning of their oil tanks. The oilmen of

Titusville refused to sell their oil to the member refiners, which probably hurt them more than it did the refiners. Eventually, in response to the public uproar, the South Improvement Company was shut down by the state, but Standard Oil continued to try to dominate the industry. Over the years Tarbell's father and brother—along with most independent oil producers in the Titusville area—were ruined by Standard Oil's schemes to gain control of the entire industry.

The education of a biographer and journalist

Ida Tarbell went to the Titusville high school, excelling in science and graduating with honors in 1875. She went on to major in biology at Allegheny College, where she was the only female student in her class. She reportedly rose at four o'clock every morning to study and was not satisfied with her work until it was nearly perfect. Tarbell graduated in 1880 and took a teaching job at a school in Ohio, but she was not happy with the career and resigned after two years. Returning to her home in Pennsylvania, she found work as a staff member of *Chautauquan* magazine, a periodical devoted to the spirited Methodist adult educational movement of the times. Tarbell worked long hours every day and was soon promoted to the position of managing editor.

Tarbell had grown up to become a tall and attractive woman with strong opinions. She had ambitions for a career, which was fairly unusual at a time when most women worked in the home. She decided early that she would never marry and that she would always support herself so she could live her life as she saw fit. In 1891 she took a daring step and moved to Paris, France, to live with some friends. She studied history at the Sorbonne (a prestigious college in Paris) and began work on a biography of Madame Roland (1754–1793), a French writer and political figure. Tarbell wrote articles for American periodicals to support herself, using the slow overseas mail to send them in for publication. Her writing gained an audience in the United States and caught the attention of Samuel S. McClure (1857–1949), who had founded the popular monthly magazine *McClure's* in 1893. He visited Tarbell in Paris and invited her to work for his magazine. In the beginning she would only agree to write articles for the magazine from France, but in

1894 she returned to the United States and soon accepted a position as an editor at *McClure's*.

Tarbell's first big job at the magazine was to write an eight-part biographical series on the French emperor Napoleon Bonaparte (1769–1821; ruled 1804–15). Readers loved the series, and it raised *McClure's* circulation from 24,500 readers to 100,000. Over the next four years she wrote a very popular biographical series on the life of President Abraham Lincoln (1809–1865; served 1861–65). To research the book, she conducted interviews in Washington, D.C., and Illinois and established a wide network of correspondents who provided her with information. Her study of Lincoln's early years was published in 1896, with a complete two-volume biography following in 1900. The Lincoln series caused *McClure's* circulation to rise again to 300,000 readers.

Exposing Standard Oil

At the turn of the century, the writers at *McClure's* turned from literature and biography and began to write investigative pieces on contemporary social issues, often revealing corruption or injustices in the practices of big business and the government. McClure, who was at the forefront of the new journalistic movement, began to restructure the format of his magazine to include more of this coverage. This was the beginning of the muckraking movement, and Tarbell eagerly joined in. She had long wanted to write about the experiences of the independent oil producers in Pennsylvania when they faced the seemingly unstoppable force of the Standard Oil Company. She proposed a multi-article series on the history of the company to McClure and he readily agreed.

In 1901 Tarbell began a two-year investigation into the giant oil monopoly, or a company that has the exclusive possession or right to produce a particular good or service. Rockefeller had always attempted to keep a low profile, and most of his complex business dealings and transactions had been conducted in secret. Fortunately for Tarbell, however, Standard Oil had recently come under federal investigation for violating the Sherman Antitrust Act by forming a monopoly and unreasonably restraining competition in the

The Muckrakers

Around the turn of the twentieth century, a new movement in journalism called muckraking emerged in the popular new weekly magazines such as *McClure's, Collier's, Everybody's,* and *Cosmopolitan.* In this form of investigative reporting, journalists intentionally set out to expose dishonesty and unfair or illegal practices in government and business. The goal of the muckrakers was to bring injustices and abuses to the attention of the public in order to bring about reforms and social changes. They attempted to use scientific methods in their research and reporting in order to remain objective or neutral about the social problems that existed in the modern industrial society.

McClure's was the first to feature muckraking articles. One of the magazine's most famous muckrakers was editor Lincoln Steffens (1866–1936), whose collected articles were published as the book *Shame of the Cities* in 1904. Steffens concentrated on the corruption in the city governments of St. Louis, Missouri; Minneapolis, Minnesota; Pittsburgh, Pennsylvania; and Chicago, Illinois. Writer and social reformer Upton Sinclair (1878–1968) used fiction to expose the ugly practices of business and government in his novels. His first work, *The Jungle* (1906), focused on the dangerous and unhealthy working conditions in the meatpacking industry. As Ida Tarbell would do a decade later, Henry Demarest Lloyd (1847–1903) chose the Standard Oil Company as the subject of many of his articles and books, including his *Wealth Against Commonwealth.* The 1894 book directly attacked the corporate monopolies, or the companies that had an exclusive right to produce a particular good or service. Journalist Jacob Riis (1849–1914) wrote articles about the slums of New York City, using candid photographs of needy men, women, and children to awaken middle-class New Yorkers to the suffering of the poor in their city.

industry. Because of the court's investigations, Tarbell was able to obtain volumes of public records to examine. Using her extraordinary gifts for absorbing and organizing hundreds of factual details, she put together the most thorough record of the company in existence up until the early twenty-first century. Despite her personal dislike of Standard Oil (which she openly acknowledged throughout her writing), critics agreed that her work was highly accurate.

Tarbell carefully acknowledged the genius and hard work with which Rockefeller handled Standard Oil. She made it clear that Rockefeller's corporation had acquired its power

The term muckraking was first applied to this type of reporting by President Theodore Roosevelt (1858–1919; served 1901–9), who feared the new movement might destroy the reputations and effectiveness of businessmen and politicians by exposing their secret dealings. In a 1906 speech Roosevelt compared this kind of journalist to a muckraker, a person who cleaned human waste from the ground. He quoted from a passage in John Bunyan's epic *Pilgrim's Progress* (1678) that described the muckraker as "the man who could look no way but downward with the muckrake in his hand, who was offered a celestial [heavenly] crown for his muckrake, but would neither look up nor regard the crown he was offered, but continued to rake to himself the filth of the floor" (as quoted by Vince Copeland in "How Capitalists Rule"). The label was originally a negative one, implying that these journalists were seeking to discredit others for their own political ends, but it soon came to suggest more favorable qualities. The muckrakers became known to reformers and much of the reading public for their social concern and their courage in fighting against the great powers of the nation to expose injustice.

From about 1901 to 1912, muckraking journalists did an effective job of achieving their goals. Articles about monopolies, child labor, politicians who took bribes, and the terrible working and living conditions of the poor enraged the public, which became much more vocal in its concerns. This in turn pressured politicians to make changes. Muckraking articles were read by diverse peoples all across the country, and the middle class, the working class, the farmers, and the factory workers all united in a desire for change. This national drive for reform was called the Progressive movement and spanned roughly from the 1890s to about 1920. The muckrakers had proved that the media could be one of the most powerful forces in the country.

Around 1912 *McClure's* changed its focus to literature, signaling an end to the muckraking movement. Muckraking journalism, however, continued to exist into the early twenty-first century.

and wealth through his unusual business talent and drive, and his choice of associates who had the same top skills and motivations. Tarbell did not oppose large corporations that followed honest policies. Her point was, rather, that Rockefeller was already so successful that he did not need to ruthlessly destroy the independents and small business owners. In her 1939 book *All in a Day's Work*, she observed of Standard Oil: "They had never played fair, and that ruined their greatness for me."

Tarbell also investigated Rockefeller's personal life. She uncovered the story of his father, a phony doctor who had once been arrested for rape, which until then had been kept secret. She even followed Rockefeller as he attended church. She painted him as a greedy, secretive manipulator, and he quickly became the man Americans loved to hate. Tarbell's readers responded with enthusiasm, and the original plan for three articles about the company turned into a nineteen-article series that ran from 1902 to 1904. In 1904 it was published as a two-volume book called *The History of the Standard Oil Company*.

Tarbell's work focused public resentment on the Standard Oil Trust at a time when the government was carefully watching the organization. Within one year of the book's release, the federal courts brought charges against Standard Oil for being a monopoly and for limiting free market competition. In 1911 the Supreme Court ordered the Standard Oil Trust to be dissolved. Most historians credited Tarbell's book as being at least partly responsible for the breaking up of the trust and for later laws that were passed to regulate the giant corporations and monopolies. Tarbell was viewed by the public as a heroine in the business reform movement, but she was rapidly losing interest in the story and was reluctant to join in other antitrust campaigns.

Life after *McClure's*

In 1906 Tarbell and some of her colleagues had a dispute with McClure, partly because his business policies were leading to trouble for the magazine and partly because his political views were beginning to change toward opposing reform. The top editors left the company to take over and operate the *American* magazine. Tarbell immediately set to work on her next series, which was on the U.S. tariff system. Tariffs are taxes placed upon imported goods that made them more expensive than the goods produced in the country where they were destined to be sold. Therefore tariffs on imported goods were useful to manufacturers who wished to sell their goods in their own country, but harmful to those who wished to sell their products abroad. Tarbell disliked tariffs since they interfered with competition and often helped industry at the cost of consumers and farmers. Her articles on the topic were released in book form as *The Tariff in Our Times* (1911). President Woodrow Wilson (1856–1924; served 1913–21) was so impressed by this work that he offered Tarbell a position on the Federal Tariff Commission in 1916. Tarbell had lost interest in tariffs and refused the position, but she did eventually get involved in creating government policy. She participated in Wilson's Industrial Conference in 1919 and in President Warren G. Harding's (1865–1923; served 1921–23) Unemployment Conference in 1921.

Some unexpected views

Because of her crusade against trusts and monopolies, Tarbell was labeled a reformer, but her opinions were not always progressive. Tarbell took an interest in factory management around 1912 and began to visit U.S. factories to observe the labor management methods of Frederick W. Taylor (1856–1915). Taylor was a machinist who advocated the use of scientific management in industry, a system in which factory managers studied a job and reduced it to a minimum number of necessary steps. Each step was analyzed to determine the most time-saving means of performing it, and each worker was assigned to learn only one simple step to be repeated quickly and efficiently throughout the workday. A standard day's output from an excellent worker could be determined, and pay rates and rewards could be used to ensure workers were motivated to meet the standards. Automaker **Henry Ford** (1863–1947; see entry) applied Taylor's methods, known as Taylorism, in his factories to mass produce cars. Ford also created a department that dictated to workers what kind of lifestyles they should lead and hired spies to make sure his employees conformed to the policies in and out of work.

Labor unions (organizations of workers formed to protect and further their mutual interests by bargaining as a group with their employers over wages, working conditions, and benefits) fought against Taylorism, arguing it took all control over the workplace away from the workers. Tarbell, on the other hand, was highly impressed with Taylorism and Henry Ford's methods. She wrote a book about the new scientific processes of management called *New Ideals in Business, an Account of Their Practice and Their Effect Upon Men and Profits* in 1916. She also published biographies of industrialist Elbert

H. Gary (1846–1947), the chief executive of the massive United States Steel Corporation, and Owen D. Young (1874–1962) of General Electric, who advocated better labor-management relations and more government regulation of big business. These books were vastly different from her articles on Rockefeller as they tended to limit themselves to the most flattering views of these men and to endorse big business. However, Tarbell had always held that she was not opposed to big business, she had only opposed the unfair practices of Standard Oil.

In another series of articles begun at the *American,* Tarbell expressed her views about the rights and roles of women. These were published in two books, *The Business of Being a Woman* (1912) and *The Ways of Woman* (1915). At the time she wrote the articles, Tarbell was one of the most successful women in the country, having become a well-respected journalist and a participant on government committees. By 1912 the movement for women's suffrage (the right to vote) had grown very strong, and many of its leaders looked to Tarbell to participate. Tarbell surprised many by declaring she did not support women's suffrage or even the concept of women working outside of the home. Although she herself had decided never to marry and to have a public career, she believed that a woman's most useful role in society was as mother and wife. In her writing, she urged women to tend to their homes and to value their domestic role.

Tarbell left the *American* in 1915 at the age of sixty, but she continued to write for a variety of magazines and to lecture and participate in government conferences on industrial problems. She traveled to France in 1919 to report on the Paris Peace Conference after World War I (1914–18; a war in which Great Britain, France, the United States and their allies defeated Germany, Austria-Hungary, and their allies), and in 1926 she visited Italy and interviewed dictator Benito Mussolini (1883–1945; ruled 1922–43), on whom she wrote a highly favorable report.

In 1939 Tarbell published her autobiography, *All in the Day's Work*. She continued to work, teaching classes in biographical writing and serving as consulting editor of a Tucson, Arizona, magazine called *Letter* until she died of pneumonia in 1944 at the age of eighty-six.

For More Information

Books

Brady, Kathleen. *Ida Tarbell: Portrait of a Muckraker.* Pittsburgh, PA: University of Pittsburgh Press, 1989.

Chernow, Ron. *Titan: The Life of John D. Rockefeller, Sr.* New York: Vintage Books, 1998.

Tarbell, Ida M. *All in the Day's Work: An Autobiography.* New York: Macmillan, 1939.

Tarbell, Ida M. *The History of the Standard Oil Company.* New York: McClure, Phillips and Co., 1904.

Tarbell, Ida M. *More Than a Muckraker: Ida Tarbell's Lifetime in Journalism.* Edited by Robert C. Kochersberger. Knoxville: University of Tennessee Press, 1994.

Tomkins, Mary. *Ida M. Tarbell.* Boston, MA: Twayne, 1994.

Periodicals

"Ida M. Tarbell." *The Bookman,* vol. XVI (January 1903). This article can also be found online at http://etext.lib.virginia.edu/etcbin/browse-mixed-new?id=AnoTarb&tag=public&images=images/modeng&data=/texts/english/modeng/parsed (accessed on July 7, 2005).

"Ida M. Tarbell, 86, Dies in Bridgeport." *New York Times* (January 17, 1944). This article can also be found online at http://www.nytimes.com/learning/general/onthisday/bday/1105.html (accessed on July 7, 2005).

Web Sites

Copeland, Vince. "How Capitalists Rule." *Workers World Service.* http://www.etext.org/Politics/Workers.World/Series.capitalist.rule/capitalist.rule.21 (accessed on July 7, 2005).

Cornelius Vanderbilt

Born May 27, 1794 (Port Richmond, New York)
Died January 4, 1877 (New York, New York)

Shipping executive
Railroad executive
Financier

"I for one will never go to a court of law when I have the power in my own hands to see myself right."

When Cornelius Vanderbilt died in 1877, he left an estate valued at $100 million. Vanderbilt's astonishing fortune ranked him as the richest American in his lifetime, and his wealth had seemed to grow right along with the rapidly expanding new nation. Known as the "Commodore," he made his first fortune in shipping and went on to own a large section of the railroad tracks that connected the East Coast to Chicago, Illinois. Vanderbilt had a skill for recognizing coming changes and trends, and his talent for investment opportunities made him one of the American Industrial Revolution's leading figures. His estate also created one of the country's great family fortunes.

An early start in the shipping business

Born in May 1794 on Staten Island, New York, Vanderbilt came from a Dutch farming family who lived in Port Richmond, on the north shore of the island. His great-great-great-grandfather, Jan Aertson, came to New York in 1650 as an indentured servant, a common form of contract labor in the era and a way for poor men and women to try their luck in the New World. In exchange for promising their labor for a number of years, the

Cornelius Vanderbilt. *(© Bettmann/Corbis.)*

indentured servant was provided with transportation to North America and food and shelter during his work years. Aertson had been born in a village called De Bilt in the Netherlands, and the *van* ("from") added to it gave the family its surname.

Vanderbilt was the fourth of nine children in his family. His father had a boat business, and as a youngster Vanderbilt grew to love the sea and sailing. He left school at the age of eleven to work with his father, and by the time he turned sixteen he badly wanted his own boat. He struck a deal with his mother, who lent him $100 in exchange for plowing eight

Robert Livingston lost his steamboat ferry monopoly after Vanderbilt improved a competitor's business. *(Courtesy of The Library of Congress.)*

acres of rocky soil on which she wanted to plant crops. Vanderbilt then turned to his friends for help with the job, offering them rides in his new boat as payment for their labor.

Using that boat Vanderbilt started his own transport and freight service that carried goods between Staten Island's farmlands and New York City's Manhattan, an emerging center of commerce. In time he repaid his mother the amount of that first loan plus an extra $1,000. When he was eighteen years old, the War of 1812 (1812–15) erupted between the United States and England over a variety of complaints, including the capture of American sailors for enforced duty in the English Royal Navy. Vanderbilt profited during the three-year conflict after winning a government contract to carry supplies to the numerous military forts along the New York and New Jersey shorelines. With the money he earned from that project, he built a schooner, a ship with at least two masts that was capable of carrying a much heavier volume of cargo. His ship serviced the communities located on the shore of the Long Island Sound on the Atlantic Ocean, and he soon added two more schooners to his fleet. By 1817 he had saved up $9,000.

In 1818 Vanderbilt sold all of his boats. They were all sailing vessels that relied on the wind to power them, and he was convinced that steamships were going to dominate the shipping industry instead. A little more than a decade earlier, a wealthy New York lawyer and politician named Robert Livingston (1746–1813) had joined with American inventor Robert Fulton (1765–1815), and their first steamship made the trip on the Hudson River from New York City to Albany, New York, in record time. Their next vessel made its maiden voyage from Pittsburgh, Pennsylvania, to New Orleans in

1811. Vanderbilt wanted to learn as much as possible about the new technology and went to Thomas Gibbons, a steamboat ferry operator. Gibbons's boat ran between New Brunswick, New Jersey and New York City, and Vanderbilt promised to increase its profits in exchange for a salary of just $1,000 a year.

Epic legal battle

Vanderbilt delivered the profits as promised. He revised the schedules to make the service more reliable and made the boats more comfortable for passengers. After convincing Gibbons that a larger ferry was needed, he learned to captain the new vessel himself. But Vanderbilt's time with Gibbons was important for another reason, and one that had a far more lasting impact on the American economy: the newly successful Gibbons line came into conflict with Fulton and Livingston, who believed they had the rights to all steam-ship travel on the Hudson River. A generation earlier, states commonly granted monopolies (the exclusive possession or right to produce a particular good or service) to companies or individuals. This dated from the first years of the new nation, when lawmakers and leaders wanted to encourage invention and investment in their communities, but had no funds to do so yet. Granting monopolies in certain indus-tries and sectors was one way to promote business and innovation.

Some years earlier the New York legislature had granted a monopoly for steamboat travel to **John Fitch** (1743–1798; see entry), whose version of a steam-powered boat came before Fulton's. Fitch even demonstrated it before the dele-gates at the Constitutional Convention in Philadelphia, Pennsylvania, and Livingston was one of the attendees. Fitch died in poverty, and Livingston later managed to secure his New York rights, probably through political connections. Gibbons took Livingston to court over the monopoly rights, and the case advanced all the way to the U.S. Supreme Court. The landmark case, *Gibbons v. Ogden,* was decided in 1824 and eliminated all state monopolies. It also gave Congress some authority over interstate commerce (commerce that crossed state lines), a legal first that would later play a significant role in a wave of regulatory laws for American corporations in the early years of the twentieth century.

Vanderbilt managed to prosper during the years he worked for Gibbons, with some credit going to his wife, Sophia Johnson Vanderbilt (1795–1868), whom he had married in 1813. In the town of New Brunswick, which was the halfway point between Manhattan and Philadelphia, she ran a hostel for travelers on the Gibbons ferry line. In 1829, after a decade working for Gibbons, Vanderbilt decided to start his own steamboat line. With the immense sum he had saved—around $30,000 by then—Vanderbilt began a service that ran between New York City and Peekskill, New York, a Westchester County town on the Hudson River. This project sparked his first business battle with another transportation owner, Daniel Drew (1797–1879). Vanderbilt beat his competitor by charging much cheaper rates, a practice that Vanderbilt would continue for the remainder of his career.

In his next venture, a steamship line that ran to the state capital of Albany, Vanderbilt went up against the Hudson River Association, a group of boat operators that set rates amongst themselves. Again Vanderbilt's line charged a much lower rate, and the association finally decided to pay him to keep out of the Hudson River traffic. Vanderbilt agreed to give up his Hudson River line for the next ten years and earned $100,000 plus another $5,000 annually from the deal. For the next several years, he concentrated on shipping and ferry services along Long Island Sound and up the Atlantic seaboard to towns in Connecticut and on to Providence, Rhode Island, and Boston, Massachusetts. Vanderbilt's passenger ferries were known for their safety and their somewhat fancy interiors, and they also used a more efficient boiler that saved on operating costs by burning much less fuel.

Profited from California gold rush

By the time Vanderbilt celebrated his fortieth birthday in 1834, he possessed a fortune worth $500,000, a huge amount at the time. His lines prospered and later the following decade he moved into long-distance travel. The California gold rush, which began in 1848 with the discovery of a gold nugget near Sutter's Mill in the northern part of that state, caused a massive migration of prospectors hoping to make their fortunes in gold mining. There was no transcontinental railroad (spanning the country from one coast to the other) yet, and New England and Atlantic seaboard residents who planned to move to California to prospect for gold had two sea transportation options. One was to board a ship that sailed around Cape Horn, the southernmost tip of South America, which was known for its dangerous storms. The other involved booking passage to Panama in Central America, and then making a trek over land through the Isthmus of Panama. This was a tropical jungle, and newcomers were at risk of contracting malaria (a sometimes deadly disease spread by mosquitoes that causes chills and high fever). When they made it across, they had to wait for another ship that would carry them up the Pacific coast to San Francisco, California.

Vanderbilt found a shorter route, through Nicaragua, and charged half the price of the leading company's rate for both legs of the journey. In 1815 he made the first trip on his new Accessory Transit Company (ATC) venture himself to oversee its smooth operation. He also began meeting with wealthy London, England, bankers with the hopes of obtaining financial backing to build a canal through the Isthmus of Panama. In the end the English bankers declined to get involved, though by 1880 construction had started on what would become the Panama Canal, originally financed by a French consortium.

In Panama Vanderbilt learned that the two executives, Charles Morgan and Cornelius K. Garrison, whom he had put in charge of ATC had betrayed him through a stock manipulation that resulted in their gaining a controlling interest in the company. Realizing that a lawsuit would, at best, result in monetary damages the two men were unlikely to pay, he vowed to ruin them instead. He formed a rival company to the ATC and managed to put the ATC out of business within two years. Known for his competitive streak and ruthlessness in dealmaking, Vanderbilt sometimes paid New York state officials and judges to help him out. He was known to have many contacts inside the Tammany Hall political machine (power structures identified with political parties that were led by a boss and his associates) in New York City. Similarly stubborn in his personal affairs, he treated his wife and twelve children poorly.

Moved into railroads

Vanderbilt soon sold most of his fleet and left the shipping business altogether. In the early 1860s he ventured into railroads. His first purchase was the New York and Harlem Railroad, which again put him into competition with Daniel Drew.

Railroad executive Jay Gould competed with Vanderbilt for control of the Erie Railroad. *(© Bettmann/Corbis.)*

Known for his stock manipulation schemes, Drew attempted to block Vanderbilt's purchase by selling short, or selling stock shares that did not technically exist under law. Vanderbilt managed to win this battle by buying the stock anyway, using his political connections to have the stock declared valid, and thereby gaining a controlling interest in the railroad. Furthermore, the price of the shares rose from $90 to $285 in five months. Drew lost that confrontation badly and was determined to take revenge on Vanderbilt at the next opportunity.

In 1864 Vanderbilt bought the failing Hudson River Railroad, which ran from New York to Albany. His next purchase was the New York Central Railroad in 1867, which connected Albany and Buffalo, New York. He merged it with the Hudson River Railroad and then leased the Harlem Railroad to it. He called the new company the New York Central and Hudson River Railroad. In 1866 he tried to purchase the important Erie Railroad line. Drew was the treasurer of this company, and the business rivalry between the two men became known as the Erie War. Again Drew issued fraudulent stock, teaming with financial backers Jay Gould (1836–1892) and James Fisk (1834–1872). And once again Vanderbilt kept buying up as many shares as he could, but this time he nearly went bankrupt doing so. Drew, Gould, and Fisk fled to New Jersey but eventually surrendered to authorities. Vanderbilt used his political connections to have the fraudulent stock authorized as valid shares. Gould and Fisk later betrayed Drew in their own financial scheme, and Vanderbilt's major business rival, Drew, had lost his fortune by the time he died in 1879.

In 1873 Vanderbilt achieved a legendary feat in American railroad expansion by extending his New York Central and

Hudson River Railroad all the way to Chicago. He did so by acquiring other regional lines, such as the Lake Shore and Michigan, the Canadian Southern, and the Michigan Central. Vanderbilt's trunk line, or major railroad route that operated across a large geographical area, was the second largest in its day and spurred major growth in the New York cities of Syracuse, Rochester, and Erie, as well as in Cleveland, Ohio, Toledo, Ohio, and South Bend, Indiana. Only the Pennsylvania Railroad trunk line, which connected New York, Philadelphia, Washington, D.C., Chicago, and St. Louis, Missouri, was larger.

Early corporate raider

Like Drew and other wealthy company owners in an era when American business was largely unregulated by the government, Vanderbilt also manipulated the stock in his own companies by issuing stocks at an inflated price—that is, a price not warranted by the company's real assets. But his were successful operations that usually returned large dividends (sums or bonuses) to their shareholders. He was known for sometimes buying properties at a price that was considered far too high but then making them quite profitable due to his cost-cutting measures. A century later such corporate strategy became known as the leveraged buyout. Even during the Panic of 1873, when the country's leading private bank failed, causing a financial crisis in which nearly a quarter of U.S. railroads went out of business, Vanderbilt managed to prosper.

Vanderbilt died in January 1877. After Sophia died in 1868 he had married Frances Crawford of Mobile, Alabama, who was more than forty years younger than he was. She encouraged him to donate some of his wealth to good causes, and he gave $50,000 to the Church of the Strangers in New York City and $1 million to Central University in Nashville, Tennessee, which was renamed Vanderbilt University in his honor. The rest of his estate, estimated at nearly $100 million, was left largely to his son, William Henry Vanderbilt (1821–1885), whom he had put in charge of one of his railroads. Vanderbilt believed that of his four sons, William was the only one with a talent for business, but he regularly mocked him with nicknames that included "beetlehead." Another son of Vanderbilt's died of malaria, and the other two were disinherited. There

The Vanderbilts

When Cornelius Vanderbilt died in 1877, his last will and testament left $95 million, or the majority of his fortune, to his son William Henry. By the time William died in 1885, just eight years after his father, he had managed to double that amount to nearly $200 million. His was the generation of Vanderbilts that was finally granted entry into elite New York society, which had been dominated by older money, such as the fur-trading fortune of the Astor family, before then. Unlike his father, William H. Vanderbilt was a generous patron of the arts and one of the founders of the Metropolitan Opera in New York. William was perhaps best remembered, however, for uttering the famous line, "The public be damned." This was his answer to journalists who asked him if he was running his railroad for the public benefit or not. In the second half of his retort, which is rarely quoted, Vanderbilt reminded the reporters that he was more concerned about his stockholders and their investment in his company.

William H. Vanderbilt had nine children. His second son, William K. II (1849–1920), inherited a fortune of $60 million after his father's 1885 death. William K.'s daughter, Consuelo (1877–1964), a noted beauty, was forced into a loveless 1895 marriage by her ambitious mother. The groom was Charles Spencer-Churchill (1871–1934), the ninth Duke of Marlborough, which made Consuelo the first American woman to marry a titled noble from Europe.

Another of William H.'s sons, Cornelius II (1843–1899), left much of his fortune to his son, Reginald Claypoole Vanderbilt, a notoriously immoral man who died at the age of forty-five in 1925 from liver failure after years of heavy drinking. Reginald's second wife was Gloria Morgan (1904–1965), another woman of exceptional beauty. Their daughter, also named Gloria, inherited most of her father's fortune. She was just two years old when he died, and at the age of eight she became the focus of a bitter and highly publicized custody trial between her mother and paternal grandmother in the early 1930s. Her aunt, Reginald's sister Gertrude Vanderbilt Whitney (1875–1942), took custody of her for a time. Gertrude was a well-respected patron of the arts and the founder of what became New York's Whitney Museum of American Art.

Gloria Vanderbilt, who was a successful clothing designer during the 1970s and 1980s, married several times. With her fourth husband, writer Wyatt Cooper, she had two sons. One of them, Carter, committed suicide in 1988. The second son was Anderson Cooper, a Cable News Network (CNN) anchor during the early twenty-first century.

were eight Vanderbilt daughters, and each received about $500,000 from their father's estate. Two of them joined with a brother to contest their father's will, but they lost in court. One son, Cornelius Jeremiah, committed suicide in 1882.

Vanderbilt's influence in nineteenth-century America was a profound one. He made his fortune by investing in new technologies when they were still mostly untested and others remained skeptical. His skill at turning any enterprise into a profitable one played a key role in the expansion of the transportation industry in the greater New York City area and beyond, and that expansion helped make Chicago the second-largest city in America shortly after Vanderbilt's death.

For More Information

Books

Auchincloss, Louis. *The Vanderbilt Era: Profiles of a Gilded Age.* New York: Scribner, 1989.

Periodicals

Klein, Maury. "The First Tycoon." *Forbes* (October 22, 1990): p. 44.

Web Sites

"The House of Vanderbilt." *Vanderbilt Mansion National Historic Site.* http://www.nps.gov/vama/house_of.html (accessed on July 7, 2005).

Booker T. Washington

Born April 5, 1856 (Franklin County, Virginia)
Died November 14, 1915 (Tuskegee, Alabama)

Educator
Activist
Writer

"No race can prosper till it learns that there is as much dignity in tilling a field as in writing a poem."

Booker T. Washington was the first national leader for millions of African Americans at the turn of the twentieth century. The founder of an all-black school in Alabama called the Tuskegee Institute, Washington urged the South's eight million freed slaves and their descendants to continue to farm and do manual labor. Through hard work, he believed, they would prosper and someday enjoy the same rights and privileges as white Americans. He cautioned blacks to avoid political and civil rights battles, but to work instead to become property owners and merchants, and to create their own thriving, self-sufficient communities.

As Washington recounted in his well-known autobiographies, *Up from Slavery* (1901) and *The Story of My Life and Work* (1901), he was born into slavery in 1856. He was not the property of a wealthy plantation owner but belonged instead to James Burroughs, who had a small farm near Hale's Ford, in Franklin County, Virginia. Washington's mother, Jane, was a cook in the household, and his father was an unknown white man. Washington had a brother named John, and when his mother married another slave, Washington Ferguson, they had a daughter together named Amanda.

Booker T. Washington. *(Courtesy of The Library of Congress.)*

Work in the mines

Washington turned five the year the American Civil War (1861–65) began. The conflict between the Union states of the North, who were opposed to slavery, and the Confederate states of the South, who were in favor of slavery and had seceded from the Union, lasted for the next four years. In the midst of it U.S. president Abraham Lincoln (1809–65; served 1861–65) issued his historic Emancipation Proclamation, which freed all slaves. Like many other blacks, Washington and his family were suddenly free, but while they had no master now, they also had few resources, no income, and no place to go. Many freedmen stayed on with their former masters, but Washington's stepfather went to work in coal and salt mines in West Virginia. The family soon joined him there, making the ten-day trip with a wagon that carried their few possessions. The children had to walk alongside it for much of the way, and at night they slept outdoors.

In Malden, West Virginia, Washington and his brother went to work in the mines as well. Slaves had been prohibited by law from learning to read and write, and now that all slaves were free and these laws no longer applied to them, Washington was eager for an education. He convinced his stepfather to let him go to a new school for black children for a half the day. Washington was surprised to learn on his first day that most people had two names. His family called him "Booker," and so when the teacher asked for his last name, he took his stepfather's. His mother told him later that he did have a last name, which was Taliaferro, and he made this his middle name.

Eager to escape the difficult work in the mines, Washington was fortunate to find a job as a household servant for a wealthy family. The Ruffners had prospered earlier in the nineteenth century by supplying the salt needed to cure pork at Cincinnati, Ohio, meatpacking houses across the West Virginia border. Lewis Ruffner had also served as a major general in the Union militia that was charged with the restoration of order in the South in the years immediately following the Civil War. Washington joined their household around 1867 and spent several years with them. It was a very different environment from the dirty, unhealthy area near the mines, where blacks and the poorest whites lived in rundown cabins with nearby outhouses.

Education

When Washington learned about the Hampton Institute in Hampton, Virginia, he became determined to enroll there. The institute was a school for former slaves run by the American Missionary Association. It had opened just a few years earlier, in 1868, and Washington knew that he could enter on a work-study plan to pay his tuition. He left Malden in October 1872 and traveled to Hampton. He had to walk part of the way and had no money by the time he reached Richmond, Virginia. The Hampton Institute became a turning point in his life, and the school's founder and principal, Samuel Chapman Armstrong (1839–1893), became a mentor to him. Like Ruffner, who had been a slave owner, Armstrong believed that blacks were intrinsically different from whites, and fit only for lesser roles in society. Ruffner had been a Republican Party member, a party founded on the abolition (ending) of slavery, but he supported the idea of colonization, which called for sending the freed blacks back to Africa. The views of both Ruffner and Armstrong played an important part in shaping Washington's own beliefs about the role of African Americans in the newly reunited nation.

Washington earned his degree from the Hampton Institute and went back to Malden with it. He taught school there from 1875 to 1877 and then spent a year at the Wayland Seminary in Washington, D.C. He was then hired as an instructor at the Hampton Institute and began teaching there in January 1879. Two years later he was invited to Macon County, Alabama, where a school similar to the Hampton Institute was being planned. He eagerly accepted the job as the new school's director and set out for a part of the South that he had not yet seen. Unlike Virginia, Alabama was deeply isolated from the rest of the nation and far more rural. Attitudes were different, too, and some whites strongly objected to the idea of blacks attending school at all. But in 1881 the Tuskegee Normal and Industrial Institute officially opened on the Fourth of July holiday. Though the Alabama legislature had set aside some funds to pay the teachers—part of a deal to attract new black voters—the institute had no facilities when Washington arrived. His first students built the school themselves, after classes were dismissed at a nearby African Methodist Episcopal Zion Church, and even made the bricks. For food they grew their own produce.

Tuskegee was set up as an industrial school to train students for manual labor or the skilled trades, but it also offered training for future teachers. Industrial classes included carpentry, farming, mechanics, shoemaking, tinsmithing, and blacksmithing. The school also served female students, who learned various domestic arts such as sewing and canning. The principal of the women's students was Olivia Davidson, who became Washington's second wife in 1885. His first wife, Fanny Norton Smith, died in 1884 just two years after their marriage, leaving him with a young daughter, Portia. He and Davidson had two sons together, but she died young as well, leaving him a widower in 1889. His third wife was Margaret James Murray, a Fisk University graduate

George Washington Carver

In 1896 Booker T. Washington hired George Washington Carver (c. 1864–1943) as a teacher at the famous Tuskegee Institute in Alabama. Born near the end of the American Civil War (1861–65), Carver spent his early years in Missouri on the same farm where his family had been slaves. Known for his love of plants even in his childhood, he was desperate to get an education and overcame many obstacles to attend school. During his years at Simpson College in Iowa, Carver's passion for horticulture (the science of growing plants) impressed his teachers, and he went on to the Iowa State College of Agriculture and Mechanic Arts, becoming the first black student at the school, which later became Iowa State University. He earned a graduate degree, taught there as its first African American faculty member, and became known in scientific circles for his published papers.

Washington knew of Carver's work and invited him to teach at the Tuskegee Institute. Carver spent the remainder of his career there, and after Washington's death in 1915 he succeeded his former boss as the country's most prominent African American. He was one of a handful of respected black scientists in his era, and his best-known laboratory work involved the peanut. These experiments came out of his determination to find a better source of income for poor farmers across the South. Cotton had been the mainstay of its agriculture for generations, but a boll weevil insect epidemic in the early twentieth century destroyed the crops for several years.

Carver realized that the peanut plant did not rob the soil of its needed nutrients as cotton did. Instead, legume plants like peanuts and soybeans enriched the soil by adding nitrogen to it, and Carver found that alternating these crops with cotton resulted in stronger and healthier cotton plants. Legumes could also be a source of protein for the farmers' own diets. He wrote pamphlets for farmers that provided information on how to plant and harvest these crops and ran a soil-testing service and a mobile educational unit. At Tuskegee he set up an industrial research laboratory to find new uses for the peanut. Under his supervision the laboratory came up with some three hundred uses for the plant, including printer's ink, paper, shampoo, leather dye, glue, and even insulating board.

whom he wed in 1892. Murray would play a vital role in Tuskegee's success, and like her husband became a mentor to the students.

Washington's philosophy of self-sufficiency

In addition to his duties as head of the school, Washington also worked to raise donations to keep its doors open, and he was successful at collecting contributions from whites as well as blacks. Many whites viewed Washington as a man who

The Wheelwright Shop at the Tuskegee Institute, which was founded by Booker T. Washington. *(© Bettmann/Corbis. Reproduced by permission.)*

represented all the virtues to which the poor should aspire—cleanliness, dignity, and a certain degree of humility. He rose to great prominence in the 1890s and lectured and wrote articles for newspapers and magazines about race relations in America. Whites approved of Washington's message to black audiences, in which he urged African Americans to seize any available opportunity and not devote their energies to protests and civil rights issues. Washington believed that blacks should create self-sufficient communities with their own businesses and property. In this way, he asserted, they could achieve equality with white Americans.

While Washington championed home ownership and farming, the situation for blacks in the deep South (a region of the southern United States that included South Carolina, Georgia, Alabama, Mississippi, and Louisiana) outside of peaceful Tuskegee was difficult. Many worked as sharecroppers, tilling land for white landowners. A sharecropper is a tenant farmer who works the land for an agreed share of the value of the crop, minus the deductions taken out of his share for his rent, supplies, and living costs. The black men who did own property were often the focus of hostility and even violence. White mobs regularly targeted blacks suspected of wrongdoing and even carried out death sentences outside of the court system. Many blacks were hanged or set on fire by such mobs, and a suspiciously high number of victims were black property owners. In 1892, a year when 161 lynchings (hangings) occurred in the southern states, an African American journalist named Ida Wells-Barnett (1862–1931) began a campaign to raise public awareness of the issue. Three of her friends who were black entrepreneurs in Memphis, Tennessee, had been slain after opening a grocery store that competed with a white-owned business in the city.

Wells-Barnett was one of Washington's toughest critics. Along with writer and educator W. E. B. Du Bois (1868–1963), she objected to Washington's policy of what the educator's foes called "accommodationism" with white America. The Tuskegee founder had become one of the most prominent African American leaders in the country, but he rarely voiced any criticism of whites or of establishments and institutions that excluded blacks. It was a time when many blacks were unable to vote in Southern states because of certain laws passed by whites who wanted to prevent them from exercising that right. These included the poll tax, a fee to vote that did not have to be paid if one's grandfather had been a registered voter—which effectively barred the descendants of slaves who could not afford to pay the fee—and literacy tests. Furthermore, in 1896 the U.S. Supreme Court ruled in the landmark *Plessy v. Ferguson* case that states could indeed enact laws that segregated (separated) blacks and whites in public facilities and on modes of transportation as long as the facilities were "separate but equal." These statutes were known as Black Codes or Jim Crow laws.

The Atlanta Compromise

In the midst of such deepening segregation and racial tension, the defining moment of Washington's career came on September 18, 1895. On that day he was a featured speaker at the

Cotton States and International Exposition held in Atlanta, Georgia. Before an all-white audience at the event, which was held to showcase the achievements of the South since the end of the Civil War, Washington argued that eight million blacks had a place in the South, and that place was as its labor and agricultural force. "Our greatest danger is that, in the great leap from slavery to freedom, we may overlook the fact that the masses of us are to live by the productions of our hands and fail to keep in mind that we shall prosper in the proportion as we learn to dignify and glorify common labor," he declared that day, according to the *American Reader.* He asserted that equality would come through hard work, and that fighting for political power and equality was the wrong strategy for African Americans. "No race that has anything to contribute to the markets of the world is long in any degree ostracized [excluded].... The opportunity to earn a dollar in a factory just now is worth infinitely more than the opportunity to spend a dollar in an opera house."

Washington's speech became known as the "Atlanta Compromise," and it was viewed by some as a turning point and even a tremendous setback for the civil rights movement. It did, however, force other African American leaders to adopt new tactics, and a determined anti-Washington faction met ten years later at a 1905 meeting of the Niagara Movement. Their mission statement called for an end to racial discrimination against blacks in America and for the granting of full civil liberties, including a political voice. Led by Du Bois, the Niagara Movement organizers went on to form the National Association for the Advancement of Colored People (NAACP) five years later.

Washington strongly believed that blacks were corrupted by the urban environment, and his distaste for city life had come from witnessing the overcrowded conditions in Malden, West Virginia, and Washington, D.C. Keeping close to the land, he believed, and working the soil as farmers was better for African Americans. Many blacks in the South disagreed with him and fled the cotton states for the cities of the East Coast and Midwest when urban factory jobs became plentiful from 1914 to 1918. This population shift became known as the Great Migration. It lasted well into the 1950s and permanently altered the racial makeup of the nation. This had a long-lasting social and cultural impact on African Americans of the twentieth century and would help millions of them prosper.

First black to dine at the White House

Washington enjoyed immense prestige during his lifetime, and newspapers called him the "Leader of His Race" and "the Wizard of Tuskegee." U.S. president Theodore Roosevelt (1858–1919; served 1901–9) even invited him to dine at the White House in 1901, making Washington the first African American ever to do so. He served as an adviser on race matters to both Roosevelt and his successor, William Howard Taft (1857–1930; served 1909–13). He continued to seek wealthy white benefactors for the Tuskegee Institute and his other projects and received money from such prominent business-men as steel industrialist **Andrew Carnegie** (1835–1919; see entry); George Eastman (1854–1932), the founder of Kodak; and Julius Rosenwald (1862–1932), a partner in the Sears, Roebuck retail empire. Washington also tightly controlled any donations he made to black causes or institutions, giving funds only to those who agreed with his own ideas.

Washington fell ill in New Haven, Connecticut, in October 1915 and died a month later at the Tuskegee Institute from arteriosclerosis, or hardening of the arteries. At the time the school had 1,500 students, as well as the largest endowment (money or property donated to an institution as a source of income) of any black college or university. The school later lent its name to the Tuskegee Airmen, a group of African Americans in the Army Air Force who trained there to become the first all-black fighter pilot squadron.

For More Information

Books

Harlan, Louis R. *Booker T. Washington: The Wizard of Tuskegee, 1901–1915.* New York: Oxford University Press, 1983.

Periodicals

"The Atlanta Exposition Address." *American Reader* (Edition 1991): p. 185.

Web Sites

Booker T. Washington National Monument. http://www.nps.gov/bowa/home.htm (accessed on July 7, 2005).

"History of Tuskegee University." *Tuskegee University.* http://www.tuskegee.edu/Global/story.asp? S=1070392 & nav=PBo8PBpC (accessed on July 7, 2005).

Where to Learn More

Books

Bagley, Katie. *The Early American Industrial Revolution, 1793–1850.* Bridgestone Books, Mankato, MN: 2003.

Calhoun, Charles W., ed. *The Gilded Age: Essays on the Origins of Modern America.* Wilmington, DE: Scholarly Resources, 1996.

Cashman, Sean Dennis. *America in the Gilded Age: From the Death of Lincoln to the Rise of Theodore Roosevelt.* New York and London: New York University Press, 1984.

Clare, John. D. *Industrial Revolution.* San Diego: Harcourt Brace & Co., 1994.

Faler, Paul. *Mechanics and Manufacturers in the Early Industrial Revolution: Lynn, Massachusetts, 1780–1860.* Albany: State University of New York Press, 1981.

Foner, Philip S., ed.*The Factory Girls.* Urbana, IL: University of Illinois Press, 1977.

Hindle, Brooke, and Steven Lubar. *Engines of Change: The American Industrial Revolution, 1790–1860.* Washington, D.C. and London: Smithsonian Institution Press, 1986.

Kornblith, Gary J., ed. *The Industrial Revolution in America.* Boston, MA: Houghton Mifflin, 1998.

McCormick, Anita Louise. *The Industrial Revolution in American History.* Berkeley Heights, NJ: Enslow Publishers, 1998.

Olson, James S. *Encyclopedia of the Industrial Revolution in the U.S.* Westport, CT: Greenwood Press, 2002.

Orleck, Annelise. *Common Sense and a Little Fire: Women and Working-Class Politics in the United States, 1900–1965.* Chapel Hill: University of North Carolina, 1995.

Rivard, Paul E. *A New Order of Things: How the Textile Industry Transformed New England.* Hanover, NH: University Press of New England, 2002.

Ruggoff, Milton. *America's Gilded Age: Intimate Portraits from an Era of Extravagance and Change, 1850–1890.* New York: Henry Holt and Company, 1989.

Smith, Page. *The Rise of Industrial America: A People's History of the Post-Reconstruction Era.* Vol. 6. New York: McGraw-Hill, 1984.

Summers, Mark Wahlgren. *The Gilded Age, or, the Hazard of New Functions.* Upper Saddle River, NJ: Prentice-Hall, 1997.

Web Sites

"The Industrial Revolution." http://www.bergen.org/technology/indust.html (accessed on July 8, 2005).

"Rise of Industrial America, 1876–1900." *The Learning Page.* http://memory.loc.gov/learn/features/timeline/riseind/riseof.html (accessed on July 8, 2005).

"Technology in 1900." *Way Back: U.S. History for Kids.* http://pbskids.org/wayback/tech1900/ (accessed on July 8, 2005).

"Transcontinental Railroad." *American Experience: PBS.* http://www.pbs.org/wgbh/amex/tcrr/index.html (accessed on July 8, 2005).

"Wake Up, America." Webisode 4 of "Freedom: A History of US." http://www.pbs.org/wnet/historyofus/web04/ (accessed on July 8, 2005).

Index

Bold type indicates major entries.
Illustrations are marked by (ill.).

3/06 $55.00

LONGWOOD PUBLIC LIBRARY
Middle Country Road
Middle Island, NY 11953
(631) 924-6400
LIBRARY HOURS

Monday-Friday	9:30 a.m. - 9:00 p.m.
Saturday	9:30 a.m. - 5:00 p.m.
Sunday (Sept-June)	1:00 p.m. - 5:00 p.m.